may be cut off from ...
which is so terrible and ...
babe may grow up ...
knowing her and without
knowing me. It is difficult
to face. And I know your life
without me would be a dull
blank. Yet you must never let
it become wholly so. For to you
will be left the greatest charge in
all the world; the upbringing of
our baby. God bless that child,
she is the hope of life to me.
My darling, au revoir. It may
well be that you will only have to
read these lines as ones of passing
interest. On the other hand, they
may well be my last message to you.
If they are, know through all your life
that I loved you and baby with all
my heart and soul, that you two
... things were just all the
world to me.

I pray God I may do my duty,
... I know, ... that may ...
... should not lose its otherwise.

To Fight Alongside Friends

To Fight Alongside Friends

The First World War Diaries of Charlie May

Edited by Gerry Harrison

WILLIAM COLLINS

William Collins
HarperCollinsPublishers
77–85 Fulham Palace Road
Hammersmith, London W6 8JB
www.WilliamCollins.co.uk

First published in Great Britain by William Collins in 2014

Copyright © Gerry Harrison 2014
Foreword copyright © David Crane 2014

Gerry Harrison asserts the moral right to
be identified as the editor of this work

A catalogue record for this book
is available from the British Library

ISBN 978-0-00-755853-7

Set in Dante MT by Palimpsest Book Production Limited
Falkirk, Stirlingshire

Maps © John Gilkes

Endpaper images courtesy of the Regimental Archives

Printed and bound in Great Britain by
Clays Ltd, St Ives plc

MIX
Paper from
responsible sources

FSC
www.fsc.org

FSC™ C007454

FSC™ is a non-profit international organisation established to promote
the responsible management of the world's forests. Products carrying the
FSC label are independently certified to assure consumers that they come
from forests that are managed to meet the social, economic and
ecological needs of present and future generations,
and other controlled sources.

Find out more about HarperCollins and the environment at
www.harpercollins.co.uk/green

Captain Charlie May, in the summer of 1915,
before his departure for France.

Gerry Harrison is the great-nephew of Charlie May. Born in India, he grew up in England where he later became an actor. Finding life behind the camera more fun, he then worked in television and film. Contacts as a politician working with the Irish community in London led him to write a history, *The Scattering*, published in 2004. Now living in Ireland, where he had a second-hand bookshop, he is a contributor to the *Irish Times*. He is completing a biography.

Contents

List of Illustrations

Frontispiece
Portrait of Captain Charlie May (Photo courtesy of family)

Plates
Charles Edward May (Photo courtesy of Jason Bauchop)

The steamship Wastmeath (© National Maritime Museum, Greenwich, London)

Port Chalmers, Dunedin, 1880 (Photo courtesy of Museum of New Zealand Te Papa Tongarewa, Ref: O.24194)

Princes Street, Dunedin, 1885 (Photo courtesy of Museum of New Zealand Te Papa Tongarewa, Ref: C.011756)

The May-Oatway Fire Alarm (Photo courtesy of Dunedin Fire Brigade Restoration Society Inc.)

The May Family in London, about 1905 (Photo courtesy of Susan and Charles Worledge)

Lily May's wedding, 1909 (Photo courtesy Susan and Charles Worledge)

Trooper May at camp, King Edward's Horse (Photo courtesy of family)

Charlie outside tent, Salisbury Plain (Photo courtesy of family)

Private Richard Tawney (Photo courtesy of LSE, Ref: LSE/Tawney/27/11)

Captain Alfred Bland (Photograph courtesy of Daniel Mace)

Lieut. William Gomersall (Photograph courtesy of Victor Gomersall)

Private Arthur Bunting (Photograph courtesy Adrian Bunting)

Maude with Pauline in her christening robe, 1914 (Photo courtesy of family)

Maude and Pauline in leather-bound case (Photo courtesy of Regimental Archives, Ref: MR4/17/295/4/4)

Maude, Pauline and Charlie, perhaps on leave, Feb. 1915 (Photo courtesy of family)

Maude (Photo courtesy of the Regimental Archives, Ref: MR4/17/295/4/4)

Pauline, aged about four with Teddy bear, c.1918 (Photo courtesy of the Regimental Archives, Ref: MR4/17/295/4/4)

Charlie's personal diaries (Photo courtesy of the Regimental Archives, Refs: MR4/17/295/1/1-7)

Pencil sketch by Charlie, 'Our Camp in the Bois' (Photo courtesy of the Regimental Archives, Ref: MR4/17/295/5/1)

Charles Edward May, seated, at Imperial School of Instruction camp, Zeitoun, Egypt, 1915 (Photo courtesy of Susan and Charles Worledge)

Dantzig Alley British Cemetery (Photograph courtesy of Derek Taylor)

Charlie's headstone, Dantzig Alley (Photograph courtesy of Derek Taylor)

Frank Earles, early 1920s (Photograph courtesy of Rosie Gutteridge)

Pauline, a friend and Maude in Fontainebleau, France, 1922 (Photo courtesy of family)

Pauline's wedding to Harry Karet, 1950 (Photo courtesy of family)

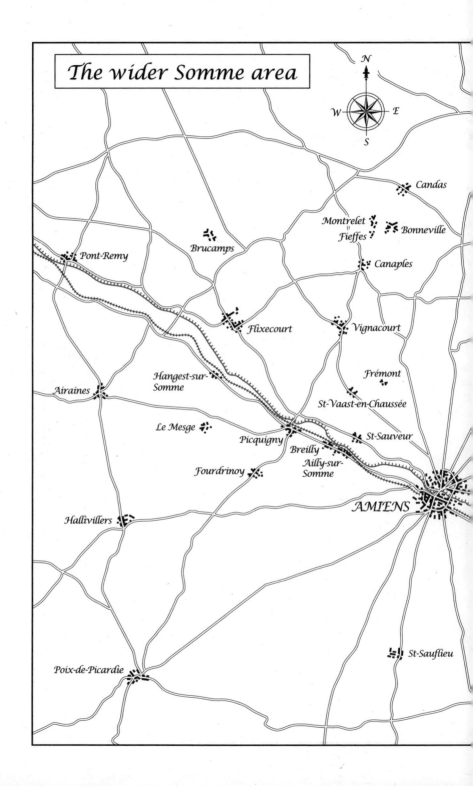

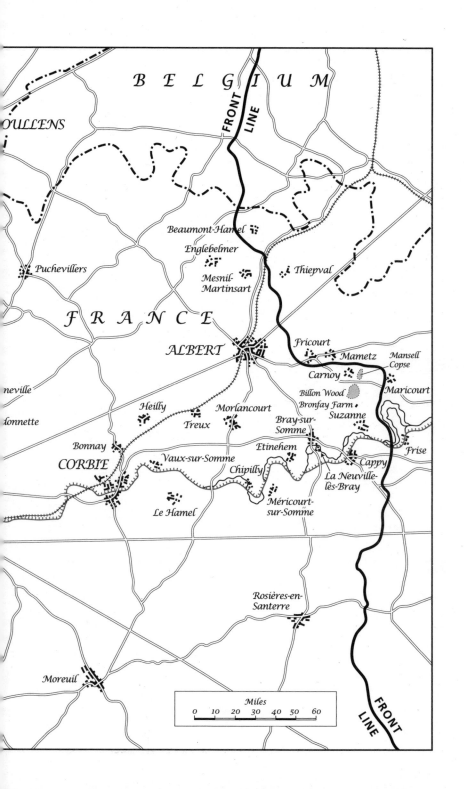

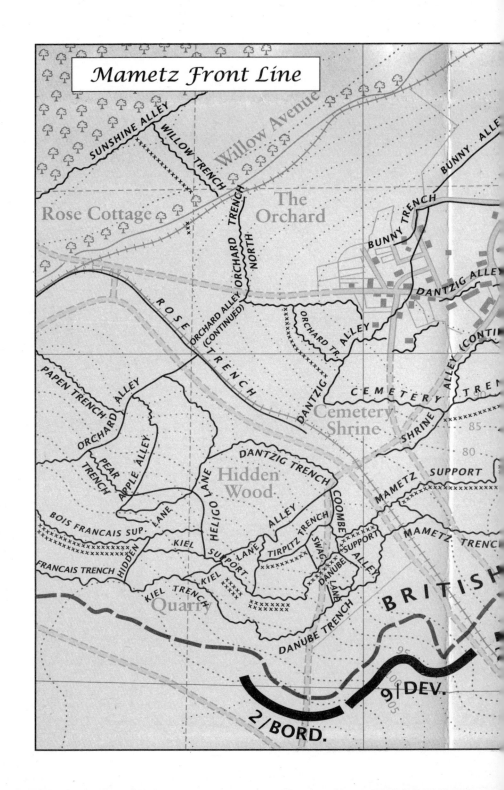

Mametz Front Line

TRENCH

RIGHT LANE

TRENCH

BEETLE ALLEY

POMMIERS
REDOUBT

DANTZIG ALLEY (CONTD.)

BUCKET TRENCH

POMMIERS

Mametz

BULGAR ALLEY

105

100

95

BLACK ALLEY

120

POPOFF LANE

BUND

THE
TRIANGLE

BAY LANE

TRENCH

Black
Hedge

BLACK

TRENCH

AUSTRIAN
JUNCTION

BAY TRENCH

SUPPORT

AUSTRIAN SUPPORT

BAY
POINT

BULGAR TRENCH

BULGAR
POINT

AUSTRIAN TRENCH

LINE

FRENCH

RONT

1/S. STAFFS.

22/MANCH.

2/QUEENS.

FRONT LINE

21/MANCH.

100

95

20TH
EVON

Foreword

What is it that makes one diary live and another simply die on the page? Nine times out of ten it is down to the intrinsic interest of the material or the quality of the writing; but every so often one comes across a diary where it is the sense of personality behind it that lifts it out of the ordinary: such a diary is that of Captain Charlie May, killed in the early morning of 1 July 1916, leading his men of B Company of the 22nd Manchester Service Battalion into action on the first day of the Battle of the Somme.

There is nothing very remarkable about Charles May, and that is the point about him: from the first page of his diary to the last haunting entries he feels so utterly familiar and recognisable. That is partly because his war was the war that a million men like him knew and endured and has become part of our historic consciousness; but more than that it is because Charlie May is 'England' as England has always liked to imagine itself, the England that stood in square at Waterloo and would stand waist-deep in water at Dunkirk, the England of a hundred 1940s and '50s films, down to his English wife and his English baby daughter and the English batman and the Alexandra rose that he sports into battle – the unassuming, modest, enduring, reliable, immensely likeable kind of Englishman, with his kindness, his tolerance, his loyalty, his certainties, his prejudices, his pipe, his fishing rod, his horse, his good jokes and his bad jokes and his un-showy patriotism, that if you had to spend your war up to your knees in clinging mud you would be very grateful to find next to you: and he is absolutely genuine.

I do not know if it is odd that someone so quintessentially English should come from New Zealand, or if that is part of the explanation, but Charlie May was born in that most stonily un-English of towns, Dunedin, on 27 July 1888, the son of an electrical engineer who had emigrated five years earlier. His father made his name and the foundation of a successful business with a patent for a new kind of fire alarm device, and on their return to England, Charlie had entered the family firm of May-Oatway, acting as company secretary before moving with his new wife, Maude, from the Mays' family home overlooking Epping Forest to Manchester where, just two weeks before the outbreak of war in 1914, a daughter, Pauline, was born. It is clear that the Mays did not lose sight of their New Zealand lives – their Essex home was named 'Kia Ora' ('be well' in Maori) and Charlie would call his new home 'Purakaunui', after a pretty coastal settlement, near Dunedin – but in 1914 there would have felt nothing odd about such a double identity. It was famously said that sometime between the landing at Anzac Cove and the end of the Battle of the Somme the New Zealand nation was born, but in the late summer of 1914, before Gallipoli was ever dreamed of, many of the thousands of New Zealanders who volunteered to fight in a war half a world away would have seen themselves as part of a single imperial family, one corner of the great Dominion 'quadrilateral' of Canada, South Africa, Australia and New Zealand, on which the British Empire rested.

While still in the south May had been a member of King Edward's Horse, a Territorial unit of the London Mounted Brigade with strong Dominion links, and, daughter or not, it was only a matter of time before war put an end to his short married idyll. On the outbreak of hostilities five divisions of a small but highly trained British Expeditionary Force had immediately been embarked for France to stem the German advance, but Kitchener for one never had any illusions that this was going to be a short war over by Christmas and within the month the first 300,000 of a New Army had responded to his call for volunteers.

By the end of September another 450,000 had volunteered, in October a further 137,000, and in the following month Charlie May enlisted into the 22nd Manchester Pals battalion – the '7th City Pals' – and added his name to the five million men who would wear uniform of one sort or another before the war was over. The idea of the 'Pals battalions' had first been put to the test in Liverpool by Lord Derby and the city of Manchester enthusiastically followed suit, embracing the patriotic and civic ideal of a battalion made up of friends from the same street, pub, factory, profession, warehouse or football club, joining up and fighting together – 'clerks and others engaged in commercial business,' as Derby put it, 'who wish to serve their country and would be willing to enlist in a Battalion of Lord Kitchener's new army if they felt assured that they would be able to serve with their friends and not to be put in a Battalion with unknown men as their companions'.

It was a sympathetic initiative, if a double-edged one as time would bitterly show, but in the late summer of 1914, as towns across Britain competed with each other in displays of civic pride, the slaughter that would engulf whole tightly knit communities in grief still belonged to an unimaginable future. Within hours of the Lord Mayor of Manchester launching his appeal in the *Manchester Guardian* on 31 August, volunteers were besieging the artillery barracks on Hyde Road and by the end of the next day 800 men had been sworn in and the establishment of the first of the Manchester Pals battalions, the 1st 'City', or 16th Service, was complete. Over the next four days another two battalions were added, and after a late summer lull in recruiting caused by the frustrating long queues, a further three battalions in November, the 20th, 21st and Charlie May's 22nd under the command of Lieutenant Colonel Cecil de C. Etheridge.

It would be exactly a year before Charlie May and his battalion embarked for France, and in that time an enthusiastic but improbable bunch of men drawn largely from the cotton industry and City Corporation – 'mostly town bred', wrote May, with a rare whiff of the King Edward's Horse and the Empire – had to be turned into soldiers. In these early stages before their khaki uniforms arrived, they wore the 'doleful convict-style' 'Kitchener Blue' and 'ridiculous little forage cap' so deeply resented among the New Army, but over the next twelve months, and in the face of the universal shortages of uniforms, weapons and ammunition and every provocation and indignity an army could dream up to frustrate, bore or disillusion a civilian volunteer, the job was at least begun.

It would be as late as October 1915, by which time the 22nd were at their final camp on Salisbury Plain as part of Major General Sir William Fry's 30th Division, before the artillery could even start firing practice or their Lee Enfield rifles and machine guns arrive. If May's diaries from France are anything to go by, he would have taken the frustrations in his stride. With six years' experience in the King Edward's Horse behind him he had received his commission back in January, and he was a company commander when, in the middle of November 1915, after a last few days' leave to see his wife and sixteen-month-old daughter, Captain Charlie May and the 22nd Battalion finally embarked from Folkestone for Boulogne.

The war that Charlie May had been trained for was not the fluid conflict of retreat and advance that the BEF had known in 1914 but the war of trenches that is how most of us now think of the First World War. In the popular memory the year 1915 seems almost like a pause between the heady optimism of the opening weeks of war and the slaughter of the Somme, but while May and the 22nd were shuffling from camp to camp – Heaton Park, Morecambe Bay, Grantham, Lark Hill – and progressing from longish 'walks' to bayonet and bomb practice, the bloody failures of Aubers Ridge, Festubert and Loos were teaching a bereaved nation the appalling reality of warfare along the 475 miles of earthworks and trenches, stretching in an unbroken line from the Channel to the Swiss border, that we know as the Western Front.

It was to this static, troglodytic war of attrition, mud, rats, sleeplessness and endurance that May was bound and it is as they finally set off for France that his diary begins. In the last two or three years of peace Charlie May had begun to establish himself as a journalist and writer, and the diary is unmistakably the work of a born story-teller, a man with a lyrical sense of place, an ear for dialogue, a gift for rapid and vivid characterisation, a taste for the incongruous and a *need* to record what he saw and experienced. 'One gets into a habit, quite unconsciously at first, of any hold it may subsequently get on one,' he was confessing less than a month after landing in France. 'For instance, here did I set out, gaily and with no foreboding, upon this diary, never thinking it could become a tyrant that would 'ere long rule me, and here I am reduced to impotence when evening comes round, unable to refuse the call of these pages to be scribbled in ... But fill it I must, this habit has me so in its grip.'

Charlie May's war diaries survive in seven small, wallet-sized pocket books, written in faint pencil in his neat but tiny, italic hand, as a rich and vivid testament to this compulsion. At one level it seems rather curious that an officer of his dedication should indulge in something so defiantly in breach of King's Regulations, but we can be grateful that he did because the result is an account that had never seen the censor's eye, a vivid picture of battalion life in and behind the trenches during the build-up to the greatest battle fought by a British Army.

The friendships and tensions, the homesickness, frustrations, delays and endless postponements, the fog of ignorance, the combination of boredom and terror that every man who has ever fought could testify to, the relationship of officer and batman, the almost incomprehensible contrast of the pastoral world only miles behind the fighting and the scarred and pocked ugliness of the front line – all familiar enough, perhaps, but seen and recorded here with a freshness that brings them home as if for the first time. 'This war, I am sure, is one of the most peculiar the world has ever known if, indeed, it is not the most peculiar,' he writes of the surreal experience of facing an enemy you might never see,

> In no other can it have been possible to soldier so long, to witness such evidence of the presence of an enemy and of his ability to injure without ever catching sight of beast, bird or man belonging to him . . . Except through my glasses, I have never yet seen a Fritz – an experience in no way peculiar, since it has been experienced by many a thousand others of double my active service.

There is a visceral immediacy about a war diary – a question mark hanging over each entry, the unspoken possibility that it might be the last – that no retrospective account can quite match. But the main fascination of these pages remains Charlie May himself. There is material here – details of units, movements, coded map references (which have been omitted from the text) – that would plainly never have got past an

Army censor, but it is the absence of *self*-censorship that makes these diaries so compelling and disarming a portrait of the archetypal English 'Everyman officer' – 'a truly ordinary sort of clout-head' as he describes himself – shorn of all the reticences and defences behind which he traditionally hides.

There is no cynicism or pretence in these pages, no attempt to make things sound better or worse than they are, or to dissemble the depth of his feelings for the men under his command or the wife and daughter to whom his diary is addressed. In Robert Graves's *Goodbye to All That*, any talk of 'patriotism' was fit 'only . . . for civilians, or prisoners' and any new arrival would soon have it knocked out of him. Underscoring every page of May's diaries, however, is an unembarrassed pride in his country and an almost maternal affection for the Englishmen with whom he is privileged to fight.

It has its 'little Englander' side – 'I can't imagine why the Germans want this country,' he quotes one of his messmates on the irredeemable squalor of the 'hairy, dirty, baggy-breeched', sabot-wearing French peasant; 'If it was mine, I'd give it to them and save all the fuss' – but in nothing is he more an Englishman of his time than in his less attractive prejudices. He can write very movingly of the shattered lives and homes that they come across in the villages behind the front lines, but he only has to see or smell another French midden to feel a sudden, nostalgic, humorous tug of affection for 'Dear, old, tax-ridden, law-abiding England!

> How I would delight to see one of your wolf-nosed sanitary inspectors turned loose in this, our Brucamps. How you would sniff, how snort, how elevate your highly educated proboscis! . . . And how masterly indifferent would our grubby people be of you, how little would they be impressed, how hopelessly insane they would think you, and what grave danger there would be of a second Revolution if you or any untold number of you essayed to remove from them their beloved dung-heaps.

It is the same with the 'British Tommy'. He might lose his kit as soon as look at it, he might need 'booting along' or a good 'strafing' – May's favourite word – he might get drunk, he might be 'something of a gross animal', but 'God knows he has enough to put up with. And I cannot help but love him.'

'Men dropped by the road side exhausted,' he writes in one wonderfully evocative passage,

Others staggered pitifully along in bare feet, the mud having snatched both boots and socks from them. Others again went strong, chattering and laughing whilst among the lot the officers, those of us whose strength was equal to it, went in and out carrying a rifle for this man, giving a cigarette to another, helping a lame duck up on to his poor, swollen feet again and chaffing or cracking feeble jokes with them all . . . It was a dark night. Men were but shuffling shadows against the chalk mud of the roadway except when the lights went up from the lines all about us. Then you could see the huddled forms of tired, mud-caked Englishmen shuffling home from their labours. The war is a war of endurance. Of human bodies against machines and against the elements. It is an unlovely war in detail yet there is something grand and inspiring about it. I think it is the stolid, uncomplaining endurance of the men under the utter discomforts they are called upon to put up with, their sober pluck and quiet good-heartedness which contributes very largely to this. All the days of my life I shall thank God I am an Englishman.

It does not stop him grumbling at all the usual targets of the infantry officer – the staff officer with nothing but a public school to recommend him, the deliberate idiocy of the censors, the base camp shirkers who would be all the better for a week in the trenches, the public at home querulously wondering why the Army isn't 'moving' – but nothing in the end can dent his faith. It is possible that had he lived to see where his blind confidence in the build-up to the Somme led he would have shared in the general disillusion, but any man who can extract comfort out of Loos or the disastrous fall of Kut or 'Thank God for the Navy' a week after Jutland is probably proof against anything that even the Great War can throw at him.

There was nothing abstract about May's patriotism; that was the strength of it. It was embodied in the men he was fighting with – in Bunting, his loyal batman, who had pulled him out of the canal when drunk one night in Manchester; in the puzzling Richard Tawney who, for whatever reasons of his own, went on refusing a commission; in the 'pitiful sight' of 'Poor English soldiers battered to pieces'; in 'Gresty . . . a good man and one whom we liked well . . . his poor body full of gaping holes' – and it made May want to *fight*. 'Do those at home yet realise how their boys go out for them?' he asked,

> Never can they do enough for their soldiers, never can they repay the debt they owe. Not that the men ask any reward – an inviolate England is enough for them, so be it we can get our price from the Hun. Confound the man . . . But one day we'll get at him with the bayonet. The issue <u>must</u> come at last to man to man. And when it does I have no doubt as to the issue. We'll take our price then for Gresty and all the other hundred thousand Grestys slain as he was standing still at his post.

It needs to be remembered that the 22nd was also the '7th City Pals', and the strong friendships and loyalties around which the whole concept of the Pals battalions had been initiated made such losses seem more painful still. By the time that the Battle of the Somme began, the battalion formed in November 1914 had of course changed with time, deaths, promotions and new arrivals out of all recognition, but one only has to look at the parallel accounts of May's old comrades from the Morecambe, Grantham and Lark Hill days – fascinatingly incorporated here as footnotes to his own diary entries to add fresh perspectives – to feel how strong were the bonds formed in England in a battalion like the 22nd and how bitterly the losses were mourned. 'Tonight we had a little reunion of all the old boys,' May himself wrote just a week before the Somme began,

> There was the doctor, Murray, Worth, Bill Bland, 'Gommy', Meller and myself and we sat round a table and sang the old mess-songs

. . . It was tip-top and we all loved each other. There are so many new faces with us now and so many missing that the battalion hardly felt the same – and one cannot let oneself go with the new like one loves the old boys. I would that the battalion was going over with all its old contingent. How certain we should all feel then. Not that the new stuff is not good. But we knew all the others so well.

Above all though, for Charlie May, England was his wife Maude and their baby daughter Pauline; his diary is an extended and deeply moving love-letter to them. He had married Bessie Maude Holl in February 1912 when they were both twenty-three, but it was really only when he had to leave her and their new daughter, that they both seem to have realised – not how much they had loved each other, that never seems to have been in any doubt – but how astonishingly fortunate they had been in their brief, shared lives. 'I thought of you as we strolled there, Lizzie with her reins slack wandering where she would and at her own pace,' he wrote after one afternoon spent riding through a world of larch and birch clumps and wood pigeons still untouched by war – a passage in which images of Maude, England and a deeply felt sense of natural beauty fuse into one to take us as close as we can probably get to what it was that Charlie May was ready to fight and, if necessary – un-heroically, reluctantly but matter-of-factly – die for.

And I longed that you could have been with me, for I know how you would have loved it and how happy we two would have been. The green rides of Epping came back to me in a flash. You in that black spotted muslin dress you used to wear looking cool and lovely so that I just asked nothing more than to walk along and gaze at you dumbly, like any simple country lout gazes at his maid.

'I do not want to die,' he wrote; the thought of never seeing Maude again, of his daughter growing up and never knowing him, turned 'his bowels to water'. But as the sporadic tours in the front-line trenches and the training behind the lines intensified in the build-up to the expected great summer offensive of 1916, there became less and less room for the 'personal'. It is impossible to read these diaries and the first casual mention of the Somme without a sense of grim foreboding, and yet at the same time there is no missing the growing excitement at the approach of battle, at the movement of troops, the massing of guns in preparation for the preliminary bombardment and the submersion of the individual in a mighty collective whole. 'It is marvellous,' he wrote, 'this marshalling of power. This concentrated effort of our great nation put forward to the end of destroying our foe. The greatest battle in the world is on the eve of breaking. Please God it may terminate successfully for us.'

There had been ominous warnings for the 22nd in the weeks leading up to the Battle of the Somme – a night raid with heavy casualties that showed the German wire uncut by the artillery, dud shells and 'whispers' that 'our ammunition . . . is not all that it should be' – but the grief that the word 'Somme' would conjure up for thousands of families whose sons had flocked to enlist in the autumn of 1914 belongs to retrospect. To Charlie May the word meant only a glimmering river – 'full of sport', he thought it should be, as he set off to buy his fishing tackle in Corbie – idling quietly through a landscape of 'tiny panoramas' of bullrushes and pampas grass, of 'brown trees, blue, sparkling waters, white, brown, red, blue and purple houses clustering around their grey churches'. The larger picture, the overall strategic concerns and aims that lay behind the Somme offensive of July 1916 – Verdun, the Eastern Front, the eternal illusion of a 'break-through' – were of no concern. *His* Great Battle – the battle that would mark 'the beginning of the end', he told Maude on 15 June – would be what he called the 'Battle of Mametz', and his responsibilities were to the men around him and the wife and daughter who were never out of his thoughts.

On the morning of the first of July, after a week of preliminary bombardment, the 22nd were part of the 7th Division, and their sector lay opposite the heavily fortified village of Mametz, on the southern edge of the Germans' Fricourt Salient, east of Albert. On their left the British line stretched up northwards through names that would soon be seared into the national consciousness – Fricourt, La Boisselle, Thiepval, Beaumont-Hamel – and on their right, eastwards and south to Maricourt, the junction with the French army and the River Somme itself. But for the company commander of B Company, the war had shrunk to the '900 yards of rough ground' in front of him and the inner battle to live up to the standards he had set himself. 'My one consolation,' he wrote to his wife, in one final, simple and binding credo,

> is the happiness that has been ours . . . My darling, *au revoir*. It may well be that you will only have to read these lines as ones of passing interest. On the other hand, they may well be my last message to you. If they are, know through all your life that I loved you and Baby with all my heart and soul, that you two sweet things were just all the world to me. Pray God I may do my duty, for I know, whatever that may entail, you would not have it otherwise.

The diary would be the last word she had from him. He did his duty, and so, too, did the battalion of whom he was so proud. 'They are all so clean-cut and English as you know so well, my own,' he had written to his wife on the eve of their departure for France; 'I feel confident they'll go when the chance comes. Please God the 22nd may carry the old Regiment's name another rung up the ladder of fame.' His soldier's prayer was answered. If his optimism in the prosecution of the war was unfounded, his confidence in the courage of his men was not. He would not live to know it – his last moments are preserved here in his wife's desperate, unbearable need to know every detail of his end – but Mametz was taken and, almost uniquely, the battalion's targets all met. It had been, though, at a shocking price. Of the 796 officers and men of the '7th City Pals', 472 were either killed or wounded on that terrible 1 July, a day that would cost the British Army 19,240 dead and 57,470 casualties in all. May's Battle for Mametz was over but the Battle of the Somme had only begun.

David Crane
February 2014

Prologue
'A pippy, miserable blighter'

7–10 November 1915

Lark Hill,[i] 7th November '15

I am going to commence this book this evening because now I have seen you for the last time before going abroad and I will therefore be unable to make [a] personal confession to you again for some time to come.

I arrived back here depressed from my leave-taking from you and Baby and found little to ease the sadness of my soul. More than half our fellows are out and the mess is full of the 23rd men, come over to say 'goodbye'.[ii] You know how little I love them and tonight they put me in no mood to reconsider my affection. Some are singing ragtime with

i On 28.10.15, the 21st and 22nd Manchesters moved from Grantham to No. 3 Camp, Canadian Lines, Lark Hill. On the 4th November they paraded for a final inspection by Lord Derby, the honorary colonel, and soon afterwards received a telegram of good wishes from the King George V.

ii The 23rd (or 8th City) Bn, Manchester Regt, was raised as a bantam battalion of men whose height was below the normal regulation minimum of five foot three inches. On this same evening a concert was given by sergeants for officers, which included a performance by 'a musical quartet and scenes from Shakespeare' (Sgt Richard Henry Tawney, 7.11.15).

1

deplorably poor success, whilst the remainder talk 'shop' in loud and raucous tones. They are hateful people and I wish they would go home and allow us to make our final arrangements in peace and quietude.

Our kits have all to be on the transport wagons by 6.15 a.m. tomorrow and we follow on Tuesday. I will be jolly glad when we get on the move, as will all the rest of our fellows. We believe we are bound for St Omer. I wonder!

I wrote to you this evening but not at length because I could not. I'm such a pippy, miserable blighter that it would be a sin to convey it to you, and just when you will want bracing up.

Guillet was in this afternoon with his bride.[i] They looked very well and appeared very happy. It quite reminded me of our honeymoon. By gad, my sweetheart, what happiness has been ours! It seems wonderful to me to look back upon.

8th November '15

Had a final inspection of the men this morning, checking rifles and bayonets principally. They will get them mixed up though their innocence of any such thing is simply sublime. I had to 'strafe' them a bit come the last and have promised them the most diabolical punishments if they get up to the same tricks at the front. They seemed rather pleased than otherwise. But they are like that. Promise them a regular hell of a time in France and you can't please them better. Their keenness to go is marvellous and I trust it will hold when they get there. They are topping fellows and I do hope we can bring the most of them back with us.

This afternoon the CO declared a half holiday as B and C Company were playing off the battalion final at soccer.[ii] It was 'some' match. Rivalry ran terrifically high and we all expect to hear of several fights tonight. B lost 1–nil. It was a splendid game, the best any of us have seen on the

i A 'Miss Guillet' attended the wedding in 1909 of May's sister Lillian as a bridesmaid.
ii The 22nd (or 7th City) Bn was now commanded by Lt Col. Paul W. Whetham.

Plain. The men were simply wild about it, and I am afraid it cost a certain company commander, who ought to have known better, rather more hard cash than he cares to think about in cold blood.[i]

The mess is in great form tonight. Everyone is in except the CO, Merriman and Knudsen,[ii] who are all three spending this last evening with their wives. They have their farewells yet to do. I do not envy them, poor chaps, nor their womenfolk. Mrs Knudsen was up at the match this afternoon and I got her to give the prizes. She came into the mess afterwards and wished us all goodbye. It was rather an ordeal for her. We promised to bring [her husband] back safely for her and I sincerely trust we shall.

All our fellows are in hilarious mood, singing and joking no end. They are a grand lot and as I look at them I can't help feeling proud of our old battalion and the men who've made it. They are all so clean-cut and English as you know so well, my own, I feel confident they'll go when the chance comes. Please God the 22nd may carry the old Regiment's name another rung up the ladder of fame.

They have me on to make a bit of a speech tonight at mess when proposing the King's health. I wish they wouldn't do these things. It is one of the chief trials a senior officer has to face. I always make such a hash of speeches. Go red and hum & hah and generally look a perfect ass. However, 'faint heart never won fat turkey', so I shall have to go through with it.

All the transport has gone now with the machine gun[s] etc. Our kit has been taken with the former so we are reduced to what we stand up in and must endure the horrors of a floor-board couch for the first time for some months. There is some proverb about hard work softening the roughest couch, I believe. I am unfortunate. I have had an easy day.

i May had been transferred to the command of B Coy, having at first commanded A Coy. He clearly lost a wager on the result of the match.
ii Maj. Frank Boyd Merriman; 2nd Lt Orric Joures Knudsen.

9th November '15

We have not gone yet. That is the one and only item to be recorded today . . . Yet how near we were!

The right half Battalion paraded and marched off at 11.40 a.m. and had progressed as far as 600 [yards] from camp when a whistle blew and we were recalled.

How flat we felt and how everyone swore!

I understand that the bad weather in the Channel is the reason for the delay. It breaks the mines loose and you run on them and get blown to blazes.

I am sorry for the rest of the Brigade.[i] It has already preceded us and I can picture whole regiments lying in puddles on the quayside with only the howl of the wind and the pattering rain-drops to sing them a lullaby. That sounds quite melodramatic. But I bet it is all that and more for the poor beggars.

We now go tomorrow at 5.30 a.m. Reveille 3.30. Bow-wow! It is hardly worth going to bed and I wouldn't but that I had so little slumber last night.

The men I am afraid won't sleep at all. They are now busy singing, 'When this b..... war is over we'll be there . . .' I am afraid some of them will get drunk, which will mean a rotten tour in the morning dark for company officers. That, however, is all in the game.

Countess Brownlow[ii] has sent all the mess little pocket writing pads today. Very neat and very welcome. I am exceedingly pleased with mine. It was just the thing I wanted but couldn't find. I have already written you the first note on it and have no doubt but that I will finish the pad on you, my dear girlie.

I wonder what you are doing tonight and of what you are thinking. My darling soul, when shall we meet again. When will the time come that we can once more set up our home and recommence our life of

i 91st Bde, then a unit of the 30th Div.
ii Adelaide, Countess Brownlow, the lady of Belton House, near Grantham, where the battalion was in training.

utter happiness. Ah, Maudie, how little I realised where happiness lay till this old war came along and it was denied me. How limited is a man's mind. It does not allow him to enjoy life in the present but only to realise what moments have meant to him by looking back on them when they have passed. At any rate it has been so with me.

8.45 p.m. Fresh orders have just arrived. The 5.30 a.m. idea is now off and we do not move till 11.40. Thank heaven for its mercies and also for the forethought which led me to sneak the Second-in-Command's blankets after he had left yesterday. I look like having a warm night's sleep after all.

10th November '15

At last we are under way. But our journey is destined not to be a straight-forward one.[i]

We came like birds as far as Folkestone, even to the pier of that town. But there we stopped. A Scotch major met us with the announcement that the Channel is closed and that we must stop the night in Folkestone billets.

A long march out into the night is the result with a longer halt on the Leas[ii] where the wind blows chill and people say nasty things about the Army in whispers. The men were great. Never a murmur out of them after they had been warned that all was to be treated as night operations.

Our billets were eventually allotted and we got the fellows into several large empty houses – 150 in each. They are right as trivets.[iii] We officers dropped on a top-hole billet also. A large boarding house where guests were *non est* before our advent.[iv]

i The battalion shouldered arms at twelve noon and marched to Amesbury railway station, where trains had been assembled. It de-trained in Folkestone at 6 p.m.
ii The Leas is a flat expanse of public garden along the summit of the cliffs at Folkestone.
iii Meaning in perfect health.
iv The men were billeted in unoccupied lodgings in Marine Parade on the seafront where they had 'a very uncomfortable night without food or fire' (Tawney, 11.11.15). The officers stayed in the Devonshire House Hotel.

They hunted up steak and chips for us and what with this and a whiskey and soda to wash it down, we are happy as bugs in a blanket and quite satisfied with the war up to now. Don Murray, D. S. Murray[i] and myself share a room where we have sheets and a *cheval* glass.[ii] Corn in Egypt, I have not known such luxury since I left you, my sweetheart, and it has a most heartening effect upon one.

Especially is this so after my journey down. I came with Major Merriman and he, poor fellow, is rather depressing. I think he is obsessed with the idea that he is going to be shot. He is rather mournful about everything. I am no good in that attitude. The rest of the boys are so bright, God bless them. And yet I have no doubt but what the chances are the same for all of us.

If we don't get away tomorrow I am going to try and find Miss Carey's[iii] and see her for you. I'd be tickled to death to meet her after all you have told me of her.

i Capt. Donald Murray; Lt David Stanley Murray.
ii A *cheval* glass mirror is one in which the glass is mounted on side-swivels inside a frame.
iii Most likely a family friend who lived in Folkestone.

Chapter 1
'And all because it is war!'

11–27 November 1915

11th November '15

At last we are in France! We had no word in Folkestone of what they wanted us to do until 3 p.m. Then it came in a hurry that we were to embark at 4 p.m. A rush and a hurry and then the job was done, the whole battalion getting aboard intact. It was a good passage till about ten minutes out from here but then we ran into the rain.[i] At 3.30 p.m. the battalion finally sailed, with destroyer escort, for Boulogne.

What rain! Bow-wow. And it must have been going all day. They have put us into tents on the top of a hill and the whole place is a quag with running streams feet deep all about it.[ii]

i 'We [have] had wretched weather since our departure from England, but were lucky to have a very easy crossing, the sea being fairly calm – the only thing to mar it was the rain, which didn't half come down, and made me feel sorry for the men as the whole battalion was huddled together on the deck' (Lt William Ellis 'Gommy' Gomersall, 14.11.15).
ii After disembarking at Boulogne the battalion marched up a hill for a night under canvas at the 'rest camp' at Ostrahove. With no boards in the tents, the rainwater was able to flow through in streams.

We are soaked to the skin and cheery as the devil. Cotton, Don Murray, Bowly[i] and myself are in one tent all cuddled up close together for warmth. 10.20 p.m.

Townsend[ii] has just poked his head under the flap and asked for shelter. The CO's tent has blown down and its three occupants are hunting for homes. We have taken Towny in and he is now cheerily pessimistic, wondering why he joined the Army and expressing the wish that his mother could see him now.

We are a happy party, even though wet.

My stars, what strange creatures men are. Six months ago and half these fellows would have been half dead with less than half this dampness and now here we are happy as Larry and busily preparing for sleep. And all because it is war!

12th November '15, 8.10 a.m.

What a night it has been! Rain in torrents and a gale which sent the camp dustbins hurtling along the ground to fetch up with a bang against the sides of various tents, the occupants of which thereupon effectively contrived to make the night yet more hideous by heartfelt and lurid cursing.

Twice we had to get up and re-peg down our frail home, but at length we got it more or less secure and were able to get to sleep.

The men have stood it very well and everyone is cheerful this morning in the chill, dry breeze.

We officers are being cared for in the Salvation Army hut where the two young women in charge have proved good Samaritans indeed, getting Bowly and myself hot tea and some warm water wherein to wash. We already had gruesome shaves in our tents and now feel fit as fiddles.

---

i 2nd Lt Hugh Stapleton ('John') Cotton joined the colours after the initial records of each company had been made; Lt Reginald Walter Bowly, nicknamed 'Bubbles'.
ii Adjutant, Capt. John Edward Townsend.

I believe we leave here at 9.30 for a 48 hours train journey.[i] We hear a rumour we go to the Argonne. If so, the St Omer tale falls heavily to earth.

[Later]

Neither Argonne nor St Omer has materialized but we are here, off the beaten track, but close to Amiens and within thirty miles of the new Arras front, for which we are destined. We have had a truly awful day. It has, of course, rained but that is a minor evil now. The train journey was slow and uncomfortable but at length we got to Pont-Remy. There we started to march and there the fun began. The men were beat. A night with no sleep and soaked to the skin they had little heart for a twelve mile slog, overloaded as they were.

Then the guides took us three miles wrong and we had to about turn just at dusk. No one knew where we were for or how to get there, the guides being a pair of damn fools. However, the CO got us right at last and we went slowly forward again.

I handed B over to Don Murray and was sent to the rear with the doctor.[ii] Don Murray did well. He is a good chap for his job.

The Doc & I have had an appalling time.[iii] He is a regular nailer is the

i The following morning the battalion marched down into Boulogne to board a train. The journey for most, via Etaples and Abbeville, was in cattle trucks labelled '32-40 hommes ou 6 chevaux'. There were no ordinary passenger carriages available, except first-class, which were reserved for officers.
ii The battalion's medical officer, Lt George Barbour McGregor.
iii 'The rear was brought up by May and the Doctor mounted, and for the remainder of the march I followed in the car, the big headlights showing up all the derelicts, who were whipped on and spurred by May's wonderful personality . . . We threw a searchlight over the remains of a worn-out battalion. They were willing to lie down anywhere and die, but May pushed them up and on, and up and on they went, staggering through the mud, desperate and lost souls . . . The last of our merry troupe got in about 11.30 and just fell like logs in the stables and barns which constitute their billets' (Capt. Albert Edward 'Bill' Bland, 13.11.15).

Doc and I admire him from the bottom of my heart.

The men fell out in bunches till at last we were left on an open plain with 60 footsore men, separated from the battalion and utterly lost.

I bet there will be some grey hairs to show for the night's adventure. The men were so done that they sneaked away from us and hid where they could lie down in the wet and sleep. We dug 'em out and booted them on and in the end we got here, bringing every straggler with us.[i]

I hope I may long be spared a similar tour.

Don & I are now billeted in a large French house from which the family is absent, and are happy as Larry now the day is over.

13th November '15

A busy and a good day. It has not rained. Let that be noised abroad. Our village is small and poor on the whole but we have sorted out good billets for both officers and men. The latter for the most part are in lofts and barns with plenty of dry, warm straw to lie on.

They are well fed and rested & the trying tour of yesterday is now only a memory to be talked about to wondering friends and relatives when the war is over and the beer of peace foams in the pewters in the hostel of their local village.

Don Murray and I are in clover.[ii] This billet is all right. And we have turned the dining room into the Coy mess room, a purpose it serves admi-

i The location was Brucamps, at which the transport and machine-gun sections under Maj. Charles Moubray Allfrey had already arrived. It is unclear why May so often refers to Brucamps in his diaries with such a bitter memory.

ii The officers were fortunate to be billeted in the farmhouses. 'I am extraordinarily happy, simply bursting with riotous spirits. We are living like lords at the rate of 1/- a day. The one thing lacking is shell fire. I shall not achieve the real thrill till I get within the sound of the guns and the phut-phut of the rifle and the glorious ping of the bullet that whirrs past like a singing whipcord. This is not blather. I mean it' (Bland, 13.11.15).

rably. We are all foregathered in it this evening writing letters etc. and are a cheery party. Murray, Bowly, Cotton, Shelmerdine and Prince are all here.[i] Young Shel did jolly well yesterday, so Murray tells me. He is our Mess President and is full of eggs and the price of fowls at the moment.

I have put your photo and Baby's on the mantelpiece in our mess and they look jolly homely, my sweetheart. Tonight I have written you and am mighty glad to say I had two letters and a watch case from you last night.

This village is quite quaint and its inhabitants more so. For the most part they are hairy, dirty, baggy-breeched and in *sabots*. They have not had the English before but they evince no interest at all. Seemingly they have no interest left in life than the driving of an odd cow or two out on to the hillside to graze. Poor devils. I always understood the French were characteristically clean and neat. But I am sure you could not find a village in England where the occupants are so really grubby.

My bed I must put on record. It is wooden framed, stands against a wall and has a mattress over a foot thick. There is a lovely soft pillow and a warm quilt. The fat pillow arrangement which lies on top I have cast aside because I mistrust it. It looks as though it might work on to your face and try to smother you. Over this massive arrangement hang heavy, cretonne curtains, flowered with a mystic red and yellow flower. I think this must be native to France. Certainly I never saw such a repulsive species of flora in the British Empire. It has its advantages however because the sight of it makes me hot – and warmth is very desirable in this chilled atmosphere.

14th November '15

Sunday. Church parade at 10 a.m. in an old, broken-down Church with nothing inside it save damp and mildew.[ii]

i 2nd Lt Joseph Armitage Shelmerdine; Lt John Franklin Prince.
ii 'This ruined shell-battered church, with gaping holes in the roof and only the tumbledown walls standing. But I shall never forget the service and its

Afterwards, we toured the Coy billets and had to strafe some of the men for having them untidy. For the most part, though, they were quite good although a lot of the men are pretty sorry for themselves, thinking straw but a poor bed. They may, however, be thankful they are doing so well and I have no doubt will fully realise this before we are many months older. Many of them realise it now and are thoroughly enjoying themselves while they may.

Prince is laid up with bad neuralgia and toothache. The day before yesterday cracked him up and he is pretty dicky today. I am very nervous about him because, as you know, I never thought him strong and I am afraid he will prove a weakness if we have hard slogging to do. It is a pity, because he is such a good boy when he is in form.

We have had Bethmann, our interpreter, to lunch today. He is a very decent chap and works hard. We like him. Also he is a good man to keep in with because he has all the arranging of billets etc. – and B Company is not averse to a decent billet when one is going.

We strolled around the village this afternoon and thoroughly explored it. On the top of the hill east of the place there is a great crucifix hanging over in the wind and looking very desolate and sad. Just below it is a hovel or two standing in its attendant heap of manure. These heaps are the chief – at any rate they are the most obtrusive – features of the landscape. They assail the nostrils at every turn and are prolific to a degree. Every house has one, and the bigger the house the larger its heap. Pride of place seems to go with the magnitude of one's dung-heap. Every man to his own taste, of course. This one, however, certainly strikes a mild outsider like myself as strange.[i]

---

beauty, away over here amongst a land of strangers and so near the common enemy' (Gomersall, 14.11.15).

i 'The battalion receives orders at the last moment from the Brigade which receives orders at the last moment from Headquarters, to occupy a certain area . . . The battalion marches into or nearly into its appointed village, the Interpreter follows exhausted on a bicycle, O.C. Companies ride on and around and do their best with no French on their tongue tips, while the battalion stands

Doc, who is Scotch, calls these heaps 'middens' and curses them unceasingly. He swears we will all die of typhoid if we remain here a week. The well from which the battalion water is drawn he looks upon as chief drain to the collective 'middens' and he chlorides of lime like fury. The well, by the way, only fills a dicksie (two galls.) in four minutes, and since it takes about 100 dicksies per day to make tea for the battalion and another 100 or so to fill the watercarts, you will understand that everyone does not look on the well with the same degree of antagonism as does the Doc. It is a splendid thing to put a defaulter on to. One day's turning of that handle will cure a man of the most divers evils.

15th November '15

The ground was white as far as one could see this morning with the bare trunks standing out black against it and the frosty sunlight glistening on the snow. Three inches had fallen in the night to the sorrow of all save sundry small boys who whooped and bellowed outside my window and threw snowballs at everyone and became a general nuisance.

The battalion went out for a route march under Seconds-in-Command, leaving Coy commanders with fatigue parties to try and get their houses in order. It was a problem fraught with many pitfalls for the unwary. My own especial *bête noir* was drainage.

This village is innocent of any such modern fastidiousness as a sewer. Indeed everything drains back on you, not away as any ignorant Anglican might suppose.

I have seen sinks dug, planned gutters here and erected dams there,

---

and shivers and pretends to be happy. Then the various companies are marched . . . to various cosy nooks or draughty corners, and after considerable adjustment involving much marching . . . settle down. Then the Officers look around for the said rooms in the said houses, and are quite glad to shed their packs in the first handy place that offers . . . While the Officers are securing their billets, the men clear the village of cigarettes and chocolate. They can always find enough French for that!' (Bland, 5.12.15).

and striven generally and with moderate profanity till the impossible has been achieved. Water has been persuaded beyond a higher level and my cookers now stand on a more or less dry foreshore.

Also we have dug a bath and built seats round it and a soak-hole for the water which is no longer pellucid. So altogether we have progressed and, so encouraged, I begin to feel some confidence that, did we remain here long enough, the mud might be persuaded to leave the village street.

Dear, old, tax-ridden, law-abiding England! How I would delight to see one of your wolf-nosed sanitary inspectors turned loose in this, our Brucamps.[i] How you would sniff, how snort, how elevate your highly educated proboscis! How you would storm, how shriek and how summons! And how masterly indifferent would our grubby people be of you, how little would they be impressed, how hopelessly insane they would think you, and what grave danger there would be of a second Revolution if you or any untold number of you essayed to remove from them their beloved dung-heaps.

16th November '15

More snow greeted us this morning. It is about six inches deep now and the fall continued up to lunch time. It makes the district look very beautiful and, but for the slush underfoot, would constitute no nuisance, since the temperature remains quite mild.

I sent the Coy out under Murray for a march which warmed the men up and, having rescued an ambulance wagon and an ASC [Army Service Corps] lorry from two separate drifts away out in the country, they come back very pleased with their morning's labours and looking very red-faced and healthy withal.

It has been a day of settling claims for billet damages. I think the French peasantry have Hebrew blood in their veins in degrees of varying intensity. They claim 30 francs for firewood. You offer five and eventually after Madame has dissolved into tears, and protested by various saints

i During the march from Pont-Remy to Brucamps the guides lost their way.

her inability to supply firewood of less than two *sous* the stick, you settle for ten amid a shower of mutual protests of undying affection.

Prince is about again and looking much better. I am very glad because we move tomorrow and it would have been hard luck on him to have been left behind. Also now he can take his Platoon, which is altogether desirable.

As I say, we move. But whither I know not. It is a strange feeling this of being moved about an unknown country like pieces on a chess-board as helpless as they to control our movements and as ignorant of why and wherefore. Yet it has its advantages. It saves worry. One gets into a regular happy-go-lucky way of looking at things, conscious only that one will fetch up somewhere all right and that we will get to the trenches just so soon as the master player decides that we are wanted.

17th November '15

As anticipated we moved today and, in passing, struck some of the most vile roads one could imagine. The snow had deteriorated on the fairway to a thick slush which made the going heavy and penetrated the stoutest boots. It also has, up to now, defeated the efforts of the heavier transport vehicles to get here but we have rounded up the lighter ones and the men have been fed and are too tired to worry about the lesser trouble of an absence of blankets.

We started out for St Vaast but found that, on arrival, to be in the possession of an Ammunition Column and no room left for us. We had, therefore, to hump on to this little village [Fremont] where we have been rewarded by finding comfortable billets and a most hospitable country folk.

We B officers are billeted in on old farmhouse whose good dame is full of tender felicity for '*le pauvre soldat Anglais*'. Her son is a trooper in the *Chasseurs* and has been at the war since August 1914.[i] She is a really kindly soul and is doing her utmost to make us as comfortable as

i The French Army had raised twelve regiments of *Chasseurs à Cheval*, to form a light cavalry unit.

15

circumstances permit and now we are all sitting round the tiled kitchen with a roaring fire rushing up the chimney, thawing ourselves out and talking shocking French to the inhabitants. Shocking that is with the exception of Shelmerdine. He is very good at the game and I am afraid we will be rather lost when he leaves us and will run grave danger of obtaining lamp oil when we ask for jam.

Cotton has just made a sound remark. 'We who are nearest the firing line,' he says, 'Know least about the war.' It is sound, is that. We know nothing. And we have had no news of the progress of events for more than a week. It came as quite a shock to me to realise it. I have not thought of the actual fighting for days. How different to when we were in England and *The Times* came every morning. Then we were greatly concerned with what was going on down the road. Now we do not trouble. We are too busy.

18th November '15

Another trek today. Up whilst the moon was still in possession, with a wash in a bucket in the farmyard in water from which the ice had to be broken before we could use it. Then *petit dejeuner* of bread and butter and the finest *café au lait* one could wish for, prepared by our good friend Madame *de la ferme*. Afterwards came a ripping march over frozen roads through a freezing air to these our present quarters [at Raineville].

We rest here, I believe, for four days. It has some pretensions as a village but is only really more or less of a large collection of mud and wattle buildings surrounding an untold number of 'middens'. The men are snug enough in straw strewn barns but we officers have struck rather a bad patch as regards chambers though so far as comfort is concerned we are not doing badly. We are in a peasant's cottage, Murray, Bowly and myself have commandeered wood and are now sitting in an inglenook thawing ourselves and scratching notes by the feeble light of a tallow candle. Our rations stand on the table – some bacon, two chickens, several loaves and a tin of jam. With the candle, stuck in an empty baccy tin, shedding its flickering light on them, with Bowly asleep in his chair and Don Murray bent over his letter pad, both so familiar and yet so strange in these meagre surroundings, it all seems to me unreal and at the same time familiar. Unreal because of my comfort loving companions, familiar because so d'Artagnan soldiered as did Micah Clarke and the one and only Sir Nigel.[i]

I had a letter from you today. A very welcome letter, breathing as it did of you and Baby and home and all dear, clean English things in this new land where dirt and stinks seem the accepted companions of the populace and where comfort is not even slightly understood.

19th November '15

A more or less uneventful day in billets. Getting them in order, with all the little odd arrangements which make so much for comfort, takes a long time and considerable thought but there is not a deal to show for them afterwards and really nothing to record. One thing, however, worthy of note is the way in which the men have come on in the way of making themselves comfortable. Mostly town-bred, they were slow at first to see that men can live in comparative comfort in the most unpromising circumstances but they learn with avidity and in another week or so the oldest campaigner will be able to tell them little indeed.

As yet they still lose things – lose them at a most appalling rate – but they are now getting into trouble for it, which brings it home, and I feel sure there will be little lost from now on.

20th November '15

This has been a red letter day. Worthy[ii] and I have been to Amiens, bought some tobacco and indulged in a civilized lunch off a clean table-cloth.

i References to: *The Three Musketeers* by Alexandre Dumas, *Micah Clark* by Sir Arthur Conan Doyle and *Sir Nigel*, also by Conan Doyle, a swashbuckling story set during the Hundred Years' War.
ii Capt. Thomas Ryland Worthington.

How one appreciates such little things after one has been denied them even for the short time we have.[i]

Amiens, as a city, we were not impressed with, its cathedral, as a cathedral, we were – greatly. It is indeed a lovely edifice and one which I sincerely trust may be spared the fate of Rheims. Its altar and rose windows I can recommend to any man who has an hour to spare and desires elevation of the soul.

If he also desires bodily comfort he may go to the *Hôtel de la Paix*, lunch there and come away satisfied. It was some lunch they gave us and I record it amongst my choicest memories. Worthy ran very near to making a beast of himself on it and the waiter was obviously relieved when at length we called for the bill. Three francs fifty perhaps did not leave a great margin of profit when two hungry devils like us are suddenly introduced to a lunch. But, even so, I do not think a really properly trained *garçon* would display palpable relief at its termination. I can only think, therefore, that the French have engrained mercenary instincts.

21st November '15

A day of slight disaster. The field cashier was at Brigade HQ for officers to draw what pay they could. We all requisitioned, but when Bland came back he had everyone's cash but B Coy's. The reason is that we sent in the wrong form. I had somehow taken it down incorrectly. How, I do not know; but it is most distressing and all the more so since it reduces

i 'On Saturday the CO agreed that three officers a day may be allowed to go [to Amiens]. On Sunday was published a Divisional Order, forbidding any officer or man to journey thither except on purely Regimental business. To make it the more tantalising, on Saturday morning the whole battalion went along the Roman Road that links us to the said city, and we reached a spot where it lay visibly two miles away – and then about-turned and marched home again, our tongues hanging out of our mouths, our bones turned to water' (Bland, 23.11.15).

us to the painful necessity of borrowing from the more fortunate others. This we have done with success and are now suffering from an excess of sorrow – for those who have trusted us.

22nd November '15

Another uneventful day so far as general interest is concerned. Just the usual Brigade Route march for the battalion during the day and the usual unfruitful tour round the byways after dark in search of wood for the fire at which we are wont to thaw our feet before retiring. It is not our fault that we take the spare wood of the village in this clandestine fashion. One must be warm. That is unanswerable. Yet the people are so constituted that they will not sell their beloved *bois*. Then, what would you? To see an otherwise honest and respectable English gentleman, sneaking stealthily from one shadowy wall to another and flitting swiftly across the open spaces where the moonbeams flicker, with a large and cumbersome fence post under his arm, is not a sight one of a strict moral rectitude similar to my own, can look upon with equanimity, but when one is reduced to a choice between witnessing it or enduring the sensation of slowly freezing from the feet up, not to mention the other minor disadvantage of becoming the possessor of an enduring dew-drop, one is liable to find oneself weak. And certainly I confess that as the flame leaps joyously upwards from our stolen fuel it thaws into non-existence the last ice of my own honesty.

23rd November '15

It seems to me that one or two little remarks of the men, heard *en passant*, are worthy of record here and today seems propitious for writing them down, there being an absence of news more suitable for inclusion in this my notebook.

One fed-up one, writing home, expresses his opinion of this fair land thus, 'I can't imagine why the Germans want this country. If it was mine, I'd give it to them and save all the fuss.' Evidently a man of personality that, a man who judges from what he sees rather than from what he hears.

Overheard near the cooker, 'Well I hopes as how they'll fight the next blinking war in England and give a swotty a "chanst" to do the decent by hisself.'

The next was in answer to a young fellow who was grousing at the food, which is excellent and, for active service, plentiful. 'Rotten grub! You don't know you're alive. I once lived on potatoes for a fortnight, and got worms.' The relevance of the penalty may not be quite apparent but the retort had the wholesome effect of silencing the grouser, and of adding to the gaiety of the remainder of the assembly and must therefore be appreciated for its efficacy.

We had our first dose of gas this afternoon – and are somewhat disappointed. It is not at all exciting. One merely pulls on a helmet, which smells abominably and which causes an otherwise decent battalion to at once assume the aspect of horrible ogres near which it would be criminal to bring any highly strung infant, and walks solemnly through a house filled with a yellowish atmosphere.[i]

There is nothing in it and this fearsome 'gas', which has been held up as our *bête noir* these months past and which previously we have not been able to think of with that perfect equanimity so desirable in a soldier, assumes on close contact merely the proportions of a beastly nuisance. And that mainly because it necessitates one confining one's manly headpiece within an unbecoming and smelly flannel bag.

24th November '15

A calm day which terminated in an evening of excursions and alarms. At 5.30 p.m., when all had been dismissed, and we were busy discussing

i 'We had a lecture on gas helmets and then were deliberately "gassed", the whole battalion passing through a room filled with the strongest possible chlorine mixture, helmets on of course' (Bland, 24.11.15).

our evening meal, came orders that the battn would move in half an hour. A sudden overturning of tea tables, a stamping and a rushing, quick orders in the darkness and the sound of running feet, lanterns twinkling here and there and the sound of heavy wheels of the transport commenced to move. Then gradually dark lines of men began to form in the roadways, a quiet roll-call and a quiet proving, then silence – and we were ready. The watches stood at 6.10 p.m.

Forty minutes to clear a battalion, lock, stock and barrel from their scattered quarters into a formed body capable of being handled and able to move to wherever it was wanted. It being a first attempt, we were pleased with it, even to the CO.

In the end we were dismissed and went back to billets to discuss it all over a bottle of the wine of the country, in the emptying of which we were joined by D. S. Murray and Worthy who also stayed and shared our hash at mess.

Afterwards we held a glee party, singing all the old songs of Morecambe, Grantham and Lark Hill.[i] It made some of us feel quite homesick. One is a trifle inclined to sentimentality here. I suppose it is that we English are such home birds really and not at all the adventuresome roamers we are popularly put down to be.

25th November '15

Well, they have come at last, the definite orders to move. And, strangely enough, they have brought no excitement with them. Interest is the chief note, interest in what the work will be really like, how we shall manage and how much we shall learn. This eagerness to learn is the predominant note among the officers who are one and all keen to get *au fait* with their job.

The idea is a splendid one. The battalion splits up into four companies each of which is attached to a regular battalion for a week in the fire trenches. The main object being instruction [in trench warfare] – an

i The three training locations before embarkation for France.

object which suits us down to the ground and with which we are in the most hearty agreement.[i]

I wrote you a long letter tonight telling you all about it, but the post has suddenly ceased and you will not therefore hear from me till we are about half-way through our excursion. On the whole I am glad. You would, I know, only worry did you know I was under fire.

Tonight I censored a letter from one of my sergeants.[ii] He is distinctly a character. A Don of Balliol, a lecturer at the London Varsity, he enlisted as a Tommy. It is no doubt fine to think of but it is also 'an economical waste', as Earles[iii] used to say. Months ago I tried to get him to take a commission but he had views of his own and I doubt not but that he is happy where he is. He talks French fluently and is already great friends with the villagers. In his letter he told how sad the women are here. All their men are gone, they are within sound of the guns and all they can

i 'This afternoon after work, I have arranged a football match for the platoon, and how they will enjoy it. These Lancashire lads on the plain here in France will play a right hard game of the game they love, with no spectators to cheer – just the artillery roaring its continuous applause' (Gomersall, 25.11.15).

ii Pte Richard Henry Tawney had by now been promoted sergeant. Censorship was mandatory (by the Defence of the Realm Act, 1914) and the responsibility of junior officers. It is remarkable how the letters home of Bland and Tawney have, on occasion, clearly escaped censorship, but in Bland's case it may have been because he was sometimes the censor. Gomersall was more cautious, and May indicates here that he is a censor. The procedure was that at 8 p.m. the censored mail would be taken by orderly to Brigade HQ, then on the next day to Divisional HQ and then to the GPO in the field before shipment to England. Generally, the uncensored letters from England travelled to France in a shorter length of time, which was sometimes just two days. 'Censorship is like all things organised by England – a wonderful combination of organised effort and individual fatuity,' joked Bland (29.6.16).

iii Capt. Francis John 'Frank' Earles. His departure for France was delayed due to a minor injury, and his position as officer in command of D Coy was taken temporarily by Capt. Charles Mostyn Lloyd.

do is work on and wait. It is dreadfully sad for the women, this war and I think it is our realisation of this and of your quiet heroism that makes us love you as we do. At least I know I feel like that about you, my own.

For us the work and the excitement. For you the waiting and suspense. I know well which must be the easier to bear.

The guns are quiet tonight. It is the first time for days. There has been some little festival in the village and two weddings and the people have been indulging in a minor Morris Dance. They are simple and they are kind – when they know you, and I hope with all my heart the guns may never come nearer Raineville than they are now. Rather I trust in heaven that their war may go forward to the German border and over, that their thundering may reverberate through the streets of Rhineland towns and villages and cause the startled light of fear to leap up in the eyes of fatuous burghers that these may be repaid in kind for all the suffering their horrid country has brought to this 'fair' France and her fairer sister, our England.

26th November '15

It has been a day of preparation, of issuing the last few items to complete the company, of getting out the leather waistcoats and the skin coats and seeing all the final equipment is in order.[i]

And was ever an Army equipped like this one? My God. What we must cost the country. What taxation we must mean. How I hope we are worth it. It seems terrible, the cost. Yet, I suppose, it is really quite cheap if only it means a nail in Germany's coffin. And anything which will help our men to stick the winter well means that. The Germans don't like the snow, I believe.

We have just said good-bye to Grimwood, D. S. Murray and Wood.[ii]

---

i 'I have my large oilskin, rubber gloves, rubber trench waders which cover my legs right up to the hips, so I am all right and very warm and dry' (Gomersall, 30.11.15).
ii 2nd Lts Herbert Grimwood and John Patrick Hamilton Wood.

The battalion splits up tomorrow and will not meet again for a week – and that is rather a long time these days. We have all promised to meet in our rest billets and compare experiences. We should know a great deal more than we do now by then and our meeting should be an instructive one.

Townsend's poor brother in the 18th was killed today.[i] He was bombing officer and was put out by a hand grenade, whilst instructing a class. It is damned hard luck, I knew him well, a keen, young chap, rather delicate but a promising officer. It has rather knocked the guts out of Towny and he looks very ill on it. Poor old boy, his 'young brother' was a great chap with him.[ii]

However, Kismet. I wish he had had a chance though.

27th November '15

It made us quite homesick this morning. The motor-bus was waiting at 9.30 to take us to 'business'.[iii] It felt most strange bumping along through the frosty air with all around looking peaceful and comfortable and with nothing at all but joy in the morning and no sign of war at all. But it was cold. We lost all feeling on top of our bus and when at last we were compelled to get down had momentarily lost control of our legs.

They had intended taking us to Varennes but we were stopped three

i Lt Arthur Evans Townsend, brother of the battalion adjutant Capt. John Edward Townsend. During bombing practice a sergeant from A Coy, 18th Bn, Manchester Regt, had thrown a grenade which struck the top of a parapet and exploded into a trench. As a result Sgt Perkins and Pte Bagnall were killed and Lt Townsend died of his wounds the next day.
ii 'Poor Townsend. His brother was very brave and bore the news well, but one could see the pain caused by it. Captain Townsend and I of course are great friends – he is "Towny" to me, not Townsend. Strange to say I was only talking a few hours previous to his brother before he was killed, and knew him quite well' (Gomersall, 7.12.15).
iii The journey was made in requisitioned London motor omnibuses which had had their advertisements painted out in battleship grey.

miles short of it because of artillery in action down the road. I think, however, the government were only tired of carrying us for nothing because, though we marched for nine miles after that, we did not see a gun nor hear a shell till we arrived here, Mesnil, about 5.30 p.m.[i] B and D Coys only came on to this fair though unpeaceful spot [where they were attached to the 1st Hampshire Regt], A and C, [attached to the 1st Royal Irish Fusiliers] with battalion HQ remaining at Englebelmer,[ii] some three miles behind. Our billet is a château on the skyline. It has been a glorious place but at present looks somewhat shop-soiled since its back has been blown out, its walls and gardens are loopholed and trenched and the flower beds are interspersed with large shell-craters filled with frozen water. The officers' quarters were once a stable. They are much better than we anticipated and are warm where you miss the draught between the dug-out and the door.

We are quite comfortable and happy and have only had two shrapnel in the garden up to now. But we have, of course, lain doggo as one does after being warned that sight of a man by day or glint of a light by night will bring 9 inch h.e.s [high explosive shells] hurtling in at the back door.

We go into the fire trenches tomorrow and are keen to do so. It is remarkable how everyday and usual it all seems here. I must never breathe a word of it else will not be looked upon as heroes any more by the good people who stay at home and especially by you, my Maudie. Our only trouble are the rats. They swarm and are bold beyond description. They run over you, pinch candles, eat our iron rations and disturb one's attempts at slumber. It is, you will say, but a minor trouble yet it is our greatest up to now.

We are all jolly tired tonight though and I'll bet when we do get down it will take more than rats to disturb us.

i Mesnil-Martinsart was the base of the 1st Bn, the Hampshire Regt. The village was completely destroyed by the end of the war.
ii Englebelmer was the base of the Royal Fusiliers.

Chapter 2
'Mud caked to his eyebrows'

28 November–19 December 1915

28th November '15

I see that last evening I boasted that it would take more than rats to disturb us. I was badly mistaken. They beat us – easily. The trouble was that Bunting[i] had laid my bed across a favourite run of theirs and they did not intend being put off it by a mere intruder like myself.

They ran over my legs, body, chest and feet, and I was adamant. But when they started on my face I must own that I slavishly surrendered, fell to cursing horribly and finally changed my lying place. Thereafter I fared better but Murray dropped in for it. They ate his iron ration and, evidently liking some, which incidentally proves that they are but lowly people, knawed [sic] through Prince's pack and ate his also. I can tell you they are some rats, these.

Well we are here at last, in the fire trenches and are learning our job under the hospitable care of the East Lancs.[ii] We are in the fire trenches

i Pte Arthur Bunting, Charlie May's batman, who, with his cook Pte Richard Smith, had been transferred to B Coy.
ii The East Lancashire Regt, of which one battalion was known as the Accrington Pals.

and I can hardly express how strange it felt to stand on the fire slip for the first time, look out over the plain and see the Bosche trenches just ahead. And it has all struck one as so apparently safe. There is nothing to be seen bar sinuous lines of chalk mounds on the hill-sides. Nothing at all. One hears bangs, or the occasional popping of a Maxim, but one sees absolutely nothing and it is hard indeed to realise the danger, the more especially that our kind friends the East Lancs treat it all so jovially and in such casual fashion. I would not at first believe that the wily Germany lay tucked up just across there. It is only the fact that five men have been hit this afternoon has made me realise it at all.

The last three were out on a reconnoitring patrol when suddenly some bullets pinged past our listening post, the men heard a shriek and in a minute or two the patrol came staggering back. Quite cheerful they were, but a sergeant with a bullet through his foot made their going bad. The Bosche keeps pretty wide awake, evidently.

We are attached to B Coy [of the East Lancs] and the OC of it is a Lieutenant Salt.[i] And well worthy of his [MC] he is. He is really quite a boy and his officers more so but he is older than many in soldiering. He is anyway a great deal older than myself. He has been at it since Mons,[ii] has been three times wounded and now wears the Military Cross. Yet he is most unassuming and diffident of imparting advice. I think he is a fine young fellow and a typical example of the British subaltern.

Murray and I have a dug-out to ourselves. A most pretentious place, lined with gathered silk and possessing an iron bed with a spring mattress. Corn in Egypt. A comfort-loving Frenchman built it for himself when they held the line. They say it leaks. I do not know, since now it is only freezing. But be that as it may, I am much obliged of my unknown pal, the Parisian decorator.

i Lt Wilfred Austin Salt.
ii The first major engagement of the war, the Battle of Mons was fought in August 1914 and resulted in a retreat of the British Expeditionary Force (BEF). The town was finally liberated by the Canadian Army in 1918.

29th November '15

This has been a wet day. Some wet! They were quite right about our dug-out. It does, leak, some leak! In fact a wash out, literally a wash out. It has defeated Murray and myself and we are here in the sandbagged mess-room very cold and very much smoked from the damp wood on our fire, endeavouring to get a wink of sleep before our several turns of duty. But to return to the rain. It has teemed, the trenches are ankle deep – some places calf deep – in mud and water and the communications trenches are rushing streams of brown water. The men are wet through but stick the job like Britons and I do hope for their sake that the weather may lift with the morning.[i]

The Coy has taken over the line tonight on its own for the first time and we are all very bucked about it. The men have done Al and the East Lancs are pleased with them. I am glad indeed, because nothing tells a regiment's efficiency so truly as the unsought opinion of other regiments. The guns have been strafing today no end but up till now we have dodged the show. It may be ours again tomorrow, though. One never knows.

Tonight I messed with the CO [of the 1st Bn, East Lancs][ii] down in Mesnil. He is a fine man and seems to have the happy knack of griping without strafe. He put on a regular beano for dinner, soup, fish, joint, sweets, coffee, dessert. I haven't seen the like since our lunch in Amiens and I did it full justice. It is marvellous how the poor live!

i 'We've seen trenches – carefully built up in the autumn – reduced to a horrible mess by 24 hours' rain. We've been up and down in mud two feet deep and water deeper still. We've had rifle and machine-gun fire and shrapnel whizzing about our ears, and our own heavier shells shrieking high over our heads. We've been turned out at 3.00am. to investigate a report of a German patrol cutting our wire, and I personally have been in a dug-out when a shrapnel shell fell on the roof and burst there. Life in the trenches is just like life in the billets, only much more inconvenient. Fire trenches are wonderfully safe places, and dug-outs simply "dilly"' (Bland, 2.12.15).
ii Col. Thomas Stanton Lambert.

30th November '15

It has been fine today and the sun has even shone. The trenches have therefore dried up considerably and everyone is more comfortable. This morning I had some twenty rounds at the Bosches but whether with luck or not it is impossible to say. I did, however, find two definite ranges and was able to register these.

At this evening's 'stand to' the Germans started heaving more torpedoes at the Jocks[i] on our right and one of my fellows, L/Cpl Rodman,[ii] had the good luck to spot the place where they light the beastly thing. I at once reported it and the heavies are going to give them a dousing tomorrow morning. If it is successful, it will be most welcome and I hope, if only for Rodman's sake, that it is. This evening later there has been a regular exchange of knocks between the artillery. Ours won easily. It was some sight and I was delighted that I witnessed it.

The Bosches brought down one of our aeroplanes within their lines today. Bust 'em. Never mind, it'll be our turn again tomorrow.

1st December '15

We are out of the trenches and back in our dear, draughty but dry billet in the château stables. It has been a good day full of interest but we are all tired and weary from lack of sleep and are therefore thankful to forsake the excitement of the firing line for the quiet and comparative safety of our present sanctum.

About 11 a.m. the Bosches started on our left sector with 'whiz-bangs' and concentrated these in the vicinity of Coy headquarters. They must have dropped thirty round us before noon. At the same time, they sniped us like old boots but we gave them back as good as their own at the latter game and, when our guns commenced, they dealt it out thick and plenty to the Bosche in shrapnel, light and heavy ordnance. It was all

---

i The 2nd Bn, Gordon Highlanders.
ii L/Cpl William George Rodman.

right. The shooting of our gunners is markedly superior to theirs. We drop right on the spot every time but they invariably waste from six to a dozen rounds feeling for theirs. When the good time comes that we have unlimited shell supply, Bosche is in for a thin time indeed. Also our fellows put the wind up several of their snipers, popping bullets all about them till they felt the neighbourhood unhealthy and quitted.

It is exciting work, sniping. In fact one must curb the tendency lest it should become a fascination. The Second-in-Command of the E. Lancs[i] and myself put in a couple of hours this morning at it and had quite a bit of fun worrying the Bosches in their trenches. One fellow was walking across the open 2,000 yards off, when I spotted him and let go. You never saw a chap move quicker in your life. He ran for a tree and jumped behind it and I let him have four more there. Whether I got him or not I don't know but he didn't move for the next half-hour. I know because I waited so anxiously for him.

Last night, or rather at 1.30 a.m. this morning, I got outside the barbed wire to look for a listening post which had lost itself. Naturally I didn't find it. You seldom do, but I got lost myself instead. It was some tour and a bally Bosche Maxim which kept traversing our front added not a little to my perturbation. Three times I had to fling myself down in the wet grass, bury my nose in it and grovel whilst the damn thing went chattering over me. It is remarkable with what speed one learns to introduce celerity into 'adopting the prone position'. The bally post came in at the end of the bottom of the lines and narrowly missed being shot for its pains.

We have no casualties, are quite satisfied and very sleepy, so to bye-byes. Only one thing before we go. The post waited for us on arrival. With what joy we pounced on it. It bucked the most beat of us up into smiles of laughter. Letters from home. What a tremendous lot that sentence means to us. And as for me, your letters are like a breath of spring in that they bring joy and happiness to me. And your photo has come this time also. Thank God for it. I think it is splendid. You look your lovely self, and I feel so proud when I look at it that I can say you

i Capt. Edward Woodgate.

are mine. What with your picture and Baby's, I am happy. No man was ever blest with sweeter womenfolk.

2nd December '15

A quiet day of rest and cleaning up. And much did we appreciate it. We did not wake till 7.30, nor breakfast till 9.30 a.m. A regular treat. Afterwards we rotted [illegible] about, written letters, instituted various improvements for our convenience and generally had a lazy day. This evening three platoons went out, under Murray, trench-digging. They were shelled and it rained very heavily so in the end they came back. Bowly took a section out to put up some wire, got under machine gun fire, and very wet dodging it, so had to come in too. Altogether I am glad I was prevented from going with them. I had to see the E. Lancs about tomorrow's programme and that kept me till fairly late.

Shelmerdine and Prince have gone out to dinner this evening with the men they messed with in the trenches. So we have pinched their fire and am now sitting by it having pigged a Maconochie ration, a tin of sardines, Penau, a pound of jam, a loaf of bread and half a bottle of OO whiskey.[i] We are now fed to repletion and are sitting, well-fed and happy, before our stolen fire yarning and getting more and more sleepy. It is grand to think that you are going to sleep both dry and warm. It fairly braces you. We little appreciate in our ordinary lives what home comforts mean. A man may thank his God every night for his blankets and the good roof over him. Yet I know he won't any more than will I when the war is over and we get back to our firesides, our slippers, sheets, hot toddy, hot water, baths and carpeted floors. It is perhaps easy to philosophize when one has not got them handy but, once one is amongst them, it is damned hard not to take them as only your fair due from the world.

i Château Penau; Double OO – Old Orkney whiskey. Maconochie was beef stew with sliced turnips, carrots and potatoes in a thin soup, tinned and manufactured in Aberdeen.

3rd December '15

It is always a source of wonder to me to watch the power practical experience gives a man when imparting knowledge to others. In my little time I daresay I have been lectured as much as any and more than most by johnnies who have been entrusted with the thankless task of improving my mind. Many of these oases of boredom have endeavoured safely to pass by resort to the strengthening arm of Morpheus,[i] others I have endured with a dull eye and rebellious heart, but I do not remember ever having the faintest desire to sink so low when the man who spoke did so from knowledge born of what he had actually done himself. And Captain Woodgate was like that today when he spoke to us. Much he told us we already knew and there was much which we did not but whether he spoke of familiar or unfamiliar things, he held us just the same because we felt he had done and seen those things of which he spoke. He is a good fellow and a fine man and once again I must record our feeling for the E. Lancs. They have done all they can for us, no trouble has been too much for them and I trust we will all benefit from their example and experiences.

We have finished our paths today. They are broad brick fairways through a sea of mud and are very clean and dry and comforting. Did we stay here a week or two I feel sure the château would become something of home from home. Certainly we have an affection for our stable and as for the old rat who sports about my carcase of a night I feel that he and I would become firm friends in time were it not for his bad habit of pinching our scanty cheese. That one little failing will, however, yet prove his undoing do we but remain here long enough. There is almost an element of sadness in the thought. Sadness, that is, for the rat.

4th December '15

D Company has come out of the trenches today very muddy, very wet but quite cheery and safe. They have had rather a tough time from the

---

i In Greek mythology, Morpheus was the God of Dreams.

rain and trench mortars. The latter have pounded the trenches without cessation for two days but without effecting a single casualty. This afternoon our guns set about them in retaliation and have pounded their lines most unmercifully. I hope they have laid out a few of the beggars.

I got working parties of the Coy. going first thing this morning and cleaned up billets and lit fires for D coming in. Poor devils they were grateful for the job, the fires putting new life into them.

Tomorrow we turf out at 7.45 am to march some 15 miles back. I believe we march on again the next day to reserve billets where I trust we may stay a while and get thoroughly cleaned up.

Tonight I am going to dinner with the CO of the E. Lancs and am looking forward to it. All the other of our officers are pigging with D Company in our billet on tinned grub and whiskey. The E. Lancs fellows are coming up later to say farewell and I have no doubt if we do not watch it but that we will march out of Mesnil with fat-heads in the morning. Never mind, it's worth it when you have bumped into jolly good pals.

5th December '15

Sixteen miles march today [to Puchevillers].[i] And a long sixteen they were, what with wet great-coats, mud-laden, feet still wet and puttees hard-caked with trench clay. Still, we are here now and right for a night's rest in good billets which is a reward one gets to look forward to with amazing keenness. The men are all comfortably tucked down on good, clean straw and the officers are in various cottages with a little mess room in an old lady's cottage. We have a fire, a bottle [of] *vin blanche* [sic] and the old Madame to chatter to us about her boy who is fighting in the Argonne.

It is quite interesting, quite warm and produces in one that grand feeling of happy sleepiness which a hard day's slog always produces.

i The division was moving east and south to take a position on the left of the French Sixth Army.

We have left our good friends the East Lancs but I trust only for the time and that we may meet again one of these fine days. They were most decent to me last evening and I must once more speak of all their kindnesses to us.

Young Shelmerdine has done well again today. He always turns up trumps when it is wanted of him and I think he will do well before this job is over.

We move on again first thing tomorrow morning for another dose but I hope by then we will be finished for a time so that the men may get dry, have a bath and get their clothes cleaned. They do wonderfully, the men, putting up with every inconvenience and discomfort cheerfully and slogging along on their flat feet to the end. The battalion has had a good dose of graft ever since we landed, as good a dose as any could have had but every time it has got [at] them, and that is everything. The Manchesters are all right and the 22nd one of their best battalions.

And now to bed to the sleep of the just. I share my couch with Prince so at least we will be warm.

6th December '15

Another march today [to Candas]. It was only ten miles but it very nearly beat the men, already tired and worn out as they were. Old B got rather messed up this morning through Murray getting mixed over some order about great-coats with the Brigade Sergeant-Major. They got them off for the wagons to carry only to find that idea was off. We therefore had to put them on again, which made us late and the CO left us to follow on by ourselves. This we did to the best of our ability and eventually arrived at this village just on the tail of the battn. The Coy had been near beat but they bucked up to pass the other Coys, swinging along at a great rate and singing. Only we, their officers, knew how done the poor devils were. But they have a good sleep before them tonight and, as we are here for a fortnight at least, we hope to be right as rain and a thoroughly fit battalion before that time is out. And no doubt we shall be.

7th December '15

I stole an hour this afternoon and rode out towards Canaples for a look round and to forget the battalion and the war and for a little time to imagine that you were with me and that we had the open countryside to stroll through as so often we have done in the dear days before all the world were soldiers. It is pretty country out this road, especially to the left where the ground slopes down into a little valley the sides of which are dotted with clumps of larch and birch and other such spidery limbed, delicate trees. I turned off the highway out there and Lizzie and I strolled down the slopes to the valley's foot where we wandered along the edge of the woods cut off from all sight of man's handiwork and with only the wood-pigeons and the magpies for company. It was all damp and clean-looking, fresh and peaceful – one of the few pretty spots I have yet seen in France – and it cleared my head and made me happy and sent me back to my work refreshed.

I thought of you as we strolled there, Lizzie with her reins slack wandering where she would and at her own pace and I longed that you could have been with me, for I know how you would have loved it and how happy we two would have been.[i] The green rides of Epping came back to me in a flash. You in that black spotted muslin dress you used to wear looking cool and lovely so that I just asked nothing more than to walk along and gaze at you dumbly, like any simple country lout gazes at his maid.

It is a strange world. Here I am in the midst of men, of work and dirt and close to fire and steel and sudden death. My heart should be fired with martial ardour, I should have no thought for anything but the fighting I am paid for but instead my whole being is filled to the exclusion of all else with the thought of you, dear heart, of our darling Baby and of the happiness which has been ours.

We are here I hear for about three weeks and already seem to have returned to our wonted routine. The Army is wonderful. One day it strains and strives and fights with blood and noise and dirt predominant,

i The horses had been brought to France on the same boat and train as the men.

the next it returns to all its old starch and buckram and curses a man for a dirty boot whom the day before it had loved though he was mud-caked to his eyebrows in the trenches.

8th December '15

We are now filled with ambition as house builders. Orders have arrived that we are to look out suitable buildings and convert them into fit habitations for *L'Armée Brittanique*, which is to feed, wash and sleep in them at its own sweet will and get strong and dangerous ready for the ever-recurring 'new offensive in the Spring'. It is most interesting, and no end of a problem. We have one hammer per company, the promise of some wood, 25 yards of waterproof canvas for the battalion, a limited supply of chloride of lime, and 12lbs of nails. And thus armed we set forth, [illegible] is ordered, to produce four Ritz hotels replete with every comfort for the soldiers of the King. I ask you! Truly if it is accomplished, as I have no doubt it will be, my admiration for the Army will go up by leaps and bounds. If only we had some bundles of firewood and a screw or two the outlook might be more rosy. But 12lbs of nails, a hammer and 25yds of felt! I ask you!!!ⁱ

i 'We came here yesterday, Tuesday . . . for a few days' wood-cutting. *Encore de picnic* . . . A pleasant march of four miles to a pleasant village teeming with friendly folk. Sunshine and laughter – a holiday, in fact, under the greenwood tree. France is full of little woods, carefully preserved, and they are being most carefully cut; there is, of course, a tremendous demand for wood in the trenches. The need for it was more than obvious. And, as it happens, the stuff our lads are busy with is going to the very part of the line we were in. Nevertheless the powers that be most jealously guard their wood. It is the one commodity that love nor money cannot buy. The villagers simply will not either give or sell what they have. And so, if we need fires we have to burn our ration boxes. Most of our cooking is done with wood, eked out with an occasional spoonful of coal or coke. Here, however, we have struck homely little cottages where all are only too happy to do us any service. They make coffee at odd times;

We have been to see D Company again tonight and have gambled. Naughty boys! Yet somehow I do not feel so naughty as I might have done had I not won 28 *francs*.

9th December '15

The house building continues, but very slowly. Up to now it has been mostly talk. In a day or two, however, we really expect to do something, and, personally, I am consumed with a fiendish desire to use up those 12lbs of nails. I feel that to smite lustily upon a nail would furnish some outlet for the awful amount of energy which is fast accumulating within me and causing me, in common with the rest, to fret and fume at the idleness which is now being forced upon us.

Rumour appears to be rife in Manchester that we, their darling 'Pals', have suffered heavy casualties. Save the mark. I should think it must have originated in some poor devil in another battalion dying of *ennui*. That is the only way I can account for it.

It is raining again. It always rains here. For that reason I can never understand why they haven't a river or two knocking around. But they haven't, nor even a decent stream. I haven't seen running water, save the Somme, since we landed. It is rather remarkable when one thinks of it. They seem quite content with their village ponds, which are apparently kept going by the drainage from the 'middens', and from which the horses and cattle drink, apparently thriving thereon and so producing a somewhat pleasurable example of perpetual motion.

10th December '15

I am something of a hero today. When I have screwed up my courage to a point where it permits one to face officials, who present forms which

———

we use their stoves for our own cooking, they pass round sweets; we share our cigarettes. *C'est une véritable entente cordiale'* (Bland, 8.12.15).

I fill up and sign, always feel that I am. And today I have sent off a parcel to you. That entailed a three mile ride, which was joyous, and an interview with a postal official and yellow forms, which was not. And to think that all this writing and signing was all around nothing more offensive than the poor, little, shell-chipped and harmless statuette of St Joseph which I had brought from the old ruined château, of affectionate memory.

And I got hot and excited about it, entered things in the wrong places and had to rewrite the forms, so that I feel sure I have aroused the suspicions of the post people and it is doubtful if the parcel will ever reach you after all. Oh, dear, it is terrible, this war.

We have orders today that we are to split up as a Division and mix ourselves with others which have been out longer.[i] It is a good thing and shows wisdom in the higher command which decreed it. It means stiffening for us in action and the fillip for the older crowd which the introduction of young, fresh and keen troops always produces.

We don't know when we move yet, and it may not be for a long time but the news is something in that it shows we are not forgotten. It has bucked us all up wonderfully.

I have just heard that I do not get my company back till Monday. Two more days of this sickening idleness. It does not suit me at all. I am like a childless wife, peevish and ill content through having nothing on my hands to look after.

11th December '15

It has rained again today, the 10th day in succession. They say you can get accustomed to anything. Perhaps you can, I do not know. All I can vouch for is that we do not get used to the rain. We only strafe it the more with each succeeding day of humidity. I had your letter today in which you say you have not heard from me since Nov 30th. I cannot understand it unless the Censor has been busy at the Base and I have unwittingly been too communicative.

i This re-allocation of battalions took place on 20.12.15.

Don Murray and I went out into the country by ourselves this afternoon and forgot building operations and rest billets and every other such objectionable thing in trying to shoot crows with our revolvers. Needless to say we did not succeed. But it took us completely out of ourselves and was therefore quite a success.

12th December '15

The doctor came in to see me this morning on his way to Canaples and I decided to saddle up and go with him, the fresh breeze and stronger sunlight of the morning tempting me more strongly than the exhortations of the padre. So off we went, trotting along together down the open road, with the far-flung uplands on either side, the tempting curves of the road to lure us on, the buffeting breeze to set our blood a-tingling and the stronger sun to burn our spirits up with the joy of the morning. With such a morn as this was, with a good nag between his knees, a good friend at his side, with the merry clatter of hoofs in his ear and the open road before him, a man were surely but a common glutton if he asked more in an hour of his life?

We rattled under the railway bridge, where a picturesque but unsoldierly French territorial stood on guard, through Montrelet and Fieffes and so down the valley road to Canaples.

I found Prince there in good form but the others were out cutting wood.[i] Canaples must be noted. It has a stream, let that sink in. Also it

i 'I had to be up early to come to this forest with my men, wood-cutting. All around me is the continuous noise of the hammers, long and short saws, the felling axes and short axes, etc., and the men are not half-enjoying this change of work, which is like a picnic and a fine rest for them. A party of about ten are clearing undergrowth – which is very dense – one mass of young trees entwined in it, and then in the clearing others are sawing trees, others lopping the branches of those fallen, others sawing up trees into yard lengths. We cannot wander in the wood as there are a large number of bears about, and in any case we could not on account of the undergrowth. I have a large fire going,

is the proud possessor of a railway station, two street lamps, a milk refinery and a château. Canaples is some village in these parts and is typically French in that it has a café wherein two young ladies dispense drinks or, just as readily, photographs of themselves in the nude. Truly it is a pleasing country.

It was not possible for me to sample either of the chief wares of the café but I understand it has been overcrowded by my depraved company since the woodcutting commenced and the only reason any of its stock is still in the possession of its proprietors is the acute penury of my high-minded privates, who have not been paid for over a fortnight. I had intended paying them this morning but a wise providence decreed that I should forget the Acquittance Roll. Thus a prolonged moral depravity has by happy chance been avoided.

I have just discovered one reason why streams are so scarce. There are no field drains here, nor any attempt at ditching. Hence when it rains the water just lies on the surface till, in good time, it soaks in. Very simple and very rotten. Even the uplands are a bog.

13th December '15

The Coy has come back and I feel a happier man than I have done for days. They blew in this morning looking dirty and wet and were at once turned loose to clean up & have an easy. And not before they wanted it, I'll be bound. The big majority have not had a half-hour to themselves since they landed in France. I think it a mistake. 'All work and no play' is a very true axiom and I certainly know the men do twice the work after a day's holiday.

Tomorrow I am going to let them have the day to themselves, even

---

on which I burn all the small brushwood . . . The men have an hour off from 12.0 to 1.0, and it was quite a merry party all around the fire yesterday. We stop work at 4.0 after starting at 8.0 in the morning, and march back to our village with rifles, axes, saws and everything. Here the men thoroughly enjoy a good dinner which awaits them' (Gomersall, 16.12.15).

though the general is coming around. That may not be strictly military but it certainly is common sense, a factor one meets remarkably seldom in this game. I may be a heretic, certainly I am wrong to do so, but I cannot help but both see and feel that there is a vast wastage in this army of ours. Not, I mean, of materials or stores – for the distribution of such things is wonderfully organised – but of men and brains. Initiative is asked for, but woe to the man who displays it. Opinions are sometimes sought – but apparently with the sole idea of making an opportunity for the airing of some higher grade's scheme, already settled in his own mind. So that one feels – and somewhat resents it – that there is humbug about and that one is being looked upon as more or less of a fool. One does not like being thought a fool, even though one has no claim to genius.

If I were alone in this I might be thought that unutterable thing – a man with a grievance. But I am not alone. All our officers feel as I do. And when thirty active business brains feel like that surely it were but foolishness to deny justification.[i]

We came out here to fight, not heroically or in the heat of passion, but just to do our little bit like Englishmen should. We did not expect to be satiated with red tape and buckram or have our brains cramped into a hidebound receptacle of blank banality which those of a lad could fill.

There is still something wrong with the Army. I do not think it is with the higher command that the fault lies. Nor can I allow that it is with the company officers. It is with that vast sea of senior ranks, or climbers, that I find the fault and I cannot but believe that there the fault will be found by others more fitted to judge than I.

i Those who volunteered for the Pals battalions often came from the worlds of business, law, academia, education, and from the Officer Training Corps of Public Schools and Universities. May believed they tended to be better educated than soldiers in the Regular battalions.

14th December '15

It has been inspection of kit, cleanliness, rifles, etc. today and if one had been looking for proof of the efficacy of this time-honoured army institution he had only to have seen my dear, dirty Coy at 9 a.m. parade and then look upon them, brushed and cleaned, at 3.30 p.m. The difference in them was simply marvellous though they are by no means properly clean yet. The trenches leave their marks on a man in more ways than one.

We visited C Coy Mess this evening. It was quite a birthday party. Yet there was no real birthday. That, be it whispered, was Rambottom's[i] own unaided invention, and was used solely for the more or less base purpose of beguiling his landlady into letting him entertain his friends up till 10.15pm. Until this night he has been forced to seek his couch at 9.30, his landlady believing in the axiom of 'early to bed' and being a woman of very considerable force of character, which, in Ramsbottom's eyes, is in no way diminished by the fact that she has two charming daughters whom only very respectable young men who go to bed at very respectable hours may converse with. My dear pal Gordon is so awfully susceptible. He confided in me tonight that the young and pretty one had called him her 'cher Capitaine Gordon'. It had made his heart flutter. I advised him in future not to risk his chances by telling horrid untruths to the desired-one's parents.

15th December '15

We route-marched today as a company. The whole of B let loose on a freezing, windy morning when the sun shone and the blood pulsed and one's legs flung out untiringly. It was a most enjoyable little tour through Bonneville and Fieffes. The latter village with its twin, Montrelet, is more charmingly situated than any we have yet met in France. It flaunts red and purple roofs among the brown tree trunks in a most jumbled,

i Capt. Gordon Openshaw Ramsbottom.

picturesque mosaic and its old white church with the square tower and slate roof is quite Scotch in its simple, quaint design. Altogether a charming, little spot and one which in summer must be quite entrancing – viewed always with a respectful aloofness.

Prince very pertinently remarked, as we scrambled down the hillside and feasted our eyes on the ripping little pictures in the valley below, 'What a pity it stinks! And why is it that Art and a drainage scheme never will go together?' I did not answer him, because I could not. Such things are beyond the mental capacity of a plain soldier such as I am.

16th December '15

It is one of the many marvellous virtues of Tommy Atkins that he soon forgets. It is the thing which helps him more than all else to bear his none too rosy lot cheerfully. Therefore I suppose it is a trait everyone should be thankful for. Yet somehow one finds oneself looking upon the peculiarity with somewhat mixed feelings when one is the company officer of the aforesaid Tommy. For instance, today we went out to Auchen to do some firing on a very primal range. I conceived the idea of doing an attack, on the lines of field firing, and in due course it was duly launched.

Certainly the Company fired. There was no doubt about that. The 'rapid', simply ripped out. But as the attack of trained soldiers the manoeuvre was otherwise scarcely a success. They did everything wrong they could possibly do, and were most cheerful about it. They seemed to think they were still in the trenches. I should have strafed them, but I couldn't find the heart to spoil the really happy afternoon they were having.

At Grantham and Salisbury [Plain] their attack was simply perfect. Now they are in the real thing it possesses a hundred faults. I suppose it is just human nature. And anyway we have had a jolly good afternoon.

17th December '15

Your Xmas parcels came to me today. They made me feel a regular school-boy and I opened them with the same zest that one used to bring to bear on a tuck-box. They were ripping, the plum pudding especially being received with general cheers by the mess. Then your letter came, full of loving wishes to me. It was a sweet letter, the letter of a sweet woman.

Tonight I have had officers and NCOs out on a little cross-country march on compass bearings. Murray brought his team in all right, Prince was out a bit and Bowly became quite lost. I find these sudden reversions back to long untouched work most instructive as showing how soon men forget the little essentials which make so for success. Poor Bowly was pretty sick with himself but passed if off by soundly cursing the map.

We have the report in today from the 4th Division of the battalion's behaviour in the trenches. It was excellent, the best in the Brigade. We are very pleased about it though not unduly elated. I think we all expected it would be quite all right. Those of us who have known it from the start have such utter faith in the battalion. I feel certain it will always do well. With officers such as we have I cannot see how it can do otherwise. They are a good lot, good boys all.[i]

i 'I have been in the forest again to-day, and had another most enjoyable time, and finished up with a visit from a Captain, a Colonel and a General, who were all jolly nice to me, especially the General, who was a regular sport and very chatty. The Captain had tea with me (made by my cook on the roaring fire we have had all day). We have had a splendid report from the Regulars we were attached to, and the result is crowds better than other battalions in the whole Division, certainly in the Brigade. We were put down as a long way above the average officers, NCOs and men – well disciplined, and much better than ever expected, than other units. The report on the officers was – "Well above the average, and exceptionally keen". So you can imagine we feel very proud of our Battalion and the splendid men we have' (Gomersall, 17.12.15).

18th December '15

We went route-marching this morning, that is B, C and D Coys did. I took them and quite a little jaunt it was, the morning having cleared and the sun came out to glisten things up a bit. Especially the fog beads on the spider webs which hang about the trees on the hill between Bonneville and Montrelet.

Worthy rode with me and we chatted of home and the early days and such things and were very happy. And this afternoon his Coy played mine at football and beat them. We had a very poor team up and I must look into it before we play again.

The post has stopped once more for three or four days. We move on Monday down south another sixteen miles, to Fourdrinoy I believe. And there we become really members of 7th Division, Capper's Division,[i] a regular hard-fighting lot, now down from Flanders resting. It looks as though with them we shall be 'for it', as the men say. At any rate we should see some fighting, a nice change from this messing about and continual strafing by the powers that be.

Our own particular *bête noir* has been at it again, bullying Ramsbottom and threatening to send him to England, all because a C Coy man had lost a wire-cutter.[ii]

I think our friend is something short in his mental outfit. There is

i Maj. Gen. Sir Thompson Capper, who had gained a reputation for being a bold and decisive leader, took command of 7th Div in 1914. It landed in Belgium when the German armies were pushing forward to the sea. It resisted the advance during the 1st Battle of Ypres, but lost 10,000 men. In April, Capper had been seriously wounded behind the lines where improvised explosives were being demonstrated to him. He returned in July and led the division forward at the Battle of Loos, but was wounded by enemy gunfire and died the next day. A rumour later persisted that he had been killed while charging on horseback against the enemy. This, and his early death, may have contributed to May's estimation of him.

ii May's *bête noire*, shared with Bland and now possibly with Ramsbottom, seems to have been Maj. Merriman, who later had a successful career as an MP.

nothing else I can put his disgusting manners down to. Until I met him always cherished the idea that the name 'English officer' was synonymous with that of 'gentleman'. I am reluctantly compelled now to admit that it can mean 'bully and cad' also. It has been somewhat of a shock to me, as a disillusionment always is, and I wish with all my heart that he would go away from us and make room for some decent, mannered gentleman whom we would look up to and follow.

I cannot help feeling that an officer makes a fatal mistake in not endeavouring to win the respect and affection of those who serve under him. Men are so strange, all of us I mean. We are so ready to make a hero, and love him. Therein lies the secret of leadership, and I feel it in my bones that nothing will hold us so much when the time comes as the example of him whom we honour and love. Field punishments, CBs [Confined to Barracks] and other such minor irritants don't help in the trenches. It is only the things that a man feels within him matter there. When you are right up alongside sudden death it is remarkable how one's views alter and how you see what a man really is. And I know, I know, I know, that it is then that the man who has won respect and affection will triumph over him who has used his power as a bludgeon only. All of which sounds very dramatic and serious and not at all like me. But the truth, I suppose is seldom very humorous.

19th December '15

Today we have had a regular old-time Sunday. With the exception that for church there has been no parade. And this morning Worthy and I took advantage of the leisure to ride out down the Doullens road. About two miles from here we turned into a wood with the idea of cutting across country till we found some other road to bring us back. It was pleasant in the wood. It smelt clean and fresh in there and the sunlight made a witching chequer on the brown floor of fallen leaves, which here and there was not brown at all but green, where the new grass peeped through.

We followed a cart track at first but this 'ere long petered out and we were compelled to continue along a tiny, winding way that game, or chance wayfarers or both had made. And further on this too became ill-defined and difficult to see so that we had continually to stop and part the branches to decide which way it held. I said 'This is like the rides one reads about, where men get lost in woods but follow some such slender track from instinct and are rewarded in the end by chancing on some fairy cottage where dwells a princess.' Worthy laughed, no doubt thinking me the ass I am. But lo, a few yards further and the track widened slightly and there on its edge stood a tiny cottage wherein a little fire burned. And on its threshold stood two tiny children hand in hand looking up at us with wide, staring eyes.

It was quite in keeping with the story, quite unreal, quite romantic, quite French. How the cottage comes there, how its owner lives and how he gets into contact with his fellows I do not know. He lives in a fairyland all his own. And I prefer to think of it like that.

Chapter 3
'Our past glorious Xmastides together'

20 December 1915–13 January 1916

20th December '15[i]

Eighteen miles march between the hours of 8 a.m. and 3 p.m., with an hour off of that for dinner, is not bad going without a man falling out save four with bad feet.[ii]

The battn has done quite well today and now here we are at the end of it snugly billeted in Fourdrinoy. The change has taken place and we

---

i The 21st and 22nd Bns of the Manchester Regt, while remaining in the 91st Bde, were formally re-allocated from the 30th Div to the 7th Div. The intention was to mix both Service and Regular battalions within the division, which became known as a hybrid division. The 91st Bde also included the 2nd Bn of the Queen's Royal West Surrey Regt and the 1st Bn, South Staffordshire Regt.
ii 'I had charge of the battn sick [who usually marched at the rear], and to the surprise of all, raced the battn. with them, and got in before them, though several were almost dead before starting, and two had a boot on one foot and a shoe on the other, and all had bad feet. The Colonel was delighted, and most surprised, I don't think he expected us till midnight – instead of that, we raced him and won by a head' (Gomersall, 21.12.15).

are now fully established members of the 7th Div, having bid goodbye to the old 30th for good and all.

Our village is very tiny and slightly more dirty than usual but, as we are here for a spell, we'll put the latter disqualification to rights before many days are past.

We officers have struck the best billet we have seen so far. We are in the school-master's house, which is well-furnished and most comfortable, and we have a piano. Fancy the joy of it! A piano, music and we have not heard a tune for six weeks. It has acted upon us like a tonic. You can scarcely imagine what pleasure there can be in even such a shop-soiled tune as *Tipperary* when you haven't heard a note of music for nearly two months.

21st December '15

It has rained today with a pitiless persistence worthy of a better cause. The streets are now ankle deep in mud in their worst places and the natural drains at their sides quite full with a swift running, malodorous and evil-coloured fluid, a mixture of rain, mud and the overflow from a host of 'middens'.

We have explored the village and find it half-deserted, much in ruins, extremely dirty, and altogether an uninviting spot. We are, however, here for about a month so we must set ourselves to work to tidy up and make the place as habitable as possible. And this good work we have started on today but with somewhat indifferent success so far on account of the inclement conditions.[i]

---

i 'We are at present in a little Barn, quite happy & natty, but no stairs to climb to bed & and no feathers to lie on, but putting all jokes on one side Dear, I don't think in all the British Army there are a pluckier & more contented lot of men existing. You would have screamed when we were in the trenches at the songs they are making up & singing & kidding one another. For e.g. "It's your turn to have a look at the Phil Harmans [Germans] this time, but don't look too high or you might get your hair parted in the middle & get home for

22nd December '15

One gets into a habit, quite unconsciously at first, of any hold it may subsequently get on one, or, even if consciously and quite realising what one is doing, with no heed but that you can break from it any time at will. Alas, for human frailty. For instance, here did I set out, gaily and with no foreboding, upon this diary, never thinking it could become a tyrant that would 'ere long rule me, and here I am reduced to impotence when evening comes round, unable to refuse the call of these pages to be scribbled in. And that irrespective of whether I have aught to say or whether I have naught as is my plight tonight.

It is just the necessary but colourless routine here, and will be till after Xmas . . . Such days furnish nothing and one is forced to rack one's brain to fill the required entry space. But fill it I must, this habit has me so in its grip.

The Xmas parcels have been coming in tonight and the mess is in considerable excitement.

Almonds and raisins, dried figs, Crème de Menthe jubes, fancy biscuits and all other such delicious and dainty things are strewn about the room so that it makes us feel strangely Xmasy.

But also it causes us considerable homesickness. One always associates almonds and raisins with bonbons and paper caps and the flushed, rosy cheeks of the girl one loves. At least I do, and the memories of our past glorious Xmastides together are with me strongly tonight. My love, how I long that our next Yuletide we may see through together once more. How the lamps will gleam, the fire leap and the laughter ring. I can see the very smile in your eyes now. God, what fools we are. We never enjoy our happy moments until they are denied us. Yet, even

---

your Christmas Dinner." You dare not bob your head in the same place twice. The latest joke was one of our men said he picked up a paper that one of the Germans threw down in the trenches saying they were going to "down Arms" on the 29th of this month as they were sick & tired & that we could have the B....y Kaiser & the trenches as well. Naturally we are all anxiously waiting for the 29th' (Bunting, 17.12.15).

while I so moralise, I feel I will know how to appreciate my next Xmas day with you, my own.

23rd–25th December '15

All these three days I record in one since I have had no time at all in which to write them up separately. It has been a rush from morning to night, trying to arrange something for the men and here we are at the end of it with nothing done. There is no room for a concert. There is no beer for the men, nothing but a bar of chocolate apiece, some tinned fruit and a packet of Woodbines. It is pretty sickening and so unnecessary.[i]

By a little arrangement at HQ it could have all been so different and the battalion could have enjoyed a regular blow-out and appreciated it more than anything. Every other battalion in the brigade has done it except us. It is marvellous that the men can raise a smile at all. Yet they can and do. They are always cheery.

We officers had quite a decent Christmas Eve. I think every company in the battalion came in to see us and we sat up till midnight to see the 25th in. Then we drank to absent friends and thought pretty hard. We did the same at Dinner today. What a Christmas Dinner it was! How different from the old time-honoured institution at home. Yet we ate it with due solemnity, thinking all the while of our own, dear, clean, rosy-cheeked women across the water.

i 'Since we came here, we have, by Captain's orders, established a sergeants' mess in an empty house, where we sleep and eat. I am not sure that I think the idea a very good one, as I rather felt that on active service the sergeants ought to live with the men. Of course it means that one has rather more room and comfort (though not any more quiet, for the sergeants are, if anything, more noisy than the men). As I am supposed to know French, the begging of articles of furniture, and the getting of supplies has devolved upon me. Yesterday I was commissioned to buy 2 turkeys for Xmas, not altogether an easy task in a village like this, but I managed it and they are now hanging up in the mess' (Tawney, 22.12.15).

One good feature of this war is that it will cause many a thousand men to appreciate our England. For myself, I have groused at her and called her hard names but, when I return, if I am discontent at any time and feel inclined to rail at her I shall think of this filthy, malodorous country and call myself a fool.

The post has just come in bringing me a parcel from your mother full of almonds and raisins and dried fruits galore. Good egg. We will gorge ourselves upon them this evening and have a snap-dragon and lots of fun. A tune strummed out on the piano, a dish of snap-dragon and a jolly lot of pals around him and what more can a man want? Only one thing. The girl he loves. But never mind next Christmas will come in its time and then we shall know how to appreciate it the more.

Diversity is the spice of one's life I believe. If so I have just had an extra hamper. There was a crash in the kitchen. The three girls came running into me in a very excited and frightened state. 'Les soldats sont très malharde, [malade] m'sieur!' I go forth. Smith,[i] our cook, I find sitting on the range, our potatoes on the floor before him, an inane grin on his face the while he declares with somewhat blurred emphasis the fact that 'he doesn't believe there's a . . . German this side of the Rhine at all'.

I ordered him out to bed. He saluted, said, 'And 'bout time too, Capton', and promptly subsided in the hearth where he gave way to uncontrollable laughter. I shout for Bunting, my trusty henchman, but remain unanswered. I shout, again. The reply is a most appalling crash. I rush into the scullery and find Bunting, my trusted man, the husband of a wife and father of a family, on hands and knees in the midst of a paralysing tangle of unwashed debris. With his head beneath the drip-board, he commenced ''pologising for disgrashfell 'dition'. I cursed him for a low beast, and returned to Smith. The latter was already preparing for slumber 'mongst the cinders. With my own hands I pulled them up and kicked their posteriors out of the back-door.

Later I heard from Oldham[ii] that both the delinquents had fallen in

i Pte Richard Smith.
ii Lt Eric Oldham, who had transferred from A to B Coy.

the duck-pond. *C'est très triste.* I am afraid they will smell most atrociously tomorrow.

The British Tommy is something of a gross animal. I think he is drunk *en masse* tonight. It is terrible. Yet I cannot find it in my heart to blame him. God knows he has enough to put up with. And I cannot help but love him, even though he sits on the range and desires to slumber in the ash-pan.[i]

26th December '15, Boxing Day

A rather farcical marching [drill] competition marked the morning. The CO had ordered it, but neither B nor D Companies competed. It is likely there will be trouble for Worthy and myself. *Noblesse oblige.* Bow-wow!

The rest of the day I have spent writing, working off great arrears of correspondence and feeling much refreshed thereby. It has been quite a treat to have a slack day and we all feel twice as fit for work tomorrow. The fresh programme is out. Yet it is fresh in nothing. Only the old, well-worn routine. I must add a prayer to the soldier's Litany. It will run something like this: 'From all Routine and such like plagues, Good Lord deliver us.'

27th December '15

We have had a really useful day in the open as the first of our new Routine. We have been on an improvised range and have run a competition in rapid fire which 5 Platoon won.

i 'I had a splendid Christmas Day yesterday, and the men had a fine singsong outside the platoon billet last night which I went to, and stayed over an hour. Some sang solos, but chiefly choruses and carols. It was very jolly and I gave every man a packet of Woodbines' (Gomersall, 26.12.15). 'Our Xmas festivities were not a great success. Nearly every one in the mess got drunk too early, and were put to bed by myself and the Quartermaster Sergt., a man whom I like and respect' (Tawney, 26.12.15).

It was quite a lovely day, though cold, and lunch out there on the hillside, with the wood to shield us from the wind and with no sign of house or man in all the landscape to disturb our sense of isolation, was most enjoyable. It was quite like one of the old days on the Plain and one felt it hard indeed to realise that only a few miles off there was real war.

Bunting has come back. A bedraggled and repentant Bunting, clothed in a wonderful mixture of garments which he has conned from various friends. I had meant to be angry with him but his repentance was so deep and his condition still so sad that I had not the heart. He has now gone sick with a septic foot and is on 'Light Duty'. I wonder he has not succumbed to a combination of diphtheria and typhoid fever. Had any one less inebriated than he fallen in the pond there is no doubt but that would have been his fate.

28th December '15

We have been out today on a battalion attack and most enjoyable it was. Quite a change from the ordinary ruck, quite like an old day down Stonehenge way on the Plain. If routine continues like it has for the last two days we shall bear up beneath it quite well.

And tonight comes the rumour that we leave here in a day or two, but whether it be true or not I do not yet know. Nor does rumour say our destination, whether trenches or another village. The big bombardment, we have heard, has commenced. If so, it may well be that we move up to the firing line. If we do, I trust that this time we may go through. But I talk foolishly, the whole thing is only rumour and may well end as so many such have done.

29th December '15

Usually is rumour a lying jade, but for this once she has told the truth. We do leave here, and tomorrow morning we go to Le Quesnoy[-sur-Airaines], another training billet and not to the trenches. Not yet anyway. Perhaps the next move we will. At any rate we can but live in hopes.

I have just been reading some extracts from letters found on German prisoners. They are authentic, and, from them, one can only conclude that life in Germany is not easy to sustain just now. Some of the people seem in parlous state. So much so that until one remembers the excesses committed in the first days, when Prussia's star was in the ascendant, one can almost find it in one to pity the poor devils.

A blow has fallen on me tonight, a very heavy blow, yet one, I am glad to say, which I could, had I would, have avoided. I mean that they have asked for Garside[i] for a commission in one of the new units at home, and I have recommended him. He will, I feel sure, get the job, and his going will be the blow. As yet I do not know what I will do without him. He has been invaluable to me and to the company and I cannot imagine B without him. However, I suppose it must be. One has to look on these things from the larger rather than the personal stand-point. Nevertheless I feel very sad. One cannot have a good servant for long without getting a sincere attachment for him, and such an attachment I most certainly have for my keen, hard-working QMS.

He told the CO he wouldn't take the commission if I didn't want him to go. And, later, he said to me that he hoped he would not get the job, that he wanted to stay with me, that I was a leader of men and he would never feel the same under any other captain. Which was all rather foolish, I suppose, but which I hadn't the heart to stop him saying. Damn it, he meant it so! Please God I may always justify half such faith. It is marvellous. I cannot understand it. As you so well know, I am such a truly ordinary sort of clout-head. Poor Garside.

30th December '15

We have now moved as ordered to Le Quesnoy. That is scarcely worth recording now. It is not like the days when first we were out and moves meant endless thought and fret and worry. Now everyone is so used to it and so knows his job that the battalion just flits from one village to

---

i Company Quartermaster Sgt Robert Taylor Garside.

another as easily and with rather less fuss than a commercial traveller.

It was a fine day, a fact I am only too thankful to put down. For otherwise we should have had a bad time indeed, the roads – save the mark – being as it was absolutely atrocious and ankle deep in mud in many places.

This, Le Quesnoy, is a much better village than any yet which has suffered from us. We have good billets and the people are kind. I think we shall be all right here.[i]

It was quite a send-off from Fourdrinoy this morning. Half the village was out. Papa and the three daughters from our particular billet came right outside the place to see us go and waved handkerchiefs and shouted good wishes as we trudged off. One felt like a bedraggled Lord Mayor's Show. We must have pleased them better than the last battalion and, personally, I feel quite satisfied with Fourdrinoy. I have learnt quite a lot of French there and will remember it because of that.

Tonight I have had two letters from you, two sweet letters but so full of news and kindnesses that I despair of ever being able to answer them as I would like. My soul, you pour out your love on me, abasing yourself, in the depth of it, before me. You should not. I am so poorly furnished as an inspiration for romance that I am utterly undeserving of such a deep affection as is yours. It is I who should abase myself. It is I who am the fortunate party to our bargain. Believe me, my soul, I am fully conscious of it. And my love for you grows with the speed of the flame in stubble. How else could it be? Every day I see such evidence of your goodness, your thought for others, your bravery and your perfect woman-liness that I would be but a senseless clod did my love for you not respond as I say. May our sweet Babe grow into such another woman as her mother. It is my hope that she does.

i 'A friend of mine has found me a fine billet, a palace in comparison to every-thing I ever had – a beautiful, large room, fine bed, oil paintings on the wall, carpeted floor, wash-stand & wardrobe etc., a fine table with cloth on, a set of easy chairs, a fireplace, a large mirror on the wall, and all to myself, too, with a fine place for my servant in an outhouse adjoining' (Gomersall, 1.1.16).

31st December '15

New Year's Eve. And what a strange one. The first for six we have not been out together. I feel sad and sick at heart, for I hate the anniversaries unless they be in happy company. Don Murray and I intended seeing it through together but the D mess came in about eleven and insisted on hauling us round to C Coy. We went under protest and found many merry spirits there but mostly flushed and rowdy and quite out of touch with our mood. We, I expect, grow somewhat staid or perhaps it is that we have so much more to think about, perhaps, being married, we feel we have given up so much more than the others, that life can hold for a man such thoughts, such sweet, sad memories that he had rather be alone with them. I do not know, I am so poor a theorist, but I felt out of the throng. All I desired was to be alone with the night and to dwell on my memories of other New Year Eves with you and to think out plans for future ones. And as I came home from C Coy at 12.10am. this New Year's Day a shooting star sped right across the heavens before me. It is a good omen for our future New Years.

1st January '16

New Year's Day. And, I am glad to say, a day full of promise for the battalion. I may be slightly sanguine in saying that, but I care not in my present mood, for I am somewhat elated. We won today our first match in the Division League, beating the Queen's 2–nil. I mean no injustice to our team when I say surprise added zest to our pleasure. We had thought the 'Lambs'[i] almost too hot to tackle. No doubt they took us for more rotten than we are. Both were mistakes I doubt not. And, anyway we gave them a whacking.[ii]

i 2nd Bn, the Queen's Royal West Surrey Regt; the lamb is the emblem on its regimental badge.
ii 'We have quite a change today, for the divisional band, 37 strong, came in, and livened up the whole village. We have been lucky to get in such a splendid

57

Before the match we were inspected by Coys by the CO.[i] The men looked and stood very well and I think the colonel was pleased. They do good, these inspections. They cause men to buck-up and do their best to turn out well and so ensure really clean things being displayed.

In the evening we went to D Coy and talked and told tales and played 'vingt-et un', a feeble pastime which left me 1fr. 50c. richer at the end of an hour's listless dealing.

We do some Brigade work next week, a thing we rather look forward to, since we are rather anxious to see how we shape in the field alongside regulars.

2nd January '16

There is little to put down tonight. I have been most of the afternoon on a scheme for training patrols for night work, but there is little of that can go in here except the fact that I have devised a little formation all my own for catching our wily friend Bosche in small numbers, and only hope the CO will let me practise it with a view to getting it perfect against our return to the trenches.

The only other item worthy of record is that the battalion is washed tomorrow. The Division has given us the use of their baths and we are to put the men through at the rate of 50 per half hour. The men are pretty braced about it, poor beggars. If cleanliness is next to Godliness, I think lousiness is next to Hell. Anyway, some of the men are pretty

---

division, as we get the benefit of all their past experiences and the things they have organised during the year. The band was a fine one, and played in the square just outside the house where I live and the music carried one far from here. Our division runs a Football League, and yesterday we played our first game against the team of a regular battalion and won, 2–0. We have a church service every Sunday, and the good old C. of E. service always makes Sunday a real Sunday' (Gomersall, 2.1.16).

i Lt Col. Paul W. Whetham.

fed up about it, and one certainly cannot blame them for feeling so, little as it can be helped.[i]

Some, of course, do not appear to mind at all. In the full course of time I suppose one can get used to and even attached to anything, even a louse. It seems hard to believe, but I really think such a state of mind is quite possible.

3rd January '16

A most interesting day, laying out a complete set of trenches in the morning and going to Vignacourt[ii] in the afternoon to attend one of the most absorbing lectures it has ever been my good fortune to listen to.

Major Mansfield, of the East Yorks, talked, and all the heads were there. Generals and other red hats simply swarmed. Both Generals Fry and Congreve were present and I did not envy the major his job.[iii] He discharged it, however, splendidly, as no doubt a man would who had faced what he has.

He told us all about Loos.[iv] And a great tale it was, a tale of big deeds

---

i 'The baths are fine – hot water and shower baths are up. After washing, the men are issued clean underclothing and the old clothes collected for washing or renewal. It is a fine scheme. The things are taken from the baths next day to a neighbouring town where they are freed from anything which may show great attachment, such as lice, and then sent to a large town not far away where they are thoroughly cleaned at French laundries. At the next bath but one the men will again receive perfectly clean underclothing, that is, once a fortnight, for they are taken to the baths weekly. It just shows the advantage of coming to such a fine division and benefiting from their arrangements' (Gomersall, 12.1.16).

ii The historic town of Vignacourt was a rail centre and training area.

iii Maj. Gen. Sir William Fry had been commander, 30th Div, before the appointment of Gen. Sir John Stuart Mackenzie Shea; Lt Gen. Sir Walter Norris Congreve, VC.

iv The Battle of Loos, an assault on the German defences in Artois and Champagne, was part of a larger Anglo-French offensive. With considerable quietly done and of danger faced with wonderful coolness and presence of mind.

How near it was to complete success. What a pity we had not that extra Div handy. Yet when one thinks of the Spartan deeds performed as in the day's work by our dirty, tired and hungry British Infantry, one almost feels that one would not have the tale other than it is for anything.

For seven days and seven nights they fought and dug and floundered in the mud, and never once did the rain give up. The East Yorks, Devons, Camerons, Queen's, Wilts, Beds, and others were all in and not one can show a better record than his neighbour.

All fought as only, I believe, the British can and the heroism and devotion to duty of both officers and men was little short of marvellous. 68,000 casualties for the apparent gain of a few hundred yards on half a mile of front may seem at first sight too great a price but when one thinks how nearly through we were, how another touch and the German line had been completely broken, one feels it was not in vain and that from the lessons gained we will next time wring complete success.

One cannot attribute blame to anyone for the only partial success in this big venture but the impression left on the minds of those present was that perhaps more forethought might have been displayed by the Staff. I do not know. It is not for such as I am to have opinions on such gigantic topics. But one cannot help wondering why the fresh troops were not available sooner.

As one officer said, 'Bread is the staff of life, for the Staff is one, big "loaf".' I do not range myself on the side of such a sweeping statement but the joke is too good to allow of its being omitted.

---

losses, the British 1st Army captured the town, but the reduced support of artillery and from Reserves meant that this victory could not be exploited. When battle resumed, the Germans, now reinforced, frustrated the Allied advance: its twelve attacking battalions suffered 8,000 casualties in four hours. As a result of the failure to win the battle conclusively, General French, the British Commander-in-Chief, was replaced by General Haig. British casualties totalled over 59,000.

4th January '16

We have started on our big entrenching scheme today and this time really hope to complete the idea. Each platoon has been allotted a sector to delve in to its heart's content and rivalry is therefore keen.

One of the men made a remark which greatly tickled me, as I know it will you. He was struggling hard with some tough ground of the time. 'There's one good point about this 'ere firm we're working for. We're never b........ well out of a job.'

Considering they go from 7 a.m. to 4.30 p.m. every day without cease, I am inclined to agree with his statement. Today I have been put in charge of the patrol organisation and will therefore be pretty hard at it for some time to come. There is a big lot of ground to cover but I think with unremitting 'butting-in' we will be able to make a fair show in a week or two's time. However, here goes.

5th January '16

It is now 10.55 p.m. and I have been in exactly 20 mins. I started duty this morning at 6 a.m., so it has been a pretty good day. The Brigade, I am glad to say, stood me lunch of the château at Gissy, otherwise I should have had to go through on three beef sandwiches which are not over filling and leave an absolute void when one has done a full attack and ridden 12 miles.

The attack was a great success. The Queen's took the left and we the right with the 21st and the Staffords in reserve. These others are regulars but, without being in the slightest degree prejudiced by my own affections, I must say our fellows did their job a great deal better than did the others.

We have been to Vignacourt again today to hear a further lecture on Loos, this time by an Engineer. He was quite excellent and most interesting. General Congreve was there again and General Watts.[i] I do admire

i Lt Gen. Sir Herbert Edward Watts, CO 7th Div.

these lecturers for their pluck in carrying on so steadily with so much red flannel about.

6th January '16

My commission is a year old today. How strange it seems. If it were ten years I could more understand it. It feels to me as though I had never known any other than army life. I simply cannot picture myself as an ordinary business man, in a blue suit and a bowler hat, who just dabbled in soldiers as a pastime. Yet such I must have been once and, no doubt, will be again, 'When this ruddy war is over', as the men sing. Which reminds me that they now have a new ditty. It is rather good, making a swinging march. The last two lines express a sentiment with which I am in most hearty accord. They are, 'Oh! My! I don't want to die. I want to go home.'[i] Also they have another. This last the song of the good soldier, resigned to his fate. 'If the sergeants drink your rum, never mind. If the sergeants drink your rum, never mind. They say they take their lot, but they scoff the ruddy lot. Still, though the sergeants drink your rum, never mind.'

I hear that we are now known as 'Whetham's Flying Column' throughout the Div. This is partly due to the number of moves we have made since landing and partly to the way we went through Picquigny after doing 14 miles. They tell us the Gordons were astonished at the 'go' about the battalion.[ii] I don't know. But I know we have been christened as I say.

i 'It is amusing to read in the [English] papers on the strong resolve of K[itchener]'s soldiers. The men's favourite song – chanted to a melancholy tune – is: "I want to go home/I want to go home/I don't want to go in the trenches no more/Where the Jack Johnsons they fall by the score, /Take me over the sea/Where I never will roam,/Oh my!/I don't want to die,/ I want to go home"' (Tawney, 9.12.15).

ii 2nd Bn, Gordon Highlanders.

7th January '16

Troops have been passing through here all today. Where they have come from and whither they are bound I do not know, but there are plenty of them. We have also been given mobilisation orders today, i.e. what we are to do in case the Div suddenly desires to move in a hurry. I hope they don't. I hate doing things in a hurry. Men get stupid and everyone else excited and the ensuing strafing makes the whole army miserable for days, more or less.

Tonight the battn is out on night ops. I had the patrols only and did some elementary work with them. They are very keen, but most thick-headed. The dear, old English Tommy only has, and I expect, will ever only have, one idea of warfare. That is, to walk up to a johnny and stick a bayonet into him. In the aggregate, that is his sole aim and object. He cannot dissemble, has no cunning and only a canteen interest in strategy and only then as an excuse to blither with a friend over a can of beer. He cares nothing for the idea of stealth. He is not really built for quietly stealing on an unsuspecting foe. As proof you need only put one tin can in a sixty-acre field and turn two Tommies loose in that field to do a silent night march. I will guarantee that in three minutes one has stumbled over the can and that in a further three both have kicked it. There must, I think, be some magnetism between ammunition, boots and odd cans which unknown people have discarded in out of the way places.

So long as I live and can think of night ops, I will think of my silent patrols kicking tin cans.

8th January '16

Lloyd, Bowly, Cushion[i] and myself have been into Amiens today, and an enjoyable little time we have had of it. We had to ride four miles to Hangest and get the train from there, leaving Finch[ii] to bring the gees

i Capt. Charles Mostyn Lloyd; Lt William Boston Cushion.
ii Pte Harold Cecil Finch.

back. He also met us with them in the evening after, as he told me, having no end of a tour with them. They had never been led before, and resented starting. Also, when they did, they both kicked and bit each other and took their male chaperon more or less where they listed. However he got there in the end and I've no doubt but that the experience did him no harm.

Amiens improves on acquaintance. It has some really fine boulevards and the shops are quite good. Also the *Café de la Paix* puts on a most excellent lunch. I feel quite a *gourmand* to be always talking so eulogistically of food but, really, one gets so tired of ration beef and potatoes that a proper meal does assume somewhat undue proportions in one's ideas of the general scheme of things. I managed to get a little souvenir for you, a little item to put in the *bric-a-brac* cupboard when this war is over and we again set up our own home. It is delightful to think of, that resetting up of our own tiny castle once more.

The trains were full of young Frenchmen proceeding to mobilise. It is the 1917 class they are calling up and a fine, set up, good-looking lot of material it was so far as we saw it. They were all whistling, singing and wildly excited, but I saw none drunk. How different from our own stubby, round-headed beggars on similar occasions! I suppose one should prefer the French way, yet I, for one, cannot. I like our boys too well.

A colonel I met today told me a rather good story. There was a big review up north a bit a little while ago in honour of an illustrious personage whose name must go unrecorded by me. Three divisions were out with cavalry and guns and a real slap-up fight was conducted. When it was all over, the big man was most displeased. 'But I have seen nothing,' he declared. 'Do it again. I want to see the troops rush and the cavalry charge.'

And so it was done again, but not as previously. This time the infantry advanced in mass formation, brigades in line, bayonets fixed and men cheering. They rush to the onslaught so, *à les Allemands*. Then the cavalry charged, all waving sabres, plunging horses and yelling men.

It was a grand sight, as unlike war, as incorrect in both theory and practice and as utterly mad as one could well imagine. But the big man was delighted. He said, 'It is magnificent.'

'*Certainment,*' thought many, thinking of friend Nap. '*Mais, c'est ne pas la guerre.*'[i] However I believe a certain gentleman, who wears red on his lapels, has received another decoration and has salved his conscience with it. Ever so does the way to success lie.

9th January '16

Murray went into Abbeville, Bowly on a course and Shelmerdine to the bombers – as you were, 'grenadiers' – for we must not call them the former now. Prince and I were therefore left to keep each other company, a happiness we achieved quite successfully.

The first match of an inter-company, knock-out, football competition was played this afternoon: B Company against the Machine Gun[ners]. We beat them 6–nil and I trust it means our team may go through the whole competition successfully.

Burchill[ii] made a bit of an ass of himself – but then he usually does. He is a perfect example of the clever young fellow whose personal conceit has produced that effect popularly summed up in the phrase 'a tile loose'.

10th January '16

We have had a most enjoyable afternoon of battalion drill. It was much needed and everyone was pretty rotten for the first quarter of an hour. But after that it all came back and the work went well and smartly.[iii]

i '*Magnifique, mais ce n'est pas la guerre . . . c'est de la folie*' is attributed to Gen. Pierre Bosquet at the time of the Charge of the Light Brigade in 1854.
ii 2nd Lt Vivian Burchill.
iii 'This morning we went to a ravine about a mile away where we could safely practise shooting with ammunition (ball). We got a whole crowd of tins on wooden stands, after the style of a coco-nut stall, in the ground at the foot of one side of the ravine, and then got one hundred yards away and shot ball ammunition and tried to imagine we were shooting some Huns. The company

These sudden changes back to old ground-work stuff are, as I have often said before, most useful. One is so liable to forget that they are very likely to take you off your guard. And so they make everyone buck up and think quickly – a faculty I am afraid the Army is apt to dull.

The Coy did well. Sgt Major Knowles,[i] being in his element again, was excellent and the CO quite strafeless and cheerful.

I had a sweet letter from you last night, full of excitement at the prospect of my leave. My sweetheart, you cannot be as wound-up about it as I am. I simply long for it, for the sight of you and Babs again. Only one thing mars it – that is I do wish I had seen some more real fighting. However, those older at the game out here tell me not to be a fool but to take joy when it offers and I doubt not but that they know best.

11th January '16

We have been out and fought an advanced guard action today, and found it most enjoyable if somewhat tiring.[ii] It was quite a success, the battalion coming along Al. As for myself, I had quite an experience, being put out among the wounded. Presumably a 'whiz-bang' had smote me lustily upon the stomach and my lack of sadness at missing the last spurts across heavy plough was only equalled by the absence of pain. Yet I took it that, with such a serious wound, a man could be excused if he lay up beneath a haystack and smoked a pipe. And this I did, excusing my lapse to the major on the ground that my anguish was such that I was likely to cry out with it before the men unless I had something – such as a pipe stem – whereon to clench my teeth. He concurred and, indeed,

———

thoroughly enjoyed the novelty and it was quite an agreeable change. I did some revolver shooting as well as rifle shooting at them [the tins!] This after-noon, for the purpose of smartness and discipline we had a very strenuous afternoon's drill from 2.0 to 4.0' (Gomersall, 10.1.16).

i Sgt Maj. Frederick Charles Knowles.

ii This was a military exercise.

thought my action so well-advised that he decided to follow it, and did. So together we sat and watched the attack mature, cheering lustily, in spirit, the gallant efforts of the hale and hearty ones who were left to bring the action to its victorious conclusion.

A year ago I should have fretted greatly of being thus early put out of action. But the year has been full of instruction. I have learned many things. One is that running over newly ploughed land is not altogether unalloyed enjoyment and that, perhaps, it will be time enough to be keen about it when there are real Germans the other side of it.

12th January '16

A Coy played the officers this afternoon in the knock-out soccer competition – and lost. It was a good match and enthusiasm begins to run high as to what teams will be in. at the final. The battn team plays the 21st in the League match on Saturday, and we are keen as mustard to beat them. It will be a top-hole match to watch.[i]

I had tea at HQ this afternoon – quite an event. Everyone was most affable – almost hearty. The CO was quite chatty, quite like an ordinary man. It is most remarkable. He seems to have suddenly changed completely and for no apparent reason. Perhaps someone has told him that his battn is not quite the collection of evil-meaning blackguards he has hitherto supposed it. Anyway there is a decided improvement and we sincerely hope there will be no relapse.

I saw a strange thing this afternoon. Nothing less than a shepherd boy leading his flock by the strains of a sweet-toned pipe. It was quite an idyll. I never realised before that those pipes of Pan were anything more than fantasies conjured up by the brain of the author of Peter of that ilk,[ii] or some such clever dreamer.

i There were some football stars in the battalion, including Pte Joseph Lamb of B Coy, a former footballer with Newton Heath Lancashire FC (renamed Manchester United FC in 1902), who lost a leg at Second Ypres in late 1917.
ii Meaning J. M. Barrie, the author of *Peter Pan*.

Ramsbottom was not impressed. He is so utterly modern, so utterly Manchester. He said the man came down the street, tootled on his pipe outside a barn and waited for the sheep to appear. This they shortly did, made a similar noise in reply and went back again. This occurred twice and the man then sent in his dog to fetch them out. I do not believe him. Neither does Cotton. Cotton said, 'They must have been very clever sheep to make a noise like that.' I quite agree. But perhaps French sheep may be much more clever than our old Southdowns.

13th January '16

I have a letter from you tonight in which you ask me if I love you. You must surely be depressed, my own, or else very lonely and desirous of someone to cheer you up. My dear, dear girlie, how can you ask me such a question? To me it seems so impossible that you could ever think otherwise. And yet I expect my letters are somewhat matter-of-fact and contain little reiteration of my affections. I must try and write more softly. Yet I never meant to do aught else. When I write I feel just as with you as if we were talking together and I was recounting the day's experiences, as was my wont in the days before men had to come and fight these bally Germans. But I can understand that often enough you hunger for letters more full of unadulterated love, more truly personal missives, less everyday and plain. Here, perhaps, one is liable to forget that personal outlook. We are all so absolutely in the same boat that one gets to look upon enforced separation from one's dear ones as an affliction common to all and therefore to be borne as such. But you cannot look at it like that. How could you, when all around you must see daily hundreds of wives still with their husbands as happy and contented as if no war existed? I know how you must sometimes feel. How you must feel inclined to rave and rail against it all and I love you the more that you do not do so. When all is said and done it is those others who are to be pitied, not us. They have not known life as we have known it. I will give place to no one for greater love and happiness than has been ours. For no one could ever have loved more or been more gloriously happy than we. And that we could part when it was asked of us is but proof of that. For had I not gone when I was wanted I had not been worthy of your love. And had you not let me go, like the brave little woman you are, you could not have held mine. As it is, in letting me go, splendidly as you did, you have bound me the more firmly to you, you have, as you must know, increased my admiration and love for you ten-fold. My sweetheart, bear up. Leave will soon be here now when for ten glorious days we can drink of joy once again.

I long and long to see you, to clasp you in my arms and hug you and I long with all my heart to see my Baby, my sweet, pure and precious Pauline. Her little, pert face looks up at me from out her photo so life-like that I can see her as though she were in this very room. My dear Baby. How I love her. How much she means to you and I. What hopes I have for her, what a sweet girl she will make. She is a truly God-like gift! I feel strangely unworthy of such a precious child. Please God I may always be worthy of her and of you also, my Maudie.

There, I have given myself the pip, as I knew I should. Too long dwelling on things such as these are not good for one here. It is better not to think too much if one would bear a smiling face about one's work.

Curse the Kaiser, say I, and all similar tyrants who bring war and devastation and misery upon the world!

Chapter 4
'It is the wire that is the trouble'

14–23 January 1916

14th January '16

Quite a full day. Up at 6 a.m. and marching out to Le Fayel by 7.45 a.m.
A lovely morning. It has frozen during the night but the sun came up
about 8 o'clock giving just the necessary touch to the crispness of the
air. Absolutely a marching day.

At Le Fayel we went into Brigade Reserve [for a training exercise]. This
was rather boring. We had to lay for an hour and a half on the plough,
while the wind swept over us and chilled us to the bone. But at last it came
to an end. The Colonel came running up. 'The enemy is counter-attacking
on our right. Move the battalion down the hill and advance up the valley
on his left. Double.' And we were off. These French lands are heavy going,
also valleys have nasty habits of looking hundreds but being in reality
thousands of yards broad. But we slogged on, down one slope and up the
other till when we came to the edge of the Bois de Rusicourt there wasn't
a cool man among us. There we found the enemy had retired through the
wood, and there was nothing for it but to follow him. So in we went, and
a maze it was. The French apparently do not cut undergrowth. It was one,
long, panting struggle with shrubs which pricked, shrubs which struck you
and shrubs which tripped you up. In the end, though, we got through to

Charles Edward May. An electrician, he was
a pioneer inventor of the electric fire alarm,
which much later was installed on the *Queen
Mary* for her maiden voyage in 1936.

The steamship *Westmeath*, in which the May family sailed in 1883 from London,
Gravesend – via Plymouth, St. Vincent, Hobart and Auckland – to Port Chalmers,
South Island, New Zealand.

Port Chalmers harbour, Dunedin. This photograph, taken by the Burton brothers in 1880, shows the shipping in Otago Bay at the time.

Princes Street, Dunedin, in 1885, also taken by the Burton brothers. The town's name was contrived by linking Dundee and Edinburgh, from which many settlers originated.

The contraption known as the May-Oatway Fire Alarm, which soon became a success.

The May family at home in Leytonstone, London, in about 1905.
From left to right: Lillian, Charles Edward, Susan, Charlie.

The bridesmaids at the wedding of Lily May in London, 1909.
On the left is Maude Holl, with Charlie beside her.

Trooper Charlie May in the King Edward's Horse, while at a summer camp.

Captain Charlie May outside his tent during training on Salisbury Plain, autumn 1915.

Private Richard Tawney. This picture was taken by Edwin Hadley in Grantham, 1915. He had a flourishing business photographing the soldiers training in nearby Belton Park.

Captain Alfred Bland, whose death ended a promising academic career.

Lieutenant William Gomersall, who was a Yorkshireman before he moved to Manchester. Immediately after receiving a commission, he took a course at Sandhurst before rejoining his battalion.

Private Arthur Bunting. Charlie May's widow, Maude, generously cared for him after he was taken prisoner, regularly sending him food parcels.

find the enemy entrenched about 100 yards from the north edge of the trees. We prepared to charge them, when the 'stand-fast' came along. I was not sorry. Fully 80 of that 100 yards was plough.[i]

That is all I saw of a big divisional day. Yet everything was in, horse, foot and artillery, some 18,000 men. It must be so in the real thing. One must of necessity only see a fraction of what is really taking place. The limits of one's company is about, or even more, than the limit one can possibly see. On our return to billets I found your letter with Charlie Chaplin's likeness enclosed. It tickled me to death, bracing me also. For you must have been in good spirits to send that off. Dear old Charlie, I only wish to goodness we could see him shuffling round again. I know my taste is appalling, but I think I would sooner see a good series of his films than a play.[ii] At least my present mood tells me I would.

We had Taylor,[iii] of the 21st, and D.S. Murray to dinner last night. Quite a slap-up little affair. And afterwards Ross and Pullen[iv] of the Brigade Bombing Company came in, also Bland, and we sat up till midnight talking and smoking.[v]

i 'It had been rather a hard manoeuvre, as it was practically all wood fighting, and the forest we fought our way through was very thick in undergrowth . . . It was fine to see them tearing up a hill to take up a position and the horses mad with excitement as they tore along in between us – it made it quite realistic. There were about a dozen large guns and over a 100 horses, and it was fine to see the guns tear over an obstacle, such as a bank, up and then over, and the horses madly tearing away in front, while we rushed up with our rifles to make our way through the forest to take up our position, and all the while the continual bang-bang-bang of the machine guns firing from their positions' (Gomersall, 14.1.16).
ii Chaplin's films to this date included: *Kid Auto Races at Venice*, *Caught in a Cabaret*, *Caught in the Rain*, *A Night Out* and *Shanghaied*.
iii Capt. F. T. Taylor.
iv Lt F. G. Ross; Capt. Richard Standeford Pullen.
v 'I wonder whether you resent my cheerfulness ever . . . Why? Because I am in France, where the war is and I know I ought to be here. And I don't loathe

Ross is a smart fellow, quite young, a captain and with the Military Cross. I think it likely that more will be heard of him.

15th January '16

Intense excitement this afternoon. A yelling, 'shouting', cap-waving crowd of men surrounded the football ground. It was a topping match, which the 21st won, 3–2. On the play the game was ours but our men were just putrid round the goal, not being able to shoot for toffee. The 21st are a really smart lot and the work all round was most excellent football and very enjoyable to watch. We are all jolly sorry, though, that we lost. It rather puts us down.

Half way through Bowly rolled up. He had walked in from Le Fayel, where he is at present enlarging his knowledge and having a pretty decent time on a course.

These courses are a strange feature of army life. Some are excellent, indeed all are good – for men in need of them. But so often it happens that men are sent for instruction in most elementary stuff, stuff they knew well years ago. It seems quite unbusinesslike, quite like the army. It seems to me that there are still many things could be improved in this profession.

For instance, why not treat generals as admirals are treated when they make a mess of things? Why should they not be court-martialled and the findings published? No one ever criticises the efficiency of our Navy, nor does the procedure in any way impair the discipline of the Senior Service. It is sensibly run, the Senior Service.

If a man is not in the wrong he would welcome such a procedure. If he is the sooner he is got rid of the better. I cannot help thinking that a properly informed public opinion would be greatly beneficial to our Army, splendid though it is. No matter how good the man the knowledge

---

the war, I love 95% of it, and hate the thought of it being ended too soon. And I don't yearn hourly for my final return, although I am very much pleasantly excited by the possibility of 9 days leave in March, which indeed we haven't earned by any means so far' (Bland, 14.1.16).

that he is but a servant of the public would not be brought home to him in vain.

I know I would be thought an absolute heretic by many in the Service for talking like this, but I do not mind. The New Armies I feel sure hold a big volume of opinion similar to mine. We are new, you see, we have been accustomed to the ordered ways of business, we bring business minds to bear when we think. It makes us critical. And it will, I know, have a very great effect on the management of the Army after the war.

The Army is magnificent simply because Englishmen are what they are and, when trained and disciplined, it is in them to be the finest troops in the world. With such soldiers and German organisation and staff efficiency I think the army would be incomparable.

By that I do not mean to condemn as a whole our higher commands. Some of them are most excellently filled – our own Division could not be better served – but what I mean is that there is 'room for improvement' in our service and it would surely be well if it was looked to.

16th January '16

As I slept last night there came a banging on my door which startled me into peevish wakefulness, I thinking it an alarm! But Beck,[i] the colonel's messenger, had nothing so awful in store. It was only a notice that today there would be a walking competition [marching event] and that B must enter two teams. B accordingly did it, as ordered.

The event came off this afternoon, the machine-gun team winning. They marched jolly well and thoroughly deserved the success. Afterwards Worthington and I rode as far as [illegible] to have a look at the place. We ran into a French battalion on the move there. God save the mark! Its transports, drawn by the most terrible conglomeration of decrepit horses it is possible to conceive, stretched for hundreds of yards. The men looked the usual tough and hardy French type but were all over the road, in any order and looked, but for uniformity of clothing, not a

i Pte James Herbert Beck.

great deal better than an armed mob. They must be good fighters else they could not have accomplished what they have, but I never saw troops whose appearance better belied their reputation.

17th January '16

A joke has just come to light – a joke perpetrated on New Year's Day. The Camerons[i] sent a message of goodwill for 1916 to the Brigade, coined in Gaelic. The brigade did not understand it and asked for an explanation. This was duly rendered and amused the Staff considerably. Grant[ii] immediately scented game, and caused the message to be wired to our CO, marked urgent. We all knew that the CO had been hurriedly called off parade that day and that he had left simply bursting with importance. But we did not know that he had taken the message as being a ciphered one or that he had pored two hours over it in a vain attempt to decipher it. That, rather than own to the rustiness of his knowledge of Playfair,[iii] he had sought local help, and only admitted his failure to the Brigade afterwards.

The Staff spent quite a happy day over it, as would we have had we known, but the CO has admitted the joke against himself to no one. And where we got it from cannot be told by me, even here.

Another item of passing fair general interest was told me today. Col Kentish, now of the Divisional School[iv] but lately the worshipped CO of the East Lancs, is the hero. His battalion had been having rather a thin time. So much so that the doctor became overworked and he had to go away on leave. A new man came to temporarily fill his place. The new man was very new – just out in fact. The wet, the mud and dirty, ugly

---

i The Queen's Own Cameron Highlanders.

ii Maj. Arthur Kenneth Grant.

iii The Playfair cipher used a manual symmetric encryption technique, which encrypted pairs of letters or digraphs, instead of single letters as in a simple substitution cipher. It was harder to break, because the frequency analysis for simple substitution ciphers does not work with it.

iv The 3rd Army School of Instruction at Flixecourt.

wounds distressed him. His face became long and miserable. 'That is not the sort of expression I like to see on my officers' faces,' said the CO, 'I will see the doctor at Orderly Room.' Duly the MO paraded. 'You look depressed,' said the Colonel, 'And I cannot allow my officers such untold luxury. You must smile, you must laugh. There is a barn there and here is a mirror. You will go into the barn, taking the mirror and practise hilarious expressions before it for one hour daily until you feel capable of maintaining a permanent aspect of cheerfulness.' The doctor only had one practice. He was permanently cured.

I have not met Col Kentish, but I can quite understand why the East Lancs loved him so.

18th January '16

Poor Bland is in rather serious trouble. Major Merriman has charged him before the CO with using 'insubordinate language', a most serious thing if it is true. I do not believe there is any foundation, nor does anyone else and Bland denies any such thing. The major unfortunately thoroughly dislikes the old boy and treats him abominably. He told me 'he was utterly sick of him'.[i]

i 'You will be expecting to hear something about Merriman . . . Perhaps a few characteristics to begin with. He is of the genus fox, weasel, stoat, ferret, and rat. Whether these creatures <u>are</u> of one genus or not I don't care. But combine all their more unpleasant qualities and you have him. He is cunning, smooth-faced, double-tongued, uncertain in temper, ferocious, predatory and given to burrowing underground. He is a born intriguer rejoicing in pulling secret wires, striving to undermine other people's reputations, gloating over their mistakes, making the worst of their errors, always imagining evil, always eagerly searching after vicious motives, stooping to wilful invention to cover up any mistakes of his own, and piling up damnation for others if thereby he can save his own face . . . He gets in the ear of the powers that be, and by subtle suggestion and careful deference worms his way into their confidence, and having won his way, maintains his position by deliberately artless flattery, constant court and

It is a great pity, but we all sincerely trust Bland will come out all right. The chief misfortune is that the major is no soldier, he has no idea of 'pulling together', and is filled with the conviction that he should take every petty little thing to the CO, so changing it from the petty to the serious and upsetting everyone's applecart. I believe he means most awfully well but I must also admit that he has strange ways of showing his good intentions. However, let him pass.

This afternoon I have had a topping job, being one of the Clerks of the Course for the Divisional Cross Country run, an event in which our poor old team was quite outclassed. We will draw a veil over that sad part of the day and hope for better things next time.

For myself, I met Major Dillon, GSO1, with all the other clerks at 2 p.m. and rode right round the course. The major is just a splendid fellow, the *beau idéal* of a soldier. Thank God we still have some of his type left to us.

Captain Warr,[i] of the Gunners, and I had the same stretch to divide between us and we paddled up and down it in the wind and rain till the race came along – a half-mile stream of panting, dead-beat humanity, still game and cheery after four miles but pretty well all in. The going was really awful.

———

persistent attentions . . . In fact, my dear, he is the rankest poison I have ever met. He is a pure prig, he acts as a prickly irritant on all simple, decent people, and yet he poses as a friend of the needy, the careful dispenser of good things, the father of his flock . . . What are his relations with Headquarters? He is working day and night to oust our present Second in Command and to take his place. Whether he will succeed or not, I cannot say. If he does it will be a horrible disaster. So he pays eternal court to the CO, busies himself with the Second in Command's job, very cautiously feels his way and takes every chance of improving the situation, catching up any word of criticism of his rival and hastening to clinch it with a wise head nodding and murmured agreement' (Bland, 18.1.16). It is surprising that this letter escaped censorship, but perhaps Captain Bland was the duty censor at the time.

i Capt. William Charles Samuel Warr.

Warr told me, during our wait, something of the first battle of Ypres.[i] In his words, 'The Germans came on, line after line, battalion after battalion till the whole landscape was blotted out by a sea of grey.'

'Our infantry fired and fired till men's arms became dead with the strain of holding their rifles. The guns came up close behind the foot and fired into the oncoming mass at point-blank range, literally blowing heaps of it into the next world. As fast as the gunners could load they fired and that awful slaughter went on from about 8 a.m. to 1 o'clock when the 1st and 2nd Divisions came up and took some of the pressure off the 7th. The infantry suffered little from rifle fire but were simply smothered with shell and shrapnel. It must have been a perfect inferno. The Queens came out with 30 men, the South Staffords with 75, the Royal Welsh with 50 and so on. They had been full battalions in the morning.'

Warr's own battery lost every man and every horse, also two guns which they afterwards regained. Warr himself was wounded three times.

That was the day when the 7th held the line and stopped the Prussian Guard from getting through to Calais. The German losses were more than 300,000. I do not know what ours were, but a division is only 18,000 men. Our men must have been wonderful. It makes one very modest, being in contact with them. Also it makes one very proud to be in the 7th Division.

Warr said, 'Our infantry is marvellous. When properly trained I'd back them against the world.' Please heaven the 22nd may one day earn a reputation sufficient to justify its inclusion in that opinion.

19th January '16

B Coy lost their match against C this afternoon – and well we deserved to. C had a very good team going but the same cannot be said for ours.

i In 10.1914, Ypres was captured from the Germans by Allied troops who had retreated there after the fall of Antwerp. It remained under siege for some weeks until this was finally called off. The battle was the scene of mistakes by the senior commanders of both sides, and marked the end of the much reduced British Regular Army.

However, it was a good game, rivalry ran high and the men got most excited and keen.

This evening the battn has been on night operations and I have had the patrols again with Wicks.[i] There is a marked improvement in the way the men work and I feel certain that in a very short space of time they will become quite efficient.

And today has come glorious news about leave. I am to get mine on Feby 4th, next to the Colonel, who goes first. It is a stroke of luck and I could jump for joy. The bare thought of it is most exciting. And to think that in about a fortnight's time I shall really see you and Babs again is joy untold.

20th January '16

One of the virtues of discipline is that under its hand you can be messed about, lifted to the heights of anticipation, dashed to the depths of despair, told this and told that and generally fooled around and yet learn to wear a smile and keep your temper under it all. So I felt today. Since yesterday I had walked on air thinking of my leave and the joy so soon to be mine and here today I have a cold *douche* flung over me by being told, quite casually, that all leave is off for some time and so I do not go after all. Of course one grins and says, 'Oh, never mind,' but I really would like to return to 'civvies' for just one day and be left alone with these inconsiderate blighters who do as they will with you without the slightest consideration for human feelings.

I have been off duty this morning, being a trifle dicky. It was nothing more than a filthy head and a pain in the tum but I felt pretty bad while it lasted. Smith, our cook, I believe was responsible, for I had a tour into his utensils afterwards and found them in a most disgusting condition. I told him he was a dirty beast and that I would play the devil with him but he was so repentant, so full of the assurance that it was today only that the things had even been grubby that I have agreed to his having another chance.

i 2nd Lt Frank Cowlin Wicks.

These fellows get lazy when on a soft job, I am afraid. The easier time they have, the easier they want. But friend Smith will be working some of his comfortable fat off on seven days' pack drill if I catch another spot of grease on his pots and pans.

21st January '16

We have fought in a wood, we have retired through a wood, and have advanced again through the same wood. We have done that for a whole morning and marched ten miles in all to do it. And it has made us very tired. But has taught us quite a lot – if nothing else at least what an ass a man can make of himself. One or two officers simply got lost with their men at the beginning of the manoeuvre and remained so to the end, getting very worried and quite excited in the process and a considerable wigging as a fitting terminal to their foolish performances.

These big shows, I must confess, however evilly it may reflect upon my disposition, often gratify me, or, rather, basely amuse me. One is so apt to think of majors and colonels as moons in the firmament and brigadiers as suns. Indeed oft-times they seem greater even than these – absolutely omnipotent and omnipresent. But when you come to divisional days and 'pow-wows' take place and quite big people are most politely told off and take it without a murmur to, there always comes into my mind the old Gilbert and Sullivan couplet: 'On every side Field Marshals gleamed, And Dukes were three a penny . . .'[i]

This old Army of ours causes me to recall several such little extracts. For instance, one very true saying comes into my mind time and time again. It is the old one: 'The bigger fleas have little fleas upon their backs to bite them. And these same fleas again have fleas, and so ad infinitum . . .'[ii]

Pullen, of the South Staffords, now Second-in-Command of the Brigade Bombing Company, was in to mess last night. He was telling me how

i The lines are from a poem, 'King Goodheart', by W. S. Gilbert alone.
ii From the nursery rhyme, 'The Siphonaptera': 'Big fleas have little fleas/Upon their backs to bite 'em,/And little fleas have lesser fleas,/And so, ad infinitum . . .'

much he thought of our men and that, in his opinion, they would do better than his own at the next attack from the reason that they had been together from the start, had been well trained and that both officers and men knew each other so well. His own poor battalion is now more or less of a collection of oddments with officers scratched up from any old place. It is very rough on the old Regular battalions and I only do trust the new ones may be able to take their place as well as he thinks.

22nd January '16

A quiet little day of carrying on so far as the morning went, but this afternoon 6 and 7 Platoons played for the best team in the Coy. It was a fast and furious match, not very scientific but exceedingly energetic, and ending in a draw. I thoroughly enjoyed it, it was so refreshing, all the players being so whole-heartedly in the game.[i]

And tonight has come definite news of my leave.[ii] I go on Feby 3rd. Hooray! It is truly splendid, and a day sooner than ever I anticipated. I could shout for joy.

I was talking with the Second-in-Command of the Staffords today. He had rather an idea. Nothing less than to tackle the German trenches at night. Make a night attack on them and try and break through before morning. It would be difficult but it certainly sounds feasible. I wonder. It is well worth thinking about and there would be stranger things than the maturity of some such idea.

It is the wire that is the trouble. I cannot think of any good way of

---

i 'This afternoon, Sunday – I played football – my platoon against no. 8, myself in goal, and we won. For the rest? We are going on at the same old game, drill, trench-digging, brigade manoeuvres once a week, and so on. We might as well not be in France at all. Of course it's much nicer than Salisbury Plain (except that you're further off), as I get a good deal of pleasure from talking to the people' (Tawney, 23.1.16).

ii The prospect of leave had been made uncertain by German submarine activity in the English Channel.

dealing with that. Nor, apparently, can others better able to cope with the problem. It always seems to me so hopeless to strafe it with artillery, for the simple reason that the Bosche at once smells something is up. Yet, if you do not cut it, you certainly can't get men into the enemy trench. It is the most puzzling problem of all.

23rd January '16

It is remarkable how the tiniest of causes in the army may have most momentous results. By that I do not infer that Neuve Chapelle was in any way affected by Pullen but the fact remains that it may well have been. Delay was the chief trouble there and, as I have told Pullen, it is quite possible that he may have been a contributory cause. Pullen in those days was a full blown private in the Stafford Terriers. His Brigade had marched and marched since landing but on the particular day on which Pullen first exercised the functions of field rank it had marched just a bit beyond anything it had done before. Also there were no halts. Pullen stuck it for one, two, three hours – then he said, 'Let us halt.' And those about him complied.

His section of fours was third from the leading one of the battalion and his battalion led the Brigade. Therefore it will readily be seen that when Pullen halted, the whole Brigade did also, to the consternation of its general, the confusion of its Staff and the ruination of the language of its various Commanding Officers.

Later they made Pullen a Lieutenant. I think he thoroughly deserved it and that, for a man who has wielded Brigadier's powers, he bears his honours modestly.

Cushion has left us today.[i] He has gone to St Omer, to HQ for his training. We all feel rather sad about it, and I know he was awfully sick when it came to actually going. However I sincerely hope he will

i '[Lt William] Bill Cushion has forsaken us all for the Flying Corps' (Bland, 24.1.16).

progress well in his new role and live to make a name for himself.[i]

Rather a good tale was told me this morning, at the expense of one of the gilded officers of the U.P.S. Battn.[ii] He rolled up in the trenches to take over, clad in every latest essential for the compleat officer. A compass hung over one shoulder, glasses over the other. A map-case dangled from his belt and a mighty haversack rubbed his thigh. A revolver and trench digger gave him a bellicose appearance, which a periscope and a cartridge case in no way modified. He smelt faintly of violets and he wore yellow gloves.

The habitués of the trenches gazed upon him in wonder whilst they furtively fingered the odd pieces of clammy chocolate in their breeches' pockets and cast sly, shy glances down at their tattered and mud-caked raiment. But the major, an old hand, was in no wise impressed. Rather was his knowledgeful bosom filled with a great pity. He took the

---

i 'I understand that the official view of our functions is that there will be a big offensive in March or April, and that once the Germans are on the move, we (the Division) shall pursue them in the open. At least this is what a Lt, with whom I recently had a talk, tells me. He says the Staff feel pretty sure that by attacking everywhere at once we shall break through. But then Staff nearly always are confident. I don't feel myself very happy. My own feeling is that our national mistake [is one] of relying on quantity [and] forgetting quality. The easy and impressive thing to do is to multiply men. The difficult and important thing is to get "brains" in command & to scrap ruthlessly the social traditions which make it easy for gentlemanly fools (not always so very gentlemanly, though!) to be officers. That is what France did when she was really fighting for her life in 1793 – as far as I can remember about 6,000 officers were sacked in a year, and privates promoted wholesale. Result: Napoleon's marshals, nearly all of whom were the sons of artisans & small tradesmen' (Tawney, 23.1.16).
ii The UPS, or University and Public Schools Battalion, which at first was affiliated to the Royal Fusiliers, was the idea of J. L. Paton, high master of Manchester Grammar School, who wished to encourage men with an educated background to enlist. It was described as 'the shortest way to a commission one can think of'.

resplendent one by the arm, steered him into a dug-out and there talked vaguely about lunch. Incidentally he apologised for its absence. The other rose to the bait like a trout. He had lunch, never worry. Allow him, he prayed. The Major was gracious.

The haversack was opened and out came patent foods, concentrated foods, essences of foods, compressed foods – all sorts and conditions of most appetising looking little morsels. Then a flask was produced, a most resplendent affair – all gold, cut glass and engraving. Then a miniature stove and tiny silver spoons and forks. The major smoked a Teofani[i] – from a platinum cigarette case – and never blinked an eye-lid. All was spread on the rickety table. Everywhere around was an air of moneyed comfort, that gracious air which wealth on plenty alone can produce, when all at once, Whiz-Bang!! Whiz-Bang!!!! Two of them right on each other's heels and both plumb on top of the dug-out. The major still puffed at the Teofani and only a quick vibration about his belt betrayed the fact that he laughed muchly.

The new man – a trifle white and tremulous – was sitting on a motley heap of patent foods in the wettest corner of the dug-out. On the table was a great heap of mud. One solitary silver spoon stuck out of it. Of the rest of the splendour nothing remained.

'But this is terrible,' explained the bereft one. 'Isn't it?' said the major, 'Have a bit of chocolate. I'm afraid it's a trifle clammy but it's better than nothing.' 'No thanks. But my flask – I rather valued it!' 'Shall I send for the pioneers?' said the major. The other looked up at him quickly. Then he laughed, and it had the true ring. 'You must think me an awful ass,' he said. 'Not exactly,' said the major, 'In fact I rather like you – when you laugh.'

i Teofanis were expensive cigarettes made from a tobacco grown in Greece and Turkey. By 1916 they were manufactured in south London. The favourite wartime brand was 'King's Guard'.

Chapter 5
'Full of brimming excitement about my leave'

24 January–4 February 1916

24th January '16

There is a good tale going the rounds about the new bomb of ours. It has phosphorus as one of its ingredients, and this cheerful stuff possesses the virtue of burning right through whatever it touches. The Glosters[i] – I believe it was them – ran a patrol into the Bosche front line a few weeks back. As usual they found it practically empty, but, having strafed a sentry, they came upon a dug-out from which a light gleamed.

'Anybody in?' enquired the linguist of the party. 'Yah!' 'How many?' 'Five of us.' 'Oh, good, well divide that between you!' and the humorists let loose a phosphorus grenade. I am told the Bosche did not appreciate the joke. About thirty of him [sic] were strafed altogether and the patrol then came back, bringing its wounded in safely.

Here in billets some of our lads begin to pine. The distractions of the towns attract them. But leave is scarce. Therefore one or two, I am afraid, have taken the French variety, strictly on the principle that when in Rome

---

i The Gloucestershire Regiment.

you do as the Romans do. But difficulties strew the path for the pleasure-seeking sub[altern] when his quest is unauthorised. He cannot go by train because RTOs [Railway Traffic Officers] are sometimes inquisitive and ask to see passes. He cannot walk because of the distance and no mounted officer will lend him a horse without knowing where it is going. Other means must therefore be found. Somehow someone found out that a man living in Airaines owned a motor car. He was no less august a personage than the mayor. Yet, such is the English faith in gold, that two of our brightest youths set out the other day to attempt to bribe him into aiding them in a felonious enterprise. And strangely enough they succeeded.

An hour later they bore down on Abbeville. But there an unforeseen difficulty arose. There is a road guard there, with a barricade, and no motor-cars are allowed through unless they bear a permit. The guard is furnished by the French. The car halted. Its owner was forlorn. Alas, he had no permit. The English officers had asked him to drive and he did so thinking they surely possessed a *laissez-passer*. '*Mais, oui! C'est terrible!*' 'What's the matter with John Willie?' asked he of the bright twain who had no French. 'These johnnies won't let us through without a pass.' 'Is that all? Easy, here, show 'em this.' The paper was unfolded and shown to the sentry who duly saluted it, waved a polite hand and stepped aside.

The car sped on and he who had French gazed at his companion with added admiration. 'You're a topper,' he said. The pass was duly returned to the pocket book. 'I mustn't forget to give it to the Quarter-Master tomorrow. I meant to today but luckily I forgot. The Skipper will begin to play up if he don't get his picks soon. I've had this bally indent for 'em on me a week now.'

'My son,' said the other, 'You will come to a sad end. I foresee it. But, in the meantime, we will adjourn to the *Tête Boeuf* and you will there purchase even one bottle of Perrier Jouet with which we may drink to your present health.'

And it was even so!

Rather a joke at HQ this evening after CO's orders. All OC Coys were there and we had been having a most serious discussion about various little ruses for strafing Bosche. In the end the CO evolved one. No less than to dig a deep pit, cover it with turf and brushwood and then entice a Bosche patrol on to it. How it was to be dug without the enemy seeing it and how the chalk was to be removed he did not say.

I could not help it. I said, 'Sir, if only you would put a man-trap in the bottom and bait it with a sausage, I feel sure all would be well.' There was a deathly stillness for a moment, but then came a wild burst of laughter, the CO's being the loudest of all. On the whole it was really fortunate for me that his sense of humour is well-developed.

25th January '16

Setting out at 8 a.m. and returning to one's billet at 9 p.m., makes a full day, especially when one has included in it seven miles on foot, fourteen on horse-back and fourteen in a motor-bus. We have accomplished that today, Murray and I, yet, except that we both feel mighty sleepy, neither of us are tired. That is surely proof of the fit state one unconsciously gets into at this game.

After a field exercise in the morning we have been to Vignacourt for a lecture, which did not mature, this evening. Coming back Kentish was telling me that it is likely we move up to the trenches in about ten days. Rather a surprise for all of us, also quite a worry for me. My leave is booked to begin on Feby 3rd, or ten days from now. If we move it will mean its cancellation and indefinite postponement. However I keep cheerful and hope for the best.

This afternoon Murray and I had to saddle up ourselves. He girthed up on the off side, and swore and sweated in the struggle. But in the end he conquered and we led our mounts forth. His refused to let him come near it, jibbing and backing all round the yard. In such a usually sober horse it was quite alarming – till we looked round for the cause. This was not hard to ascertain. Donald had got the off stirrup under the saddle and had girthed up so. His horse had borne that, but the weight of the round, nuggety Donald on his back to jab the iron still further into his vertebrae was just a bit more than he was prepared to put up with. No wonder he was peevish.

Major Allfrey told me of a little incident which serves to show how quick the men can be if really put to it. The firing line today startled a wild pig which careered down the line at a fine pace. A man saw it coming, whipped out and fixed his bayonet and had pointed [it] in a flash. The major said it was done before you could say 'knife'.[i]

I suggested that perhaps such celerity was in part due to the fact that the man mistook the pig for a German general. The major however missed the point of this pearl, so I was reduced to laughing at it by myself – a state of things I always find rather dull.

26th January '16

Nothing much to record today. It is the weekly half-holiday and everybody is playing football. Six and seven platoons play off in the company competition and the battalion is playing the Staffords at Le Mesge.[ii]

Both will be good matches. I am staying to see the former. I am too keen on getting a really useful team out of B to worry about much else in the football line at the moment.

We have a series of jumps going now and Worthy and I were over

i 'We have been out since this morning till afternoon on a wood fighting scheme in a forest a few miles from here which was very strenuous, as the wood was so thick with undergrowth it made it difficult to keep direction in consequence. You can imagine my surprise when slowly going through with my men behind me, to see two wild boar career past about 25 yards in front of me and disappear in the undergrowth . . . There was no danger, as they never bother with anybody unless incited . . . They are like a pig, only twice the size, with long hair and tusks' (Gomersall, 25.1.16).

ii 'This afternoon watched our battn play the 1st South Staffordshires. It was a hard game and we just lost, 2–1. I then had tea in the village with two of our officers, where we were guests of the officers of our Divisional Field Ambulance. They were a ripping lot of doctors – been out at it since the commencement, and all the time with the fighting division, and we are very proud to be in it' (Gomersall, 26.1.16).

them this morning. They are quite good and Lizzie takes them jolly well. She has come on splendidly since coming to France and I am more than pleased with her. Horses are always so companionable and knowing, but I think she is more than usually so. She seems to know exactly what I want and attunes herself to my moods in quite a wonderful way. She has little or no appearance, but she is a good, trusty, useful and sound old soul and I am very fond of her.

27th January '16

We are a most orderly battalion – or so at least we have been told, and I have not it in me to disbelieve it. We have latrines fitted up inside canvas huts, ablution stands, with tables, basins and drainage pits complete, beneath green canvas shelters. Paths made of up-ended tins let into the ground, very dry, well-drained and orderly.[i] And a great incinerator which burns all day and night and wherein every scrap of refuse from the battn is burned to ashes. All except the tins. That's our one trouble. We have on average fully 100 tins a day taken from that furnace, all cleansed and pure and clean. They are then packed in heaps and, later, buried. That seems to me a waste. The government must be paying out in one way and another some thousands of pounds daily for new tin. Well, why not collect all this used stuff, ship it back and sell it to the highest bidder. The Army is so well organised that this should present very little difficulty and by it the taxpayer, poor devil, might easily be eased of some of his burden. The Germans, I believe, already do it. And we point a finger of scorn at them and say, 'Ha-ha, see how the Bosche is feeling the pinch. See what the Navy is doing.'

I think that a wrong attitude. Navy or not, I think the Bosche is too well organised to be foolish enough to waste that which he knows he will only have to pay for again.

i Tins of 'bully beef' were notoriously unpalatable, and, unopened, were used to strengthen the floor of trenches. (See Michael Stedman, *Manchester Pals*, Leo Cooper, 1994, p. 76.)

Last evening I had the joy of two letters from you. The latter one full of brimming excitement about my leave. My darling, what happiness it is to look forward to. Your letters have put me all in the height of expectation, and I am all aflutter with eager anticipation. I am more than fortunate to get away so early and to have the sweet wife and child I have waiting for me. My God, how I long to see you both and to hear Baby talk. What a glory that child is, what an anchor for a fellow to have.

28th January '16

This is indeed a life where one must accustom oneself to sudden change. Last night, we had retired to bed, indeed both Donald and myself were asleep when there came a banging on the door and, getting up, I found Sgt Nuttall,[i] from the Orderly Room, waiting for me with orders. We were to leave Le Quesnoy in the morning for Fourdrinoy – our old billet – and on from there the next day for the region of Albert and the trenches.

Some change from the ordered life of ease we have lately dropped into, and some excitement. But we left Le Quesnoy quite happily this morning and are now back in our old billets of Fourdrinoy with orders just to hand for a further sixteen miles march tomorrow. I think we will be in the trenches again by Sunday night. It is quite cheering, quite exciting – but I do hope it will not crab my leave. That is my one fear at the moment. Of course outward mail has ceased so I do not know when I will next be able to write to you. Not that I greatly desire to until I can advise you definitely because I know the uncertainty must be more trying to you than it is to me.

I am told disturbing rumours about a big German offensive which has resulted in loss of trenches and heavy casualties.[ii] These I trust,

i Sgt James Nuttall.
ii The Germans had taken Frise, to the east of Bray, and had launched an attack on Dompierre, across the River Somme. This is within the sector of the French Sixth Army and very close: just five miles east of Bray and twenty from Amiens.

however, are only rumours and merely the outcome of a fertile brain working for reasons for our sudden move. If only I can do one more tour in the trenches and then get back on my leave I shall be happy indeed. For then I shall feel more as though I have really done something than it has been my fortune to feel up to now. The fact that the old regiment has its own, its very own, piece of the line to hold will make a great deal of difference to us all.

29th January '16   Cardonette[i]

It is now 9.50 p.m., and a very dark night. But in our humble billet we have a hanging lamp dispensing light and cheer, a table on which to write and a bed-form on which to sleep. It is moderately dirty, more like *la guerre*. Yet we occupy it for one night only and no doubt tomorrow it will appear to us as a palace of comfort far out of reach. For tomorrow we move on again, another twelve miles. Today we did 16 – through Breilly, Ailly-sur-Somme and Saint-Sauveur. A slow march it was, slogging over heavy roads.

This village is full of troops, absolutely packed out. There are Scotch, Irish and English, all on the move upwards and only resting here *en route*. It is a regular bustle all around, laughing, chattering men, stamping horses, clattering carts, hoarse words of command coming out of the darkness and sharp batches of cursing from unlucky drivers hard put to it to feel their way with restive horses on treacherous roads.

Tomorrow we leave it and move on to another unknown halting-place. Monday is spoken of as our day for taking over in the trenches. I hope it turns out so, for that would allow me a first tour of duty before my leave becomes due. Really I suppose, I should not think such things at such a juncture. One is supposed to have, as a soldier going into action, no other desire than some high-souled ambition to do or die for one's

i Cardonette is a village a few miles to the north-east of Amiens. This is the last time May identifies, whether in code or otherwise, from where he is writing.

country. Reality I am afraid falls far short. We go because it is right and proper that we should. But I do not think there is one high-souled one amongst us. On the contrary we are all rather bored with the job, the thought of the bally mud and water is quite sufficient to extinguish keenness, and we are all so painfully ordinary that we think of leave a great deal more than we do of the nobleness of our present calling. When one is tired and unwashed I think one is legitimately entitled to refuse to feel noble, if one so desires.

We hear tonight of a new gas the Bosches have been using. It does not affect you at the time provided you wear your helmet, but some eight hours later it produces chronic prostration which culminates, if exercise is indulged in, in death. Truly this is a cheery business. If only the dirty blackguard who devised such a thing could have his nose held to a tube of his infernal production, I think the world would be the better for being rid of a hateful personality.

What with gas helmets, tin hats and woolly waistcoats *le soldat Anglais* will soon be like nothing on earth. If only we could be clothed in rubber all over and fed through a tube I think some real progress in our equipment might have been made.

30th January '16

Another twelve miles today and now here we are in the substantial town of Corbie,[i] quite the most important place we have billeted in up to now. Again it is full of troops, full to overflowing – all sorts and conditions, both French and British. The streets are alive with bustle and activity, the roads blocked with transport, horsed wagons, motor-lorries, motor ambulances – these last much in evidence and each one full of shattered

---

i The small town was the largest so far visited by the battalion. It was in fields near Corbie that facsimile or dummy trenches of the German front line, which had been photographed by the Royal Flying Corps, were used for practice by the 21st and 22nd Manchesters.

humanity – cookers stacked with bundles of wood and tended by dirty men, mules laden with ammunition and limbered wagons loaded high with picks and shovels, barbed wire and boots, in fact all the vast paraphernalia of an Army on the move. And in among all the press the civil population rush and jostle, shrieking shrill cries, laughing, shouting, excitedly jabbering. It is a pandemonium out there in the streets so that one might wonder however order will be restored to the mass again.

The men are enjoying the place immensely. It is the first time the most of them have seen a French town and they are now out and about and all over it, buying the shops out of foodstuff and purchasing all their little desires. I am afraid when next the post leaves we shall have a sorry pile of mail to censor.

We move up to the firing line tomorrow, to a sector round about Fricourt. Life is somewhat uncertain there, I believe, and in some cases the trenches are not five yards apart. It is quite a lively part altogether, quite the real thing, quite a change from Le Fayel and the easy, joyous time we had there. It will be a new experience for us and one we all keenly look forward to, partly on account of the fact that to put us there shows faith in the battn and also that there it will be given a chance to earn its spurs.

I do, however, trust that the battn motors part of the way tomorrow. There is, however, no word of this yet. It will be most unfair on the men if they are shoved on to such arduous duties as trench work after a slog in full pack of fourteen miles. Yet I am afraid that it would be quite like the Staff to do this for us. It is easy to order men here, there and everywhere whilst you sit in an easy chair in a warm château. But fully half a hundred of my men have holes through their soles already. It is just such minor little things as this that make all the difference. So often, however, they are not taken into consideration by the 'gentlemen wot gives the orders'.

Later: We have now heard that we only move as far as Bray tomorrow, and into the trenches on Tuesday evening. That is good. Also I have seen the CO and have arranged that the Battalion's spare boots are issued tomorrow morning. This should do away with the worst cases. The outlook is much better. And so the world wags on.

31st January '16

Here I am again in a dug-out at long last. A good dug-out with a coke fire and wire-netting bed. It is dry and roomy and I am told remains so even though it may rain. It has been a long day, but so full of interest as not to have appeared so at all.

There was a ten-mile ride this morning, in company with the CO and other OC companies, along the Parcy road, a road full of traffic and with a most deplorable surface. Motor-wagons, horsed-transport, guns, ammunition trains crowded along it whilst here and there ramshackle country carts led back towards Corbie laden with the household goods of the refugees from Suzanne.[i] The Bosche gassed this place yesterday and shelled it heavily and the civil population have now been evacuated. Mud was everywhere, horses splashed with it, mules caked all over with it and men smothered in a positive armour of it. The original grey of the wagons was indistinguishable for dry slush. Great holes occur in the road, some from shells, others from the hard usage the surface has been put to. It was all dirty and strenuous and like the war one reads about but seldom sees.

Bray-sur-Somme is quite a substantial village, now very full of mud and just bulging with troops.[ii] We saw the Brigade there and bumped into General Fry who stopped and asked me what we were doing. His division is in on our right. Afterwards we walked the three miles uphill

i Suzanne had been used for the billeting of French soldiers. From 13.1.16, when the German artillery had found its range, the village was heavily shelled which resulted in the almost complete evacuation of its inhabitants.

ii Bray-sur-Somme was a strategic hub for both armies throughout the changing dispositions of the Western Front. It was first occupied in 8.1914 by the Imperial German Army, but during the Battle of Albert (9.1915) the town was heavily bombed and the Germans evacuated. It was subsequently under the control of British and French forces. While 'at rest' here, the Pals usually were assigned mining duties, but the 21st and 22nd Manchesters were allocated work to assist the Royal Engineers on the construction of a narrow-gauge railway to bring supplies to the front in preparation for the big push. (Stedman, *Pals*, p. 78).

to these trenches, the Bosches treating us to a burst of H.E. shrapnel en route, so adding to the interest but not to the risk, the burst taking place some hundred yards to our right.

These trenches are quite close – about 100 yards on my sector, but closing in to thirty and even to five yards on the left. Also the region is quite lively, artillery playing up on both sides no end.

We are really at the head of a salient which friend Fritz is trying to nip at the base. He has had quite a little push against the French at Frise on our right, and is now strafing Fricourt on our left. He has made no progress at the latter place, but we hear very conflicting news about the right. I trust, however, that the French hold him safely.

Our trenches are good, but open to improvement and I hope to start the company on something tomorrow night or Wednesday at latest. They are still at Bray, only the four OC Companies being in tonight with the object of getting fully conversant with the local geography before our men come along.

1st February '16

A day of explorations, spent in familiarising myself with the very intricate sector we take over this evening. I think I have got the hang of it fairly well by now but it has been quite a job.

Worthy has been kicking about with me a good deal on the same errand. His company is supporting mine. The weather keeps fine and the trenches good and I sincerely trust both may remain so.

The Norfolks go out tonight, away to rest billets.[i] I don't suppose we will see anything of them again, I think it one of the worst features of this game that one should be thrown in contact with such top-hole fellows from time to time only to lose touch with them right away. The lad, Burlton,[ii] commanding the company I relieve, is a splendid young fellow. He wears the Military Cross, has been out fourteen months, has

i The 8th Norfolks was relieved in the trenches by the 22nd Manchesters.
ii Capt. George Philip Burlton.

94

a splendid way with the men and yet cannot be more than twenty-four. He is slim and small and fair and the others call him 'Boy Blue', partly no doubt from the colour of his eyes. He is a plucky young beggar, yet looks more like a girl than a man. I should like to write a story about him.

The company is now all in. We have taken over from the Norfolks and the men are now in full possession of our really own little bit of line. It is quite an event, the best we have yet experienced.

2nd February '16

Some day! For the most of us it began by the night before merging into it, for all it commenced at 6 a.m. The company went through the night like veterans so that with daylight sentries posted we were able to get some sleep. Personally I had quite a stroke of luck in the morning. Gazing through my glasses at Fritz's line I saw a suspicious looking kind of erection, took bearings of it and asked the Gunners to strafe it. This they did with 6" How[itzer]s this afternoon to the huge delight of my company, who appear, against orders, to have climbed the parapet en masse to watch, and to friend Fritz's considerable discomfiture. The shooting was excellent, shells dropping all round till at last one lit right on the beastly thing, flinging mud and splinters sky high. The company cheer like schoolboys when a goal is scored.

The emplacement – for so it now is shown to be – is not yet done with however. Friend Fritz is a wily man and likes to feel safe. In this case he has covered himself with concrete blocks and steel plates. The latter however are now split in twain at one spot and no doubt tomorrow will be demolished.

At 5.35 p.m. I got a telephone message to say I was to proceed on leave at once, take the men with me and report in Bray at 8 p.m. Owing, however, to many minor difficulties, not altogether unconnected with mud, we did not start till 7.50. But then we ventured on a short cut across country on slender information supplied by the doctor. The result was rather disastrous. If I had not done it I could not have believed such a thing possible. Partly due to the blackness of the night and partly to the directions of a gunner officer, who had wind up to a most distressful extent, we marched a complete circle, finishing off the end of an hour just where we had started from. Thereafter I decided to risk the communication trench and this we stuck to manfully for about a mile. The mud however then became so awful that I personally decided to risk the job and walk along on top. I told the men they could do as they wished in the matter, and one and all climbed out after me.

I think the sniper must have known about the state of the trench and counted on us getting fed up about there. Anyway he put four shots past us in about as many seconds, the last whipping off a man's cap and causing him to cry out in affright. I had to order them all back in the trench and we resumed our struggle through the morass. And eventually it ended and we came out on top. And there the blighting Germans shelled us, shelled us all the way for a mile, bursting shrapnel all round the place. But we were too tired by then to worry much and by the mercy of God no one was hit.

In the end we straggled, through mud and shell-holes, into Bray at 11 p.m.

Everyone had gone to bed but Maiden[i] had a limbered wagon ready to take the men on to Maricourt. I routed out some of the other lazy devils and made them make tea for my party. That warmed them up a bit and at length they set off. Finch was also waiting with my horse but I refused to budge another inch. I am just about beaten, for the first and, I hope, the last time. However, here goes for a sleep on the Orderly Room floor and an early start in the morning.

3rd February '16

A long day. I was up off the Orderly Room floor at 6 a.m., had a sluice in a bucket, a shave in a mess tin and breakfast off a slice of ration bacon. Finch had my horse round at 7.15 a.m. and just as I was mounting up

i Lt Earl Langford Maiden, the battalion quartermaster.

came Taylor of the 21st. I was surprised to see him. They came in it appears last night just in time to miss the shelling the Bosches treated the town to yesterday. And they take over from us in three days' time.

The ride from Bray to Maricourt was most enjoyable. It was a beautiful morning. We got the train there and it left at 9.30, commencing a solid meander round northern France which lasted till we were finally deposited in Havre at 9.15 tonight.

It is blowing now, hard. I think we are in for a rough crossing and I expect all the Tommys aboard will be very sick, myself no doubt among the number. But I am going to turn in in my bunk, try for some sleep and chance it. Tomorrow, my soul, I hope to see you – at long last. What joy!

4th February '16

We did not get away after all last night. Why, I do not know. But when we woke up this morning we were still fast to the Havre quayside. We got some breakfast after a great struggle, the *Caesaraea* not being fitted for meals at all, and were mooching rather aimlessly round the deck when the AMLO [Assistant Military Landing Officer] suddenly arrived and told us we were all to clear out and go up to the Rest Camp, the which we accordingly did. We signed our names and then went down town to lunch at the Hôtel Normandie. I can recommend that hostelry to anyone. They did young [Stapylton-]Smith and myself awfully well. The Rest Camp I cannot recommend. It is very well got up but one resents being treated like a convict by a lot of top-men who never do any fighting, who never get dirty and whose two main objects in life appear to be, firstly, to look pretty and secondly, to make things as uncomfortable as possible for a lot of dirty, tired people who have escaped from the trenches for a few days. There are some top-hole fellows going back with this draft, men who have really been through the devil of a time but who have not lost in the slightest degree their innate, glorious cheeriness.

Young Smith, Stapylton-Smith[i] as you were, is an awfully decent boy in the Motor Transport. He supplies the heavies up Bray way with shells and was in the late big strafe at Suzanne, where he had a thin time indeed. Young Hickey,[ii] of the Norfolks, is also a jolly smart fellow. He tells me I can claim 15/- detention money for having been delayed here a day. That is very good. I am all over such things.

We have now come back to the quay and are shipped aboard the *Connaught* – the old Irish Mail boat I have travelled on a good many times before between Dublin and Holyhead. She is now coated in grey and fitted throughout with bunks and rifle-racks. We have spring-mattresses to sleep on – nothing else, but consider ourselves lucky. Yet I cannot help contrasting it with former journeys in the same cabin. What luxury was mine then. Yet was I not near so content. How wonderfully this job teaches one how little a man can rub along on! It is marvellous. And it is most good for us all. Of that I am sure, even though I do not always find myself particularly grateful at the actual moment of benefit.[iii]

i Driver/Mechanic Henry Miles Stapylton-Smith. The responsibility for this activity was held by the Army Service Corps.
ii Probably Lt Hickey.
iii The SS *Connaught* sailed soon afterwards and docked on the south coast of England. From there May travelled by train to London and on to Wanstead, Essex, where Maude was staying. He spent over a week there, with his wife and infant daughter, before leaving to return to the front on Valentine's Day.

Chapter 6
'What a game it is!'

15 February–6 March 1916

15th February '16

Bray again after ten days of utter, unalloyed happiness – ten perfect days of leave, with you, my own, and our darling Babe for my companions.

It has been ten days of such sweetness that I cannot express how much it meant to me. I loved every moment of it. Yet it was over so soon. It was over like a dream. And today has been strangest of all. Only last night I was in London, where life is as usual, where pretty girls laugh happily and men go about their business in peace and unconcernedly, and yet by five this afternoon I was walking down the road to this war-battered town, watching the shells burst fiercely in the valley below me. It was so strange, so unreal that I had difficulty in adjusting my mind to a due sense of proportion. That only twelve hours off should be our England still full of men who but dimly realise what this war is, seems quite impossible. In mental outlook they are as far removed from us as the Southern Pole, in fact a distance far greater than that separates us. It is strange. Yet perhaps it is as well. Because we here like our London to remain as we know and love it. I am sure it would greatly distress our leave men to find on returning home their England as chastened as the France they have left.

The battalion is still in the trenches, but comes out tomorrow night. I have orders from the CO to remain here and get billets prepared for the reception of the men when they come out. They will be done I am afraid.[i]

The weather conditions are bad and the state of some of the communication trenches atrocious. The shelling has been heavy, very heavy occasionally, but the casualties have mercifully up to now, been light. The belief that Fritz means to attack us here has gathered force since I left until it may now almost be regarded as a conviction.

The Brigade bombers have taken pity on me tonight and have fed and are sleeping me in their billet by the church. It is kind of them. D.S. Murray is now with them as 2nd-in-Command and bids fair to make a success of the job.

The house they occupy has a shell hole in its top right corner, the house across the road has a shell hole clean through it, yet are we comfy and warm and quite happy, almost as at ease as though we sat in our London, the London that is only twelve hours off, where there is no mud and where sweethearts and wives and sweet babes smile or chuckle or anon turn sad awhile when they think of us out here. Thank God for my leave! And now to bed.

16th February '16

Except the preparation of the billets, food etc. for the battalion when it comes out tonight, I have done nothing today. And accordingly I feel a slacker – though by no means a repentant one. The easy day has been too welcome for that. It has meant a gentle breaking-in for which I am grateful.

i 'We came in on Sunday evening, a lovely moonlit night, and us stumbling over grazing fields covered with shell-holes, while at every few hundred yards for 500 miles files of tired & cursing men were probably doing the same . . . we are in support till tomorrow when we go into the front line trenches for 3 days and then back to billets' (Tawney, 14.2.16).

It has rained heavily today and I can only imagine what the trenches are now like. It is always impossible to realise their real state unless one is actually in them – and then, strangely enough unless one is very tired, they never seem so bad as they do when contemplated from a distance.

Cotton has just come out. He is the first man down. I do not expect the rest till after midnight. Cotton is better again and has done this tour in the trenches. I am very glad. He is a good man, one whom we could ill afford to lose. Royle,[i] he tells me, has been evacuated to England, having gone stone-deaf. I do not know the reason of his trouble. I do not think he will be sorry. Since he lost the transport he has not been happy at all.

Fritz has shelled the village again a little today. He now seems to include it in his daily programme. All I trust is that he will have the decency to leave us alone at night. Being shelled whilst in bed is always most uncomfortable. I am told that we now have the Saxons opposite us, and I hope it is true. They are the cleanest fighters among the tribes of Fritz and are generally quite a sporting crowd.

17th February '16

Except for the ever-present, draining, fatigue parties, the battn has rested today. It has rained more or less continuously and I earnestly hope it will clear up before tomorrow and give the poor beggars in the trenches a chance. Fritz hasn't strafed the town today. I take it he is as wet and flooded-out as we are and with little heart left for strafing anything bar the elements.

The Corps Commander was coming to inspect us today but evidently the weather put him off. At any rate he didn't roll up after all.

I did a strange thing this evening. That is I started to write a story. I trust I am not going light in the head. It struck me as rather an enter-taining thing to do. I will send it to you when I have finished it so that you may judge of my sanity.

i 2nd Lt Harold Williamson Royle.

How I have dwelt on my leave this night. It has been with me awfully strongly, till I have felt quite humpy and fed up. It is such a painful contrast being here after all the glorious cleanliness and comfort of last week. Oh, my heart, how I wish this bally war could be won and finished with, so that we might be free once more to renew our old life and happy companionship.

18th February '16

The Divisional General came today. It still rained but he turned up all right in spite of it and talked cheerily to the men. He was very good with them and is a quick, alert, human soldier. He carries confidence and efficiency in his manner and one feels glad to be in his Division.

Our new Brigadier also holds a big reputation and everyone speaks most highly of him. I have not seen him yet but I hope to soon.

This blessed rain is most insistent. We hear parts of the trenches are now waist deep in water. No pumps can keep pace with a fall of this rate. I am afraid our next tour in will be a thing to be remembered. However, one must take it as it comes and we can all work up a smile even at our very pitiableness.

Cowan[i] told me today of a certain CO who suddenly turned up in the trenches on just such a night. The good man was filled with a chronic desire for efficiency. He chose an unfortunate time for it. Everyone was more or less water-logged, particularly fed up and dense. At last he met a depressed officer. 'Sir,' he said, 'do you realise that my battalion is in such a parlous state that the German could come over and take these trenches at any moment?' 'No, I hadn't noticed it, sir,' was the amazing reply, 'But, so far as I am concerned, he is certainly heartily welcome to them.' And the zealous colonel was so nonplussed that he almost forgot to strafe the apt-tongued subaltern.

I had a truly sweet letter from you tonight – the first since my return and written the night after I left. It is so full of love and longing that

i 2nd Lt William James Cowan.

my heart has ached in response to it. My darling, what a love is ours. I glory in it and can almost find it in my heart to feel thankful to this parting for causing, as it certainly has, us more clearly to realise how much we are to one another.

19th February '16

More rain today, in spasms of varying intensity. I never took such interest in the weather before. It is strange how having to live in a thing alters your degree of regard for it.

In the morning Worthington, Bland and I rode up to the battalion's battle station to have a look at it. All I hope is that there's no battle whilst we're here. The sides of the trenches had fallen in, traverses were down through whole sectors and the rest was knee deep in water. Personally I should like the fighting kept for fine weather. A sunny day must make an awful difference to one's interest in a battle.

I have just the reason for so much odd 'pooping off', as we call it, over the parapet at night. The sentries, ingenious men, endeavour to pass their time by transfixing a piece of ration cheese on their bayonet. They then lay the rifle on the parapet and stay quite still. Presently Brer Rat comes out in answer to a tickled nostril, finds the cheese and commences to nibble. The sentry then gently pulls the trigger – and another life pays forfeit to Mars.

Shelmerdine hit on an apt remark tonight at mess. Our table, be it whispered, in place of linen is spread with leaves of ancient *Daily Mails*. Shelmerdine said, 'You are requested not to read the tablecloth whilst taking meals.'

20th February '16

In the old trenches, again, back amongst dirt and dug-outs. Yet it is really not half as bad as I had expected. It has been fine today and the 21st must have worked hard to clear the worst out. The water is still fairly deep in one or two trenches but for the most part the passages are passable.

It was some tour getting in, the back communication trenches being in really a parlous state, but we managed it in the end. Fritz is quiet tonight and I trust will remain so, but over Fricourt way and also down towards the Somme there are sounds of more or less continuous heavy strafing. I trust it is Fritz who is getting it.

We have just had word that Zepps are expected over somewhere tonight.[i] Where they are off to no one apparently knows but, except as an item of interest, they worry us little here. It would be great however if one of our Archibalds[ii] could dot 'em one in passing.

21st February '16

A day of sucking pumps and squelching feet. We have pumped and scooped and shovelled the clock round and at length look forward to the moment when the last of the water has been gulped out over the parados.[iii]

It was a cold night and snowed a little but the trenches were mostly full of interest. Bowly took out a working party at 6.30 and nearly lost the lot. Fritz put up a light as they scrambled over the parapet, saw them and opened fire all round. They were got in again with no one hit but that was a mercy and I was thankful to have them in the fire step once more.

We strafed Fritz later with machine gun and rifle grenades, one of the latter falling right in one of his sap-heads[iv] where I trust he keeps a sentry group.

Burchill went out about 1 a.m. for a tour in No Man's Land. He had two men with him and they came across a dead Bosche sniper. They got his rifles, shoulder straps etc. and returned safely with these. Quite a creditable little piece of work.[v]

i There is no mention in the official record of Zeppelins flying over his area of the Somme at this time.
ii The slang term for anti-aircraft guns was 'Archies'.
iii Earthworks piled behind a trench to help prevent a rear attack.
iv 'Russian' sap-heads were trenches, usually dug through no-man's land towards the enemy and with temporary roofs, which could be dismantled quickly so that they were ready for use.
v Two days later Lt Burchill was accidentally wounded.

22nd February '16

I think I said two days ago that Fritz was very quiet. He has made up for it today. Early this afternoon he started with trench mortars on the immediate right support street [trench]. His third shot blew it in. I met Bull,[i] my runner, coming down and he told me this but reckoning that two shells never drop in the same place I carried on. There came a most appalling crash and I found myself on hands and knees in the trench bottom, smothered in mud, slightly dazed and with a nasty headache. Close acquaintance with trench mortars is not recommended. I do not like trench mortars at all.

Afterwards I got the artillery on for retaliation. This stirred Fritz up and he put H.E. shrapnel over us. Our heavies then had a fling at him and so things gradually worked up till a real ding-dong battle was in progress. And away on the left by Fricourt it reached a very high intensity, the evening sky was lit blood red by the bursting of shells in the town and the noise of it pulsed and pounded over the whole countryside. Later the rattle and roar of rifles and machine guns ripped out and a regular ding-dong scrap went on. We all 'stood-to' and hoped for a look in, but nothing came our way more than the magnificence of the spectacle.

Later we heard that Fritz had essayed an attack from Fricourt but had been badly mauled for his enterprise. Judging from what we saw of it I should think he'd had as thin a time as a fellow could want.

The trench mortar landed another hit on [trench] 62 Street this evening, half burying a working party and putting two of the men down temporarily with shock. I had to take them off and close the trench until 1 a.m., in the hope that Fritz will have gone to bed by then.

Tomorrow we must get all available artillery on it and try and smash up his machine.

i Pte William Bull.

23rd February '16

Today was to have been a day of artillery strafing but, alas for human plans, just as the first two shots went over it commenced to snow and has so continued up till now. The gunners could not see and so had to cry off, and we have been therefore left to carry on with a few rifle grenades pooped over the parapet.

Fritz is very persistent with his mortar. He has blown 62 in again today with it. We change over tonight, back into the support lines. It really means a change from sentry duty to fatigues. The men would much rather be in the fire trenches, but I am glad we are going back because of the better shelters we get there. It is pretty raw work for the men here with the trench inches deep in slushy snow water. Over the parapet all looks peaceful as a Christmas card. No sign of either Fritz or ourselves, the pure white fall covering everything.

The CO has been round this morning strafing the men like blazes. He talks to them as though they were so many mongrel curs instead of, for the most part, a lot of decent, stout fellows quietly doing their little bit. If he wasn't such a silly ass he would annoy me very much, almost as much I believe as he does everyone else.

24th February '16

I have been all round our sector today on a little tour with Prince. It is a strange line, full of bad bends and corners and enfiladed slopes. The old trench mortar has been at it again today. He blew 62 Street in more and has now dropped a 'dud' clean in the trench. We have all been to look at it but none of us will touch it. We know nothing about it and 100lbs of high explosive is a thing one gets a very high respect for here. No doubt the RE [Royal Engineers] will remove it and take it away and cut holes in it and pull out its inside and smell it and taste and burn it and do generally all those sort of hair-raising things which the truly scientific delight in. We are neither truly scientific nor in any danger of becoming so when it comes to touching 100lbs of high explosive.

We have been relieved now by the 21st, leaving them to a bright, starlit night and hard-frozen footways. We were sorry to quit, for we would sooner do the six days in and get the six days out than fob about every fourth day.

I walked down into Bray with Worthy and very pleasant it was in spite of our tired feet. He has stuck it well has Worthy. He has had a terrible cold and been far from well but has refused to leave the trenches, even though so advised. Rather a contrast to Merriman, who seems rather glad of any excuse to keep out of them.[i]

The new brigadier was round this morning and I was introduced to him. He is a topping chap, a soldier both in appearance and being and one feels glad to have him in command at very first sight. C Company tell a tale about him which even though malicious joy is apparent in the telling, is nevertheless quite true. I should hesitate to say that the CO has wind up. Certainly however he is extremely cautious. At [trench] 69 Street, which is sniped occasionally, he said to the general, 'I do not think I should go down there, sir. It is dangerous.' 'Oh,' said the general, 'Well there is no need for us all to go. You stay here if you will but I want to go and see the men.'

Bow-wow! Some gentle snub!

25th February '16

Wake up this morning after a joyful night of sleep to find the snow pelting down and covering the ground fully five inches deep. Also it was freezing hard. Br-r-r-ah! What a life! 'What did you go to Ashton for? Why did you join the Army?' as the regimental song asks.[ii] And one really does wonder why when one looks out of the window on such a morning as was today.

---

i 'Major Merriman has just returned from leave, and is sick in his billet' (Bland, 25.2.16).

ii This song is sung to the tune of one of the two regimental marches, *The Manchester*. The next two lines are left to the choice of the singer, but the final one is usually 'I must have been bloody well barmy'.

Cotton came in to breakfast with us. He brought the little bible which Burchill had taken from the body of the dead German on the night of his patrol exploit. I had a look at it. It was a kind of children's testament, filled with gaudy prints and the story told more in the nature of a series of short tales. On the fly-leaf was the name Hermann Stampa, I think, and over this in a child's hand-writing the word 'Dada'. War is very sad. Poor devil, I suppose he had a wife and kiddie somewhere filled with pride for the daddy who was a soldier and now stricken down with grief for the daddy who is 'missing'.

It brings things home to one to come upon a little human touch like that. It makes one feel that it would be well if Kaisers and ambitious, place-seeking politicians and other such who make wars could be stricken down and peaceful, home-loving, ordinary men be left to live their lives in peace and in the sunshine of the love of wife and children. Perhaps the man may have been quite a blackguard or just a hateful, bullying, swaggering Prussian and, as such, something to loathe and detest. I do not know. All I am conscious of is that somewhere in his Fatherland there is a little child who called him 'Dada'. I have a little baby too.

A regular topping parcel came today from you, full of all sorts of scrumptious things. It was received with whoops of joy and I doubt not will be but a happy memory before the week is out. Which reminds me that in my letter thanking you I included a tale from Prince which I must record here. He told it me last Sunday when we went in. He was up to his knees in mud at the time and with plenty more to come. 'Do you know,' he said, 'I had a letter from my aunt two days ago in which she asked, "Whatever do you find to do with yourself on a Sunday?"' It made us laugh, the very ridiculousness of it. It is scarcely believable. Yet it is quite true. How little people in England understand even now what war means. How modestly should everyone there go down on their knees each night and thank God for the Channel and that our home is the 'tight little island'.

26th February '16

Surprises await us all, and add savour to life, or, mayhap, the other thing. Judge of our mixed feelings therefore when of 12 noon today we were suddenly informed that we would relieve the 21st this evening. The snow still continuing, the Brigade have decided on 48 hour spells in. It is rather boring, the slog up to the line being such a labour for all concerned. I have no doubt, however, but that the restricted trench duty is quite wise during this inclement weather. So here we are once more back in our old fuggy dug-outs and slopping about trench-bottoms running with snow water.

I have taken over from Hobson[i] of the 21st, and all the Coy is in all right in support. It is jolly cold and our dug-out leaks in places but we'll improve things tomorrow by getting a better roof on etc.

Fritz has been pretty quiet as regards shelling but he keeps picking men off more or less successfully by sniping. His snipers are good and I have an idea that it is only by them that he mans his front line. Certainly I do not think he has many men in it.

We hear today that the Division takes over another 400 yards of line on our right. This means a general shift up and a weakening, I believe, of our strength. It seems the fate of the 7th Division to hold abnormal frontages with the very minimum of men. I expect we will manage all right though, and that our weakness is more apparent than real.

27th February '16

We have taken over the new line today, and some line it is being about half a mile in length and pretty bad in parts. At the moment it is a slippery way alternating between a trough of mud and a canal of snow water anything from two to twelve inches deep. A Coy is away on the right where the major seems to be taking his responsibilities very seriously. Ram is in the centre with C, and D and B remain in their old

i Capt. Charles James Mottram Hobson.

positions, which is now the left. It is a very long stretch of line for a single battalion to hold and I trust we may rise to the responsibility. I went on tour all round it with the CO this afternoon and afterwards we explored the support line and other etceteras. It was quite a journey and most interesting throughout, having to duck past enfiladed places and run like smoke down exposed slopes. When at last we got back the CO came to tea with us and we had quite a merry little party. He was most happy and natural, the best we have yet seen him. He tells me that when he goes on leave I am to stay at Head Quarters and leave the company to Murray. That is rather sad, for I had much sooner be an irresponsible, detached company commander than muck around at HQ with two doleful majors for company. Major Allfrey does occasionally smile but Merriman is unable even to raise a flicker. It is very sad. The more so because of the risk of affecting the men similarly. A laugh here is of such value.

Bland has come on so through that. He grins from morn to eve, swears he is enjoying himself top-hole and, I believe, really is. Good luck to him.[i]

At 10.30 a.m. an apparition appeared at the dug-out door. Prince and myself were just thinking of bed. 'Gas,' it cried, in muffled tones, 'Gas.'

i 'Frankie Harrison tells me that Merriman has surpassed in cowardly priggishness, lying under three blankets and two coats with a large brazier ablaze, while Harrison and all the Company shivered cokeless in the outer darkness. He is an impossible unspeakable cad. Frankie shed a tear or two this morning when telling me all about it. There is only one hope – that his nerve will give way soon. Otherwise he will probably be <u>accidentally</u> wounded. If I were up in the trenches with him I could alleviate and cheer the rest, but I might be sorely tempted to remove the cause, – a <u>dangerous</u> game, the morals of which don't worry me in the least. I would shoot him through the leg without a second's compunction. As it is, I shan't get a chance. He is feeling a worm for interfering with my leave, and of course I reassure him, but he <u>is</u> a worm all the same. Enough. He's very polite to <u>me</u> lately, so away with him and his works. I am still very happy about it all' (Bland, 1.3.16).

On with helmets and out we went, finding a jumble of men in all states of excitement. They soon got over that however, and we filed up and manned our parapet, quiet, coolly and somewhat bored. For an hour we stood to waiting for Fritz to give sign, a thing he refused to do, and in the end word came to stand down. No gas had come into our sector.

The helmet, though stifling at first, one becomes quite used to after a while, breathing becoming easy.

28th February '16

We have changed over tonight, moving up to the firing line to replace D. The trenches are parlous in the extreme, being thigh-deep in mud or knee deep in water according to the lie of the land. No one who has not experienced it can realise, what a fatiguing business movement under such conditions is. At home one asks, 'Why does not the Army move?' Out here one changes the query, with much more reason, to, 'How can it?' One's progress is a laboured wallow through a shifting quag. Yet we carry on all right and are happy, more or less. And everything carries on just as usual. Snipers fire, guns crash and grenades come over into the trench with a vicious crack and kill men and wound others, and the stretcher bearers have to wade off with their stricken fellows through the morass which eventually leads them to the Aid Post and their burdens back to the Base and dear old 'Blightie'. How the stretcher-bearers do their work I do not know. It can only be by terrible labour and a very high devotion to duty.

I had a letter from you this evening. Delivered up here it was wonderfully cheering. How really near you are, my heart, and yet what immeasurable space separates you and Babs from the life we live here. With you all is order and cleanliness, most comforting to experience. How that idea of cleanliness associated with you adds to my hunger to be with you again! Here all is grime and mud and grittiness. We come in, our rubbers covered with running mud to above the knee. Too tired to care we pull sandbags over the slime, roll under our blanket and are asleep in a trice. But we do not like it. Indeed it is our one great trouble this enforced griminess and running mud. It permeates everywhere, food, drink, papers, indeed I verily believe our very insides are coated, armadillo-fashion, with a layer of brown, French clay.

However, so be it. What can't be cured must be endured and I doubt not but that we can stick it as long as Fritz, and longer.

29th February '16

We are out again tonight. The Queen's asked to be relieved so the Brigade has changed the both of us. I am glad. The trenches are really too awful, and, though we have worked at them continuously, appear to get worse. Our men are done and without doubt a fresh battalion can do more to keep the mud under.

Water is thigh deep in places and the mud in others comes over one's knees and grips and holds one till often it is impossible to move and the unfortunate man must be pulled or dug out by a relief party. The journey down this evening was quite memorable, almost a Brucamps affair except that it was not so extended.

Men dropped by the road side exhausted. Others staggered pitifully along in bare feet, the mud having snatched both boots and socks from them. Others again went strong, chattering and laughing whilst among the lot the officers, those of us whose strength was equal to it, went in and out carrying a rifle for this man, giving a cigarette to another, helping a lame duck up on to his poor, swollen feet again and chaffing or cracking feeble jokes with them all. Over all hung a dull, wet sky. It was a dark night. Men were but shuffling shadows against the chalk mud of the roadway except when the lights went up from the lines all about us. Then you could see the huddled forms of tired, mud-caked Englishmen shuffling home from their labours. The war is a war of endurance. Of human bodies against machines and against the elements. It is an unlovely war in detail yet there is something grand and inspiring about it. I think it is the stolid, uncomplaining endurance of the men under the utter discomforts they are called upon to put up with, their sober pluck and quiet good-heartedness which contributes very largely to this. All the days of my life I shall thank God I am an Englishman.

1st March '16

A month ago today we took over our line here. It seems like six. My leave I think it is has lengthened the time so for me. It seems such ages since I had it.

Today the list has gone in for honours for the King's birthday. I have put forward my Coy Sergeant-Major and young Bull, my runner, for a mention and I sincerely trust both may get it. They have performed their duty at all times zealously and with cheerfulness. Two of C Coy have been recommended for the DCM, both for care of the wounded under dangerous conditions. The one rescued three men from a blown-in mine shaft, the other bound up his wounded comrades, though five were hit by rifle grenades and these beastly things kept coming over whilst he carried on. One knocked him down but he remains unhurt.

It has been an easy day, getting the men dry and cleaned up from their last excursion in the line.

We now hear that the French hold Fritz well in hand at Verdun and that his casualties there have been extremely heavy.[i] I only trust it is

---

i The longest battle of the First World War, Verdun was regarded by the German army as an opportunity to break out of a stalemate that existed and reach the Channel ports. An offensive was launched in February 1916, from which the defending French forces had to retreat. Enemy gains were made. In June, after shelling the French with poison gas, the Germans launched a massive assault. However this could not be fully consolidated because of the commencement of the Battle of the Somme on 1 July. German troops were diverted to face this new threat, so the French took advantage at Verdun to counterattack with some success. Territory was recaptured through October and November. Over these months the French lost 161,000 dead and 300,000 missing or wounded. German losses were 142,000 killed and 187,000 wounded. Undoubtedly

true. He 'Fritz', or his higher commander, seems a pushful fellow, always ready to attack, and that with seemingly a total disregard for casualties. Really one wonders how he goes on. These losses must be replaced somehow and his resources cannot be any more inexhaustible than anyone else's. It must tell in the end, of that there can be no shadow of doubt. And our growing Army will surely have a big lot to say when at length we make our next move. In the meantime the more Fritz attacks the better for us, so long as we can kill him in quantities at each attempt.

I don't think I have ever recorded a word picture of a dug-out. Yet I think I must, one so soon forgets otherwise. There are two which we fluctuate between, the one in the firing line, the other in support. That in the firing line we do not love. It leaks, and a leak is a thing guaranteed to damp the affection of the keenest man. Yet it is a big dug-out, roofed with the boles of trees and lined spasmodically with corrugated iron. It is about six yards long by two and a half wide. Corduroy[i] trench boards run down one side, and along the other are two bed-frames whilst a third stands across the bottom wall. The beds are oblong frames on two feet legs with wire netting stretched across them. On these we spread sand-bags with our blanket over-all and thereon we woo Morpheus when our tour of duty is not. Just inside the entrance is a round, oak, gate-leg table, a relic no doubt from some farmhouse where a Bosche shell has found a home. On this is spread the most appalling litter of week-old *Daily Mails*, *Bystanders* of last month, muddy gloves, a Very pistol and some odd charges for some, a brown-covered trench diary, odd candle stumps and one or two empty whiskey bottles, all jumbled up in a sea of pink, service message forms. The table is made clear for meals with

---

the action on the Somme distracted German resources, and the heavy French losses at Verdun were one reason that the brunt of the Somme assault was led by British troops.

i 'Corduroy' was a ladder-like implement, usually made from cut tree branches, laid flat on the floor of a trench.

pleasing celerity. Daley[i] merely thrusts all the litter back against the wall with a sweep of his arm and proceeds to set down our enamel ware in the space thus provided. We sit around for meals on up-ended, empty ammunition boxes.

In the support HQ we are more happy. This locality revels in the somewhat inelegant name of the Rat Hole, presumably from the number of human burrows in its immediate vicinity. Our dug-out there is small but it only leaks in one place. I will leave further description of it till tomorrow when perhaps I will have more time.

2nd March '16

I see I finished my entry yesterday by half promising a description of our abode in the Rat Hole and since nothing more worthy of note has happened today locally I think I will fulfil it. But, in passing, I must first record that we had today notification from Brigade that on the Ypres front our attack of 4.30 a.m. today was successful, that the Bluff was recaptured and all the objectives aimed at gained.[ii] That is satisfactory news. But to return to the Rat Hole.

I see I say that it only leaks in one place. That is an immense advantage and in this case is all the more to be made much of from the fact that the leak is in one corner where an empty ammunition tin can be placed unobtrusively to catch the drips, thus further localising the inconvenience and, at the same time, adding a tone of habitation to the abode in a similar manner to that in which the tick of the grandad clock in the hall adds a companionable note to the sounds of a household. The roof is the usual even layer of logs. A brazier hangs against the wall inside the door, a real door by the way – from a deceased

i Daley is unidentified. See note in Index of Names.
ii Although Second Ypres, notorious for the first use of chlorine gas on the Western Front, had ended in 5.1915, occasional skirmishes continued in this area. Third Ypres, also known as the Battle of Passchendaele, commenced in autumn 1917.

fowl-run. But we have tacked sacking over the hole the chickens were wont to use and so draught and dampness are excluded. The brazier is worth a mention. It is the usual trench type. That is, it used to be an oil drum. It has now, however, been extensively perforated with the pick end of an entrenching tool and is gorged daily with coke and wood and any other odd, burnable revetting material which our servants can borrow unobserved. These braziers are supposed to glow but this is a height of ambition they only achieve when they belong to Sergeant-Majors. In officers' dug-outs they merely smoke. But in fairness to them it must be said that they succeed in doing this remarkably well. One sticks it manfully until the candle is but a yellow flicker through the gloom and the fug quite unbearable and then one turfs the blessed thing out and protests to the servants. Later, when it has reached such a state of combustion in the trench that one is fearful lest Fritz, seeing the light, will commence to shell, it comes back again – and proceeds to smoke worse than before. Enough for the brazier. A small table fills the centre of our dug-out. There is a single seat at one end, a bench hewn out of the mother chalk along one side and a form, sand-bag covered, along the other. The table is seldom adorned with more than a rum jar for the reason that here we have shelves inserted in the walls wherein are thrust all odd papers. The sleeping accommodation in this case is somewhat different from the other. The bed construction is the same but they are situated further into mother earth and about two feet lower down than the floor of the main, or mess, room. It is dry and warm down there and one quite forgives it its colony of mice for that reason. So much for dug-outs.

I had a letter from Barnard[i] today, who is now out here with the 23rd. He tells me poor Reid[ii] has been killed, bombed by a Fritz whilst out on patrol. He was badly wounded but died an hour or two afterwards. 'He was game to the last,' writes Barnard. He would be. He was that sort. Quiet, keen and reliable, I liked him from the start and it was me who

i 2nd Lt T. H. Barnard.
ii Lt William Morrison Reid.

got him his commission in the old days when [illegible] and I did such things. God rest his soul, he was a good lad!

3rd March '16

All morning at the brigade office getting out a map of our battle positions and bearings from same to various points of vantage. In the afternoon Don Murray, who returned from leave this morning, and I rode all round the hills outside the town on a tour of combined inspection and pleasure. It rained slightly but was pleasant all the same. It is quite a picturesque district, with the Somme glistening in the valley and the patchwork uplands rising high either side of it and in the summer I should say would be a pleasing spot indeed. At the moment however all is sodden and overhung with a dull grey sky which threatens more rain, or snow, to come.

We go in again tomorrow for, I am afraid, another very wet turn. The spring, however, must soon be with us now and until then we must just carry on with what resignation we can.

4th March '16

In a dug-out that leaks badly. Time 1 a.m. Just in off my tour of duty. Trenches knee deep, everywhere. Snow and sleet with a biting gale the order of the night.

Sentries cold but cheerful. Fritz very quiet. Hope he is as mucked up as we are.

The dug-out drips incessantly. There is an inch of slush on the floor. I have arranged my oilskin so that it may splash the drips off the bed on to the floor. Bowly's snoring peacefully on the bed at the bottom end. He has rigged an iron sheet in a very precarious manner on four pieces of stick over him. The water dropping on this makes a monotonous not to mention doleful sound. What a life!

What a war! What a game it is! Bow-wow!

5th March '16

The surprising thing about trenches is the persistent way in which they accumulate water. You clean a place quite dry and leave it happy yet when you return in an hour's time there it is full as ever of slush. Where the water comes from the Lord alone knows, all we have time to be concerned with is the fact that it is there and that it has to be persuaded to leave there as quickly as possible. And that is what we have been doing all day. And now it has snowed again and we'll have to redo the whole job tomorrow. What a life!!

It is your birthday today. How I wish I could see you, my dearest, to wish you happy returns. Never mind, next year we'll be all over it.

6th March '16

1.05 a.m. and just in after a pretty long day. We are back in support, Murray having taken over the front line with D. That job was done with by 7.30 p.m. but at 9 o'clock the CO had arranged to call for me in order that we might prosecute a tour of inspection of the back of the line over the top and from here to the right. We started and have been on it ever since. It is extremely interesting up there. The trenches look so different from above. We found what we wanted and tomorrow night I am to try and stake a way over direct to the right. We came back to Minden Post and thence Bunting and I made our way to the Rat Hole where I now write. Minden Post is BHQ [Battalion Headquarters]. It is a most interesting spot and one I must try and find time to describe when I get back to Bray. Somehow it looks so like war, a thing which little else does here. For the most part we seem so unreal tucked away under ground.

Dogs have suddenly appeared in the trenches. Good dogs, apparently sprung from nowhere. I have given orders for any seen to be shot. It is a pity, and one feels very sad about it but I am too suspicious of Fritz. I think him quite capable of inoculating the brutes with some beastly disease and then letting them loose on us. I may be wrong but in war one cannot take chances – especially against Fritz.

Bang. One has just been shot as I write. It is whimpering out its life outside my dug-out.

Poor beast! It seems a dirty trick – but there you are![i]

---

i 'There is an order that all dogs seen in the trenches are at once to be killed, as they may be bearers of messages or poison from the Bosche lines, and are extremely dangerous. We have killed several before but never experienced anything like this. We were informed of this dog being seen while we were having breakfast in the dug-out, and the Sergeant-Major passing at the time went off to shoot it with his revolver. We heard a shot and afterwards found it had hit the dog's head but missed his brain. He fired another shot, which also hit the dog's head, and the next thing came for our dug-out, where I was sitting in my usual place near the door. It had gone absolutely mad, and was foaming at the mouth, and blood was pouring from its eyes. It was a large, black dog, and naturally gave me a shock. It was a dangerous position to be in and I got out my revolver like lightning, but found I could not shoot as the Sergt. Major was coming up behind, and I might have hit him. He also could not fire for fear of hitting me. Luckily he got hold of the dog by the tail just as I was going to give it a hard kick under the jaw, and he carried it away, much to my relief . . . The Sergt. Major flung it to the ground and gave it a kick which turned it over just as it was going to our stretcher-bearers' dug-out. It then got up again, and he put another bullet through its head, and as it appeared quite dead, it was flung over the parapet, and orders were given for it to be buried at night. An hour later, going down the trench a 100 yds. from this spot with the Sergt. Major, we heard a rifle shot, and afterwards learnt that the dog had been seen to move, and a shot had been fired which hit it all right. Almost immediately after we saw it on the parapet above us – it had come the 100 yds. quite by accident up to us again. It was bleeding and foaming as before, and sprang down over some barbed wire coils onto the trench bottom, where three rounds rapid fire from the revolver finished it . . .' (Gomersall, 7.5.16).

Chapter 7
'Dry trenches mean happy men'

7–26 March 1916

7th March '16

In order that one may keep very wide awake at night one is compelled to live a more or less somnolescent life by day here. We have all been at it again tonight and have just come in – 11.30 p.m. Bowly has been out with a party cutting gaps in our wire in front of the support line, a precautionary measure of what may be called retaliatory offence. He has done well indeed. Prince has been on company duty but, I find, has also been wandering, on his own mystic missions bent, about on top. I have been out endeavouring to peg a way to [Trench] 55 but I have met with indifferent success up to now. Also I have had to pilot the Second in Command over those dim, mysterious ways which lead about the strange land on top. It has been inky dark but we have fluked our paths aright and only one man has become detached and lost and he is now found again. We are all quite happy and beginning to feel more sure of ourselves now we are becoming more familiar with the Way over the Top. Isn't it strange, this reversal of things? To the newly initiated wayfarer it is the trenches which are full of confusion. To us who live in them it is the ordinary, above-ground paths where the snares and pitfalls lie. Especially the pitfalls. And such pitfalls! Thrice tonight I have been head over heels into shell holes. Sergt Hinsley,[i] who accompanied me, must have eyes like a cat. He dodged everything. It is quite a startling sensation, this sudden treading on nothing. Trench mortar bombs excepted, it brings one up shorter than anything I know. But I have not suffered even so much as a jar, not even a winding, and, as on one fall I found a splendid specimen of a whiz-bomb, I am quite happy and seek my couch in cheerful mood.

8th March '16

A March morning in the trenches. A white frost over everything, the air cold and crisp, full of life and vigour. Overhead an arch of blue, stretching unflecked from zenith to horizon save where, in one place, little balls of down break out suddenly to the accompaniment of dull thuds. That is where Fritz's Archibald is bursting his shrapnel impotently, in pursuit of a Vickers fighter[ii] which changes course, twists and turns but nevertheless works ahead over the enemy's lines, on reconnaissance bent. In the trench the usual litter of old tins, torn sandbags, heaps of miniature landslides from the walls with men bending amongst it whistling, their breath a tiny cloud on the morning air, as they clean up the floor and put our house in order. Just over the brink of the parapet one catches a glimpse of jagged earthenware, the remains of a rum jar, or the battered lid, rising oyster fashion, from a discarded jam tin. That is in No Man's Land, a portion of the earth where Tommy can with impunity gratify his natural tendency to untidiness by flinging to it all that endless rubbish which a battalion mysteriously accumulates even in the short span of a day.

Only birds live out there – apparently as happily as ever. A lark trills blithefully somewhere up in the heavens above it even as I write, his

i Sgt Harry Hinsley.
ii The aircraft was likely to be a Vickers FB ('Fighting Biplane') 5, known as the 'Gun Bus', of No. 11 Sqdn, RFC, based near St Omer. This was the world's first operational military aircraft.

note throbbing as though 'twould burst his throat, full of the joy of the dawning and of the promise of spring.

It is calm and peaceful everywhere, like a springtime, Sunday morning in some remote village in our own England. It is a strange war. That is a remark I find myself repeatedly making. But one sometimes finds such difficulty in realising that it is really war at all. The necessarily small limits of one's vision no doubt is largely responsible for this.

Later: We came out again this evening. Quite an easy relief, everything working smoothly and the sharp march home down the frozen road in the light of the new moon most enjoyable. The men sang to their step for the first time for weeks. A sure indication of their feelings and that they also feel the spring in their blood.

9th March '16

I think I said somewhere that a record of Minden Post[i] was worth having. I still think so but feel chary of venturing on the task of description, it being so difficult to get 'atmosphere' on to paper. And it is the atmosphere of Minden Post which one is so conscious of there. In peace time it would be merely a heap of uninteresting sandbag shelters which one would pass by with perhaps a word as to their lack of comfort, and take no further interest in. Now, however, they mean so much to us that that casual view is quite impossible. The Post occurs against a natural embankment along the top of which runs the road to Fricourt, the road we may one day march along towards the East. Partly it is tunnelled out, partly strongly sandbagged into perhaps a dozen roomy dug-outs wherein live the CO, Adjutant, Doctor, BSM [Battalion Sergeant Major][ii] and all the other hundred or so of the Headquarters personnel.

i Minden Post was a spacious dug-out. It was shared by different units when at the front.
ii Lt Col. Paul W. Whetham; Lt Roy Mellor, who was also the battalion intelligence officer; Lt Dr George Barbour McGregor; Sgt Maj. Frederick Knowles.

Along the front of the shelters runs a corduroy footpath deeply ditched on either side and ornamented at frequent intervals with mounds of scraped-up mud. The footpath emerges from a trench which comes down the hill-side, runs in the open for a hundred yards and vanishes into another trench which, commencing where the embankment ends, wanders across the countryside to the Rat Hole and other such interesting spots. Coming down the dug-outs are on your right. On the left is first a large sump hole, fenced round, then a block heap of sandbags with dark, uninviting entrances in its sides, from which continually arises a flurry of smoke. That is the cook-house for the left half battalion, or rather it was till the Rat Hole felt capable of doing some of its work for it.

This is what you would see if you strolled that way by daylight, a most unhealthy thing to do under present conditions. It is only at night one passes the Post in quantities and then all that makes you aware of its existence are a few chinks of light cutting the blackness or perhaps a hurricane lamp by a dug-out door with some dim shadow of a man beside it. You hear shuffling feet, splashes and quiet cursing, low toned words of command or anon the sound of someone singing softly somewhere in the darkness. You stand aside and become aware of a string of men, black against the lighter darkness of the night, filing slowly past you all heavy laden and laboured of breath.

These are the ration parties winding their way to the men in the front line.[i] How they ever get their loads to their destination some nights when the moon is absent and trenches knee-deep in mud I do not know. I am afraid I do little towards it. All I insist upon is that the rations do arrive. Discipline does the rest.

And Minden Post cares not one way or the other. All it is concerned in is that the wants of the firing line are despatched from it, a task it

i 'In addition to food, the ration parties distributed supplies and ammunition . . . a terrible job, as it means fetching food, coal, water, stores of all sorts, for the whole battalion from back at the railhead, all, of course, by night' (Tawney, 14.2.16).

discharges with remarkable success considering the darkness in which it must necessarily work. There are telephones there and signal rockets. All the doings of the battalion are controlled from it. It is the nerve centre of a thousand rifles and perhaps a dozen machine guns. A Post of no small importance. Yet could a careless man stumble past it of a night and never know of its existence. It is a fascinating spot, Minden Post, one which in some vague way breathes of war, focussing in perfect miniature the whole spirit of this struggle. I would that my pencil were not so halting that I might do it justice.

10th March '16

Men are so distressingly unimaginative. I suppose that is because they are British, and no doubt it is a virtue. It sometimes however produces *contretemps* which bring grave matters perilously near the absurd. One such occurred the other night when we were turned out to a gas alarm. The signaller who warned me went first to the gas sentry, whose duty it is to bang the gong and alarm the men. The man rushed at the sentry and cried, 'Gas'. The sentry was unmoved. He winked at the apparition before him. 'Chuck it,' he said. 'We don't want none of those b....y games here!'

Another similar case happened to Cowan. The CO desired a practice 'stand to'. He detailed Cowan to get his company out and decided to accompany him. Speed is, of course, the essential factor. It was about 4 p.m. The usual hour for the permanent movement was perhaps an hour later. Cowan rushed at the first sentry he saw. 'Stand to,' he shouted. The man looked at him sorrowfully. 'But us asn't 'ad our tea!' he said. The CO fumed. Cowan rushed to the next man. He was, as it happened, Jarvis,[i] the deafest man in the battalion. 'Stand to!' bellowed the captain twice. Jarvis looked at him and smiled. Then he said, 'Is it true, sir, that

i Pte William Jarvis.

the government is going to stop our rum ration?' Cowan subsided into sweating inanity. The CO spat fire and brimstone. I am afraid D Coy was not in high favour that night.[i]

11th March '16

We had a little party last night in honour of Don Murray's birthday. Practically every officer in the battalion was present and we sang and talked and played games till nigh midnight. C Company brought their gramophone which become the *chef-d'oeuvre* of the evening till Bowly in a moment of excessive admiration managed to break it and thereby brought wrath upon himself. Wood turned up, his head all bandaged, and lent quite a martial air to the gathering, crammed as it was in our little mess-room and lit by the flicker of four guttering candles stuck in empty bottles. Grimwood turned up from the Brigade and was received with joyous acclamation. He was telling me about the manner of our late General's going. It is strange how men can deceive themselves. The old boy was useless and had received the boot in no uncertain manner. Yet by the time he left he had told so many people that he was leaving

---

i 'The Colonel wanted to test the Battalion at "standing to" in case of attack, and sent an alarm signal through. Immediately all rushed off to stand to, men hurried here and there, and in less than three minutes practically everybody was "standing to" on the firestep. When we hurried along to see if all were "standing to" and everything ready, we came across a man who is used for fatigue work in my platoon, as he is deaf. (He is invaluable though as he is such a hard worker.) Naturally we enquired, "Hello Jarvis, why aren't you standing to? Don't you know the alarm is sounded?" Jarvis couldn't have heard, and drawled out to us, breathless after our run, "Oh sir, is it true that the government has stopped the Rum Ration?" He is very fond of rum. You can imagine what was said, but I roared with the officers later, after the excitement of it all' (Gomersall, 3.3.16).

in order to take over a higher command that he had come quite to believe it himself. Indeed so firmly did the conviction grip him that his final parting was both gracious and benign. Incidentally he took the new general's saddle with him and Grimwood had to be dispatched to England to fetch it back, a task which sadly marred his pleasure at the chance of a visit to 'Blightie'.

12th March '16

There is something painfully sad about war. I do not speak from the soldier's point of view. This is not really so bad. He merely takes a risk, his eyes open. If he is hit, he has lost the throw and there the matter ends. But for the civil population in a war-stricken land life must be the sublimity of anguish. Imagine an orderly-looking, small house, red bricked, with a decently pointed door, tiled entrance and well cared for windows. A comfortable-looking little place of eight rooms, with a small garden at the back, half roses, half vegetable, a stable, coach-house, hen run and all the hundred and one other domestic appurtenances which go to make the home of a well-to-do, happily minded, middle-class family. Even the cellar below is commodious and well stocked with wine, both *blanc* and *rouge* of a sound quality and elderly vintage. A few weeks ago the family lived here more or less content-edly and in as happy a state as any Frenchman in this stricken northern France can be.

Then Bosche pushed at Frise, made a momentary success and reached for a few days a point where he could turn his guns on Bray. Think of the father of the family when the shells commenced to pitch around his home. Imagine his state of mind when the barn across the way was blown to bits. One can picture the hasty scraping together of the more valued and portable of the household goods and the hurried flight from their native village to sanctuary – where?

Evidence of that fleeing is all about me as I write. Rooms in a hopeless litter, frocks, corsets, bedclothes strewn everywhere, crockery on the floor, the last meal lying unwashed in the scullery, coal-scuttle over-turned, ornaments fallen and broken. Everywhere confusion unspeakable. And through it all the marble and gold clock on the mantelpiece still ticking peacefully on.

We have taken the house, we officers who are left behind, Ramsbottom, Bland and myself.[i] It is to be the Rest House for officers left in Bray. Major Ommanney, [ii] 21st, has pruned the roses and I am having the bulbs, already sprouting in their box in the wash-house, planted out. Our servants are here and such other help as we can command and today we clean up the litter and put our house in order. I hope when *Madame, M'sieur* and *les petite filles* return their home may look none the worse for their absence. It is the most we can do for them. Pray God war may never set its horrid foot in our England!

13th March '16

A long day at the Brigade office getting out complete plans of our position. Most interesting work. I have quite enjoyed it. And to lighten it I heard a most entertaining story. It hung on the shortage of coin in Berlin and the rumoured bartering in iron in substitute. A man called at a paper shop, lifted a fender off his car, plonked it down on the counter and said, '*Daily Mail* and *Comic Cuts*, please!' The shopkeeper tendered the papers then looked with speculative eye on the fender. 'Sorry I've no small change,' he said. 'Here, take this anvil.'

Bland is not at all himself and still keeps near his bed. Ram and I therefore strolled by ourselves along the Somme this evening. There was a glorious sunset, all flaming pinks and greys stretching the full extent of the heavens and the broad, smooth waters of the river reflected this

i 'I am having 4 full days of irresponsible indolence, together with May and Ramsbottom, in a fresh billet – a cosy, sweet little place, abandoned in a great hurry by a dear old lady (I believe) who left behind furniture, glass crockery, wine and underclothing, of all which we make full use where possible. It has been really cheery to have a touch of something familiar' (Bland, 13.3.16).
ii Maj. Francis Frederick Ommanney.

till the world seemed alight with a soft, still radiance most peaceful and witching to behold.

It is very lovely here, but I can see will be painfully hot when the spring really does come in on us.

Tomorrow we go to Corbie, and we are going to buy fishing tackle there. The Somme should be full of sport and the mere thought of fresh fried fish for breakfast is tantalising in the extreme.

14th March '16

We have been to Corbie – a most enjoyable ride along the high road from where glimpses of the river valleys on either side could be caught occasionally. Tiny panoramas these of brown trees, blue, sparkling waters, white, brown, red, blue and purple houses clustering around their grey churches. Last year's forests of bull-rushes and pampas grass now stand across the swamps in ordered lines of corn-gold, and the new shoots for the coming year show the greener by comparison. It is all very lovely, if you look at it in the distance and forget about the jagged shell-holes by your feet, and it seems an awful pity that such a fair land should be torn and scarred, its people slain, its villages destroyed by war. It makes one feel very annoyed with Fritz. One can't help thinking him a swaggering, thick-headed, bullying fellow with no thought in his head for what is beautiful when one sees the ravaging brand of his army across this countryside.

But these abstract dreams I suppose carry one nowhere. The war is too full of hard, unpicturesque facts to allow of over indulgence in them. One cannot help, however, feeling them – and what I feel I like to record.

15th March '16

Two new officers arrived last night.[i] They were hungrily waiting on the threshold of my billet when I returned to it about 8 p.m. Bland was

---

i 2nd Lts Henry Lander Faulkner and Albert Victor Dowling.

entertaining them rather frigidly. Afterwards I found that he did not like either of them. We fed them and gave them drink and then Bland deliberately set about the task of making their flesh creep. I protested to him as well as I could but it had no effect. He took them as fair game and would not be persuaded otherwise. Afterwards I also, I am half ashamed to say, fell. But both became rather too knowledgeful – always a thing to be instantly checked in a subaltern – and for their future good I was compelled to ally myself to 'Blasé Bill'.

I am afraid we have been rather cruel. They went away very silently to sleep and, I doubt not, had the distance considerably curtailed by the fact that as they left our door Fritz commenced to strafe Cappy with heavies. It sounded very near on the still night air. What a game it is!

16th March '16

Ram, Bland and I spent the afternoon fishing. We didn't catch anything – a quite superfluous statement – but we quite enjoyed ourselves for all that. It was very pleasant down on the marshes in the sunshine or meandering along the river bank. In the middle of it Fritz commenced to strafe Jean [illegible] whose trenches are on the hill about a mile away. It was some strafe and presently traversed quite near us. We watched it with interest. It is remarkable what an impartial view one takes of such things out here. One is foolish enough not to think even of taking cover. Ram remarked, 'Some strafe. And they've such a nice day for it.' Thereupon we continued fishing.

The battn came out this evening. Quite a fresh battn, singing and whistling. What a difference the sunshine makes. If that could only be whispered in the ear of the Clerk of the Weather I'm sure he'd do his best to 'shape a bit', as S-M. Knowles always says.

I have arranged a new canteen, [in] a one-time butcher's shop. Have got in beer and all the nick-nacks for the 'dry' bar and we are all fit and ship-shape for a roaring trade in the morning. We'll do it I know. And I also know that the men will be braced as blazes with the chance of buying a pint of beer.

17th March '16

Dowling has come to me as an extra officer. He is rather gross, somewhat blatant and quite rhinoceros-like of hide, but I trust he will turn out all right after a bit.

The Major seems to have made some trouble for himself this last tour in.[i] All his NCOs have asked to be allowed to revert to Private *en bloc*. It is rather pitiable. Indeed it would be wholly pitiable and, to some extent, humorous, if it was not so serious.[ii]

The net result up to now is that his Sgt Major has been transferred to C and C's sent to him. He has easily the worst of that bargain. I understand I am to take one of his sergeants – Thompson – a good man and one whom only last week he recommended for a 'Mention' – and give one of mine in exchange.[iii] Gladly would I have Thompson but not at all ready am I to part with one of my men to him. He would break any good man's heart and I am too fond of all mine to let them suffer that fate lightly. He is the picture of a man who has made a mess of it. He is a silly ass. And for the good of the battalion I wish he would go home. This is no place for incompetency.[iv]

i Maj. Frank Boyd Merriman.

ii 'The battalion came out of the trenches last night in a state of absolute rebellion. M. had been more impossible and more ridiculous than usual and had got the whole Coy by the ears, Sgt Major and the Sergeants in a state of livid revolt, and the men fed up to the teeth, except that they were partly convulsed with laughter at his antics. It is pitiable and tragic . . . I feel absolutely helpless. I don't know what I can do. I believe I ought to denounce him to the CO, but in the Army you never know what sort of wired hole you are stepping into when you begin to criticise superior officers. You may get a VC or a Court Martial for the same action, according to its success or failure. We'll see. I'll consult May' (Bland, 17.3.16).

iii Sgt William Robert Thompson was first of 2 Platoon, A Coy.

iv 'I've taken refuge with May since teatime . . . We have been sitting in the garden which runs down to the River Somme – swiftly flowing and full of water. We have watched the day die in a gentle bloom of yellow and mauve

18th March '16

I do not think I have ever mentioned the French interpreters[i] – that very efficient body of men who act as mediators or buffers for peppery colonels reduced to blasphemous impotency in dealings with the civil population.

They are nearly all of officer's rank, quiet, gentlemanly and indefatigable in one's service. They take a joyous view of life and are fond of both their dinner and their wine. Their dress is plain khaki riding kit, well-cut and finished for the most part, picked out with blue tabs at the turnover by the throat, with brass Sphinx heads set on this. The Sphinx is their badge though its exact relation to their calling I have been unable to ascertain. I was always under the impression that the Sphinx was the emblem of silence.

Up here near the line they wear the street *casque*[ii] and to meet one riding, happy visaged and thus clad, on his stock-built charger about the [illegible] of the Somme or over the upland roads is to be flashed back to the living pages of the *Three Musketeers*. For just such others as these were, I know, d'Artagnan, Porthos and Athos.[iii]

Ewald is our man. He is attached to the Brigade. An Alsatian by birth, German by name, happy by nature, polite by intuition and indefatigable by the Somme, that is Ewald! As jolly a free-lance as ever clanked a spur in saucy defiance past the gates of My Lord, the Red Cardinal.

He has been with the English from the start, won the DCM on the advance from the Marne and fully intends to win another and as good a time as he can when the Army goes forward and he is able to trot his stock old dobbin down the broad high-ways of the Rhineland. Ewald is a sample, a *vignette* of a type. I am glad I have recorded him. I should have been sorry to forget *l'interprét[eur]*.

------

and pale blue and pale green, the light soft through the innumerable poplars that France loves so dearly . . . I am happier for the moment' (Bland, 8.3.16).
i Ewald. May had in fact mentioned the interpreter, Bethmann, on 14.11.15.
ii A helmet.
iii May has forgotten one of the original musketeers, Aramis.

19th March '16

Sweet letters from you today, letters full of love and kindness and of hunger for the summer-time, so be it we could spend it together. My own, if it but could be so. What joyous times have been ours in other summers. Derby Dale always comes back to me when I think of you and summer.[i] The long valley, knee-deep in luscious grass with which the yellow-eyed dog-daisies struggled for mastery. The old Derwent gurgling along whilst I whipped it and you knitted, in toleration of my madness, or struggled to make the kettle boil. Why I should always come back to Derby Dale I do not know. It was little enough time we spent there. It must be the dog-daisies the swaying grass and the smell of the new-cut hay hangs in my fancy so.

Leave has started again. All hope it may continue to run on. If it does my next turn home should come about the end of June. 'Flaming June', is it not? We must go away from the towns then and spend some part of the holiday in the open.

20th March '16

A day spent over the uplands explaining the Brigade defences to the new officers. Very enjoyable and healthy. I met Warr of the 106th, up there again, full of work. He is building new emplacements. Then some heavies dropped rather close to us and we had to fling ourselves flat to avoid trouble. Later we scraped up a few fragments as souvenirs and came away laughing.

This evening we had a concert for the Company in Whiz-Bang Hall. Most enjoyable it was, the strains of lively music and lilting choruses putting life into us all. It was quite a top-hole gathering. Picture a long, dim hall filled to overflowing with an excited mass of eager men. A stage at one end with a badly daubed representation of the local railway station

---

i May refers to the Derbyshire Dales, not far from Withington, where he and Maude were living before the war, and through which flows the River Derwent.

for background, the footlights supplied by a dozen candles in sconces of their own grease and a piano and plain deal form thrust up in one corner as its only decoration.

From a little room at the side the turns came on and sang or played or recited according to their talents. All were good but had they not been their reception I am sure would not have been a whit the less hearty. We were out to enjoy ourselves everyone and come what might we intended we should. Such choruses were sung as did your heart good to listen to, such clapping and shouting for encores as would have flattered a premier prima-donna. It was top-hole all through. The best thing we have done for a long time.

Prince has gone on a course of instruction. Murray goes on one on the 26th, both for a month. This Army of ours is marvellous. An ordinary man might think that when after months of training an officer at last gets his command in the firing line that he had attained the ideal and that what further knowledge was necessary for him he would gain in the best school of all – that of actual experience. But then if you thought that you would not know the Army. The Army is marvellous, so utterly marvellous that no ordinary person can ever hope to understand it. That is why we never try. We just take things as they come and keep smiling. It is the only way!

21st March '16

This war, I am sure, is one of the most peculiar the world has ever known if, indeed, it is not the most peculiar. In no other can it have been possible to soldier so long, to witness such evidence of the presence of an enemy and of his ability to injure without ever catching sight of beast, bird or man belonging to him. To look out over our parapet is but to see a stretch of apparently deserted countryside straggled across with what appear to be aimless mounds of earth. Only the crack of a rifle and the whistle of a bullet close to his head serves to show the lengthy observer that the vista is deserted in appearance only. Yet this utter absence of the sight of man certainly gives the game that touch of unreality of which I have previously written. Except through my glasses, I have never yet seen a Fritz – an experience in no way peculiar, since it has been experienced by many a thousand others of double my active service.

Judge of my surprise then this morning to see a real, live, grey-clad Fritz marching up the Rue Corbie between two gleeful, khaki-clad privates whose bayonets gleamed ready on their rifles. The man was a prisoner of the 62nd Regiment Saxons. He was young but big and well-made standing about six feet and being proportioned to match. He seemed cheerful, and certainly looked both well clad and fed.

Where he came from I do not know but I hope he is but the fore-runner of many of his tribe.

The men were quite braced with the sight and would have run after him in a mob, like the crowd following a Saturday night drunk in any of our big cities, had they not been ordered about their business.

I am told that I am to go in tomorrow as Second-in-Command, the colonel going on leave. You've no idea how appallingly august I feel in consequence. I can picture myself living like a bloated aristocrat, gourmandising on expensive delicacies in the HQ mess at Minden Post, all for the princely sum of 1 franc per diem, that being the limit set by our Spartan CO. In addition I can see myself strolling round the trenches, freshly washed and shaved, flirting a 'whanger' and pointing out obvious defects in their organisation, sanitation and general management to jaded Company Commanders who have hitherto been my friends. What a life!

22nd March '16

Patrols – a word as to them. They are the fashion with us just now. Everyone patrols. To patrol properly you require a dark night and two, or at most three, companions. With these you crawl on your stomach over noisy jam tins, beneath snakelike and scratchy barbed wire, roll into shell holes or wriggle through grass. All the while your body seems bigger than an elephant's and you labour under the obsession that every Fritz in the line has seen you. You hate it at the time but endure it if only for the power it gives you to swank to lesser men afterwards. Fritz is more sensible. He hardly patrols at all but contents himself with pooping off untold lights which illuminate the whole countryside and cause our crawling unfortunates to press themselves into mother earth and devoutly wish that they had been better boys. The chief reason for patrols is that the Staff likes them. Their value is more or less problematical. In actual advantage up to now I can reckon my company has gained on Fritz to the extent of 8½ yards. This minor success was achieved by an unimaginative corporal who took it[i] off the body of a dead Frenchman, out in front of [Trench] 62. Another of the same patrol brought in the fellow's shin bone saying it would make a splendid club. Bowly called him a low person and ordered him to cast the trophy away.

I am writing this in my dug-out of Minden Post – the Second-in-Command's dug-out, which I have to myself. Some 'bleed'. Bow-wow!

23rd March '16

I was once round the line last night – getting in at 3 a.m. – and today I have been round it twice, the second time with Duke[ii] of the brigade. The result is I feel sore of feet and somewhat tired. Our line is a long one and very undulating.

It has been a quiet day, Fritz strafing the hill behind Minden Post and also F113[iii] being the only items of real interest. No one was hurt on either occasion and as this evening I have dug up two good nose-caps I am personally quite satisfied.

This evening young Robertson[iv] of 104th came into mess. He is a nice young fellow and very keen on his guns. For his sake, I wish they shot better. He, however, can't help that.

The Doc is in great form, as is Tawney. They make it a pleasure to be here.

i It is possible that May is referring to an advance to the Frenchman's body.
ii Maj. Jesse Pevensey Duke.
iii F113 is an artillery target area on a map.
iv Maj. Alexander Winton Robertson.

24th March '16

Two letters from you today, my sweetheart, the first containing photos of you and Babs in a leather case. It is a sweet treasure for me to carry with me and I am overjoyed to have it. I love it already.

This morning we woke up to find five inches of snow over everything and a thaw going strong. It made us all give way to bad language. It is so disappointing – and just when the trenches were getting decent. However, it cannot be helped and all we can do is set about clearing up again with a good spirit and assiduously as possible.

There is little to record except the gurgle of water as it runs down the hill through Carnay Avenue past my dug-out door, and the swearing of men who fall into the sea at the bottom as they stagger along through the inky blackness.

I have quite a little gag this afternoon. A new trench mortar machine was being tried up in [Trench] 60. I came upon it unseen and found Shelmerdine and Oldham gazing anxiously over the top to see where the missiles dropped. Everyone was at a tension – trench mortars are impartial in their destructiveness. I took a handful of snow, rolled a ball and threw it at Oldham, at the same time yelling 'Mortar'. It grazed the back of his neck and hit Shelmerdine's head and you never saw two more scared officers in your life.

Shelmerdine fell off the step and Oldham leapt a foot in the air. Both swore most horribly. I was sorry afterwards. I know it would have put my heart in my mouth had I been the victim.

25th March '16

The Doc, Mellor and myself employed ourselves all the morning filling sandbags and building with them a dug-out for the officers' servants. It was quite topping working in the sunshine and productive of a fine healthy glow. We didn't make a deal of progress with the dug-out but we 'sweated considerably' and so were quite happy.

I didn't go round the line again till tonight but I have now just finished the whole length and am at present sitting in lonely state in the mess quaffing hot tea from a Thermos – time midnight. It was quite a good tour, the men all working well. They are quite brave. I came upon poor Carr, the Battalion's right half,[i] lying on the floor of the trench with a bullet through his leg. He was cheerful and the other men calm. They had been out wiring and a sniper had hit Carr, but the others carried on. We have put up a lot of wire these last two nights, in spite of heavy sniping. It speaks well for the men. A got a man badly wounded last night and C a man hit lightly. A had a sentry killed this morning and now Carr is hit. Four in two days to Fritz's snipers. We must stop him. He is getting too successful.

26th March '16

We had a young Staff captain into lunch, a GSO3 [General Staff Officer Grade 3] and another has passed with a brigadier. I have been talking to Townsend about them. We cannot make it out – the system, if there is any system, by which these appointments are made. The chief essentials appear to be a Public School education and an ingratiating manner. Any such things as strength of character, military knowledge or leadership apparently do not enter into the contract at all. Influence I am afraid must play a large part also. It strikes us as a great pity, if not more serious than that. Any one who has been here any time and has met men could name dozens who would fill positions with more authority and command respect and men to a far greater degree than the majority of our Staff. I speak generally, of course. Our own Brigade is a pleasurable exception to the above, the Brigadier, Major and Staff Captain are all topping officers, radiating authority and knowing their job, but there are hundreds of others less fortunate than we are and since efficiency must apply to the whole before success can come, I think there is a lot to be done in the way of sorting out 'ere our Staff deserves its august position.

What we seem to lack is driving force along the right lines, i.e. to the

i Pte George Carr was right half in the battalion football team.

end of strafing Fritz. At present internal economy seems the be all and end all of our Top Men's endeavours. Internal economy, a determination to have as good a time as possible and a bent for scandal about higher men still sums up the ideals, any rate of our junior Staff, as near as I have yet been able to get it.

But to turn to happier topics. Faulkner – one of our new subs – has caused a battalion smile today. When he came off duty last night it was from a very damp tour in the trenches, not a bad tour but one with just sufficient water about to make things a little uncomfortable. Cowan was awake as he pulled off his gum boots thigh and Faulkner confided in him in all seriousness the following, 'Do you know, sir, I's afraid this wet won't suit me.'

Chapter 8
'Pushes and rumours of pushes fill the air'

27 March–13 April 1916

27th March '16

One really does not want to record too much of one's own personal experiences because a diary to be of any interest later must more or less hold news of greater moment. But I just can't help putting in about that damn trench mortar this afternoon. It made too big an impression on me for it to go entirely unrecorded.

Also it was only by the mercy of God that both Bowly and I were not blown to blazes. We had just gone up the little trench of 62 Street to have a look at a dug-out Bowly had found. I happened to glance up and saw it coming. For a second we couldn't see where it would drop but then I decided and started to run, Bowly following. My gum-boots of course slipped and I went down and 'Bubbles' fell with me. It landed with a thud on the parapet just where we had stood a second previously. We grovelled flat, there was a terrific explosion and the both of us were buried. 'Are you hurt?' said Bowly. 'No,' said I. 'Neither am I.' Then we both got up and scooted, with the earth falling from us as we went. But Bowly had forgotten his pipe and coolly returned for it a minute later. After that we walked on smoking, but for myself, badly shaken indeed.

I trust however that the men didn't see my grin was feigned only and that really I was in the deuce of a funk.

Bowly brassed it out quite successfully but I know it had given him a turn. He was quite shaky when we got back to the dug-out. It is my second squeak from a trench mortar. I hate them.

Last night I hear there was a big strafe on our left. We put 1500 shells into Fritz in the course of two hours. There was some row I believe and everyone here was up except the Doc and myself. We, like two unemotional pigs, slept through the lot.

28th March '16

From 4.30 a.m. to 11 p.m. makes a long day and one rather tiring when it includes two tours round the line and the slog down to Bray later. But it is always worth it on relief day. One really looks forward to the spell in Bray after six days in. It has been a lovely spring day, quite warm in the sunshine, and Fritz has been quiet in spite of the fact that we have intermittently shelled him the whole time. But tonight it is black as pitch and cold as the deuce. The men, however, are all now safely in and quite warm and cosy with big dicksies of hot cocoa, jolly good stuff. Grady,[i] my corporal cook, asked me to taste it when I went round and I drank the whole mug, to his considerable pleasure.

Yet at the moment I feel quite stunned. Bowly and the Sgt Major[ii] have both been arrested by the 21st at Minden Post for 'drunkenness'. It is a terrible, hard blow to us all. But as yet we know nothing except the ugly fact.

What a curse drink is and what an awful thing it is, not to be able to trust. In that I refer to Bowly. He was in charge and his destiny was therefore in his own hands. The Sgt Major is only a soldier and a soldier will always drink if drink is given him. But he has never fallen before

i Cpl Frederick Grady.
ii CSM Frederick Charles Knowles.

and I could curse the thoughtlessness that has broken him now. He and Garside have been my right and left hands from the very beginning. Yet I should not take the personal view. Not that I mean it personally. It is the trouble to the company that worries me but when I think of myself I mean the company. I always feel with it as Napoleon must have when he said, 'L'état, c'est moi.'[i]

Poor Knowles. I am sorry for him from the bottom of my heart. For Bowly, at the moment, I have only anger. Yet he will pay for it heavily, poor devil. How I wish to God Don Murray had not gone. You can trust Don, trust him with your life and with what is more, your men.

29th March '16

Bowly has now come down. Oldham was sent for him and a Sgt Major for Knowles. The whole black business is now before the general and I expect it means a court-martial for Bowly and either one for Knowles or voluntary reversion to the ranks. It has cast a gloom over the lot of us, it being so likely to reflect on the good name of the battalion.

However, it is done now and there is nothing left but to grin and bear it. Bowly, of course, is quite bowled over by what he has done and now, in his sober senses, is pitifully down. What his poor mother will do I shudder to think. It is sad, so very sad.

30th March '16

Mellor and I rode out to Happy Valley this morning for lunch with 'Bottom'[ii] and Whitham of the 104 Battery.[iii] They live in Happy Valley,

---

i This quote is commonly attributed to Louis XIV of France.
ii The nickname of Lt Aubrey Harris, bombing officer with 21st Bn.
iii (First name unknown) Whitham of 104th Battery, XXII Brigade, Royal Field Artillery.

an aptly named locality when the sun shines, as it did today, and the broad dip laughs up at you where you stand on the bush clad eminence where the battery is hidden.

In front the next ridge makes the horizon so that you see nothing of Fritz and only the scarred and holed slope opposite, where lurk many dug-outs, brings one's mind at all to the fact that war in all its ugliness is just beyond the hill.

Both Mellor and I fired a round, directing each one at the trench mortar position of Fritz's. I pray we may have landed close. What joy it would be to blow that fellow up.

After lunch we hunted rats. Whitham has a patent way. You burn bromide in one hole and wait with a stick at another ready to smite any rodent who bolts from the fumes. None bolted today but Whitham said they must have died from the fumes. He is an optimist. Personally I think Brer Rat merely lay low and said nuffin' as he is so wont to do when men in holiday mood set out to slay him.[i]

31st March '16

The Sgt Major was court-martialled today, a rotten business indeed. But all right in the end, as he deserves. His was a case of pure misfortune.

I feel that I should record our mess here. It is in a small five-roomed house in the Rue de Jean-Jacques. The entrance is at the back and the garden runs down to the Somme, the which we can see gleaming from the mess room door together with the trees on the further bank and the stretches of flat across to La Neuville les Bray. It is a pleasing scene with the party-coloured village – all reds, blues and whites – showing through the grey boles. The mess room is quite large. A door nailed flat on four legs makes an ample table and covered with white American cloth looks clean and sweet and attractive. Beneath the window is a smaller table littered with papers, a rum jar of beer, an occasional whiskey bottle and

---

i A reference to the *Uncle Remus* books, in which the stories are based around characters such as Brer Rabbit, 'Br'er' being a syncope for Brother.

stray tins of tobacco. The mantelpiece is also strewn with the latter but is rendered considerably more attractive by two jars of wild primroses which adorn it. One or two pipes and a book or so are other features. In one corner stands a waste-paper basket and in another two fishing rods with a net. There are five chairs, reseated in sacking, but quite comfortable and sacking is also evident in the windows of the wall and of the door. In these cases it stops gaps in the panes which shell-shock has caused. It gives us rather a patch-work appearance.

The walls are papered with some dark, patterned stuff and sketches by Bairnsfather, maps, pictures by Kirckner – rather unspeakable some of them – extracts from *La Vie Parisienne*, and one or two of Lawson Wood's efforts adorn or disfigure it according to your taste.[i] The floor is tiled in red and the ceiling white-washed. Our bedrooms lead off this apartment, the first being occupied up to now by poor Bowly and me, the further by Don Murray and Dowling.

For illumination we have an acetylene lamp, a ripping affair but the ASC have been unkind to us lately and have brought us no carbide. We have therefore been compelled to fall back on candles and three of these we have down the centre of our white table-cloth – of which, by the way, we are very proud it being the only one in the battalion and the others still relying on the daily paper – stuck on the top of empty bacca tins and gleaming quite cheerily withal.

Tonight we had another concert – a regular topper. It was most enjoyable. Now, 10.17 p.m. The 'Alarm' has just been given. Bow-wow, off we go. What the hell is up?

i These officers carried with them a variety of artwork. Captain Bruce Bairnsfather was a cartoonist, whose 'Fragments from France' was published in the *Bystander* magazine, popular reading among soldiers on the front. Ernest Ludwig Kirchner was an artist who was a founder of German expressionism. *La Vie Parisienne* was a French weekly magazine which combined a mix of writing and art, some of which was mildly risqué. Clarence Lawson Wood was a painter whose work featured animals, including a chimpanzee he called 'Gran pop'.

1st April '16

All Fools' Day, and when I think of last night's tour I have an uneasy feeling that the major was anticipating a little. It was a regular tear round. Perspiring, shouting sergeants, sarcastic officers and confused, stumbling men still dull-witted from their heavy slumbers. But the battalion moved all right and was ready to march out, fully equipped in battle order in twenty-one minutes. That was good and we are quite pleased about it. It was, of course, only a test – a valuable one.

Prince has come back today I am glad to say. He makes another officer for B, a real help and one I badly needed because Dowling, though he tries, is still somewhat raw and rather an anxiety than otherwise. He improves however.

Knowles's court martial was promulgated this afternoon. He is only reduced to sergeant. It is a surprisingly light sentence and comes as quite a surprise. I am very glad, though, and hope I will soon be able to have him back in his old rank. That, however, depends upon the CO and must rest in abeyance until his return.

There is no further word yet of Bowly's trial.

2nd April '16

A happy day. One that took three of us clean out of ourselves and blew away the cobwebs of care and anxiety, which have lately been depressing us, completely. The Doc, Worthy and I rode to Heilly – Corps HQ – via Morlancourt, Ville, Maricourt and Ribemont all along the river valley and across country the whole way.[i] It is right out of the war there, peaceful, clean and soothing. We lunched at a house whose owners have seized their opportunity and turned the large conservatory into a restaurant for officers. There madame sits at the receipt of custom and two

i Located on a railway line, the village of Heilly was also a casualty station. The horse ride was in a westerly direction, along the picturesque valley of the Ancre.

clean, nicely dressed, English-looking daughters wait upon you and serve you with a first-class meal on thin china and in dainty glasses all resting on spotless linen. It was like a breath of home. After lunch we walked in the garden and lay down beneath a willow with the stream rushing past our feet and the sun bronzing our faces. It was completely restful – a little spell to be thankful for, the which we all were. Afterwards we rode back getting in the cool of the evening, very tired and saddle-sore but happy.

Worthy goes on leave tomorrow. I do not envy him, but how I wish I was going. How I long to see you, my sweetheart, and our darling Babe once more. I long till I am sick with it. Thought of you both fills my very being till it is almost a physical sensation.

Today we have heard that we come out of the line on the 6th. Pushes and rumours of pushes fill the air but whether we are to do so or not I do not know. Events begin to move, however, and activity is evident everywhere. If we do, God send that this time we are entirely successful. We want no more failures. We want this war to end.

3rd April '16

The CO has returned from leave today full of beans and ideas. Otherwise there is little to report save that my erstwhile Sgt Major has gone from me, in the humble rank of sergeant, to Ramsbottom in C Coy. It is very sad but quite inevitable – the only thing for discipline and he lucky indeed to have got off so lightly.

This afternoon I think nearly every officer in the battalion has been round at our mess and we have laid out by the river and Prince, and Gomersall and Pullen have been in it swimming. It was quite summer-like.

Our much talked of 'move' has fallen slightly flat. We don't move at all. Only the 21st and the Staffords do so – back to rest. This rumour business is really most trying.

4th April '16

Back in the old Rat Hole dug-out again with Fritz pooping over quite a few whiz-bangs and chattering away with machine-guns intermittently. He seems quite lively. The reason no doubt being that last night the South Lancs dug 250 yards of new fire trench connecting up two minor salients of ours and carrying our main line some 100 yards nearer to his at that point. I've no doubt but that he was quite surprised when he woke up this morning.

The 21st seem to have worked quite well. The fine weather has given them a chance of which they have made the most. I hope we will be able to continue it so that in the end we may get our holding into [a] thoroughly satisfactory condition.

Prince is in with me and Dowling. The former sleeping in the bunk in CHQ and the latter relegated to the spare dug-out down Minden Avenue. It has turned cold again and feels like rain if not snow. If either transpires I think the battalion will curse *en masse*. We do really want to get a lot of work done this time.

5th April '16

A decent enough day, threatening to rain on and off but holding fine to the end and so allowing us to get on with our work. And work enough we have to do, with more to follow with a vengeance. For today has come the great news that we are to attack – with the 25th as a tentative date. We are to go away and practise it for a bit and then come in and get on with the job. The 22nd is to be in the first line on the right of the Division and to B Coy has fallen the luck of being the right first line Coy of the battalion. So old B has at last got its job and may God grant that we perform it well, that we bear ourselves like English soldiers and that the whole scheme is successful and results in victory for us all.

The line is considerably livelier lately. There seems quite a spirit of expectancy in the air. The men do not know the full news yet but I know it will buck them all up when they do. There is no other news tonight beyond that – it seems to dwarf everything else.

6th April '16

We have had a minor bombardment today in that Fritz has strafed our new trenches with heavies and searched round the support with H.E. shrapnel and other such obnoxious stuff. And the battn has had hard luck. D Coy suffering especially. One shell claimed three NCOs and wounded three men. It is a nasty jar and has set the battalion by the ears, particularly B and D Companies. We all feel wild to get at the beast, and rumour having it that he may try some minor stunt against the new trenches tonight, we hope he will that we may string him up on the wire. I saw the killed go down the line. It was a pitiful sight. Poor English soldiers battered to pieces. Poor boys, shell-fire is a horrid thing.

Gresty – a lad who was a sergeant of mine before he went to D, a good man and one whom we liked well – was about the worst.[i] His

---

i 'I came in these trenches with seven NCOs and one shell during the strafe . . . has taken five of them away, and I have to borrow two from another platoon to carry on, for the time being. Towards the end of the strafe I had been talking to them, cracking jokes and generally making light of the whole thing in front of the men, although I felt much different really, myself. I then had occasion to leave them, and during the few moments I was away, one ripping fellow, a Lance-Corporal, passed me and went to them, and picking up a chunk of shell, quite hot, which had just dropped beside him, said – "Nearly got a 'blighty' that time, Sergeant," and then burst into laughter at his escape. At the same time another Sergeant, a public school boy, also joined the three, accompanied by a Private, and then right bang among them burst a high explosive shell. I returned a few minutes later to find my Platoon Sergeant, Sergt [George Kinsey] Gresty, killed outright, two Corporals, [John Edmund] Helliwell and [Alfred] Heathcote also killed, Corporal [Thomas Moreton] Gandy and the Private wounded, and my other Sergeant, Sergt [George] Benson, an absolute nervous breakdown, suffering from the terrific shock' (Gomersall, 6.4.16).

147

poor body was full of gaping holes. It was very, very sad. Do those at home yet realise how their boys go out for them. Never can they do enough for their soldiers, never can they repay the debt they owe. Not that the men ask any reward – an inviolate England is enough for them, so be it we can get our price from the Hun. Confound the man. He fights with iron and steel against poor, brave bodies. It is what a German would do. But one day we'll get at him with the bayonet. The issue must come at last to man to man. And when it does I have no doubt as to the issue. We'll take our price then for Gresty and all the other hundred thousand Grestys slain as he was standing still at his post.[i]

7th April '16

It is a terrible thing to have one's faith shaken, to have the world one knows suddenly so dashed across with new and totally unexpected happenings that one finds it different, changed so that one feels one has lost one's grip on it and is, in consequence, unsteady. It has been even so today with us and it is our dug-out in the Rat Hole which has occasioned our distress. We had, as you know, faith in that dug-out. We liked and we trusted it. We used to seek shelter in it when Fritz strafed, and felt happy in the full knowledge of its strength. Alas! Today it became necessary to revet that part of Minden Avenue which runs past the back

i Tawney's poem 'To G', published in *The Nation* publication, appears to have been inspired by Gresty's death: 'At noon he chattered frank and gay,/At one I saw him borne away,/One hideous formless wound./A sandbag held his shattered face,/Feet, hands & chest at every pace/Slipped crimson on the ground./ He has left this world of beautiful things,/The hawk that hovers, the lark that sings,/In the smoke of the bursting shell./When he fell its sweet song did not cease./He has left all these; he has left me peace./Once more – Pass, friend all's well.' In a letter to his wife, Tawney added: 'It is not a poetic fancy about the hawk and the lark. I have watched the former hover for rats and mice when shells must have been passing within 50 yds of them, and larks sing continually when it is fine' (22.4.16).

of the burrow. During operations one man, more careless than his fellows, flung his sand-bag rather heavily on the new revetment. There was a thud, the deadened sound of a landslide and then the very clear voice of a man raised in anger, and saying naughty words indeed.

Yet you couldn't blame me. I know you couldn't. A man with his world about his ears is to be excused a short lapse into profanity if his reason is not to be endangered. And I had cause enough! Cause? I ask you! That blessed sand-bag had come right through our wall and smothered the foot of Prince's and the head of my bed in about three inches of chalk stone. Not that we minded that. It was the shaken faith we hated. All along we had believed that wall thick, fully splinter if not actually shell proof. As I said before, Alas! Really I should be pleased that the weakness has been discovered. Actually I am not a bit. We lived in but a fool's Paradise I grant you, but it was such a pleasant one.

8th April '16

It was poor Bowly's court-martial today. The CO, Tawney and I left the trenches for it at 6 a.m. Our horses met us over the hill and then we rode the five miles across country to Morlancourt. There was a regular crowd of officers there, quite a terrifying spectacle to Bowly I am sure. Brig General Devereux [Deverell] was President with all sorts of Colonels and Majors and people to help him.

The court was held in the church, up on the altar dais; the altar having been lately removed. It reminded me of tales of Cromwell and the billeting of his men and stabling of their horses in sanctified buildings.

It was quite an old church, with high narrow pews and, in one row, pews with neck-rests cut out in an overhanging board, presumably to allow the elite of the village to slumber the more comfortably. The place makes swift strides towards decay. Lumps of plaster have already fallen from the ceiling and there is that cold, mouldy smell in the air which invariably attends upon the death of an ancient edifice. At the bottom end of the aisle was a bar with shelves behind and on this were piled packets and tins of Gold Flake, Woodbines, Navy Cut, together with

Oxo packets, Huntley and Palmer's biscuits, packets of Price's candles, buns, doughnuts and a tumbled crate of oranges. Indeed all the ordered conglomeration of colours and smells which go to the making of a dry canteen. For when the church at Morlancourt is not doing duty as a Hall of Justice it is a YMCA store. And I doubt not but what it does its work now – as a refuge for tired and hungry men – as pleasingly in the eyes of the Lord as when its roof, in pre-war days, was filled with the hot scent of burning incense.

After the court, the Doctor and I went on to Heilly to lunch. The CO told us to go. It made a most pleasant break in our 8 days in and it was decent of him indeed to let us have the treat. Back in the trenches by 5.30 p.m. in time to find the company changed over all complete by Prince. We now hold the firing line.

9th April '16

Going round the line we have taken over from the Queen's I came upon the following today. It was cut in chalk beneath the carved crest of the regiment:

> *This is a famous regiment*
> *And one with a tale to tell*
> *Of how we fought at Ypres*
> *And then at Neuve Chapelle.*
>
> *We met him on the Marne,*
> *We licked him by the Aisne,*
> *We drove him back at Festubert*
> *And now we're here again.*

I thought it showed a height of confident optimism on the part of the composer and altogether it is so soldier-like in its sentiments that I felt it were a pity to miss jotting it down.

10th April '16

Rather a successful little patrol scheme last night. Sgt Whitehead[i] went out in charge and reached Fritz's wire. There the patrol was seen, fired upon and compelled to dive into a shell hole for safety. And whilst there they discovered a most peculiar weapon. Nothing less than an aerial 'torpedo' intact. They brought it in, a most fearsome object. Oldham loved it at once and immediately proceeded to delve among its highly dangerous intestines to ascertain how it went off. This he found without accident and the missile now reposes outside our dug-out as a warning to all men to henceforth tread the path of the righteous and shun the sorrowful way of the evil doer.

There is nothing else of import to record. We are working hard and satisfactorily. There is a deal done, but one ocean more is required and we have really but little time in which to work. However, 'it's dogged as does it' and we'll make a good show I know before we are finished.

11th April '16

Some strafe this evening! It started away on our left but drew considerably nearer later and so kept us standing to for over an hour awaiting our turn. This, however, did not come. What the row was about we none of us know but it was a real good one. There is little else to record. We are working the clock round and making good progress, a source of satisfaction to us all.

Thornton,[ii] of the Queens, was in today. He takes over from me tomorrow.

He seems a good chap and one who will work. I am glad if it is so since it will be a considerable happiness to have a pushing fellow working on the same lines as ourselves.

i Sgt W. Henry Whitehead.
ii There is possibly confusion here between Thornton and Thornycroft. (See diary for 12 April and Index of Names.)

Prince has put the name of our new abode up, we having shifted to entirely fresh quarters on the right of our line.

A.F. 143.

WERFER VILLA AAA[i]
NO TRAMPS, HAWKERS OR HUNS
The one in the Rat Hole we have left we called HATE HOUSE. These are very mild little witticisms, you will say, but they quite amuse us in here.

12th April '16

Relieved today, and glad we were. Eight days is just long enough in the line even though one has a whole host, as did we, of interesting things to do. The Queen's took over from us, their D from me. Thornycroft,[ii] the Company Commander, is a fine stamp of a man and all their officers appear to be a decent crowd.

It rained fairly hard and relieving was therefore a somewhat lengthy affair but we were all in by about 1 a.m. and in bed by half past. Then at 3 a.m. Fritz commenced shelling us and we had to turn out and get the men down in the cellars where they 'stood to'. This lasted till 5 a.m. and one had to be up at 8. Sleep, at this game, is a thing one must learn to look upon as a luxury, a thing to be done without.

We have taken over the B Mess of the Queens. It is a sorry affair and not a patch on our late little house by the Somme. That, however, is nothing but Madame is. Madame apparently does not like us, an antipathy evidently shared by her father. Madame turned up last night, abused Bunting, flung our valises out in the mud and then smashed chairs, tables, windows and the door. Quite a New Cut Saturday night affair I believe. And really most unpleasant for us all. And to crown it, this morning *le père* rolled up, called us *les cochons anglais* [English pigs] and nailed up

i *Werfer* is translated from the German as 'thrower' or 'pitcher'. A *Minenwerfer* was a 'mine thrower', or mortar. It was primarily intended to deliver poison gas and smoke, although a high explosive shell alternative was also developed.
ii Lt Edward Charles Thornycroft.

the side door. Dearly would I have liked to have taken him by the ear and kicked his bottom down the street. But one mustn't do that. We soldier in a friendly country and we must respect the rights of the inhabitants – even, I suppose, to the extent of allowing them to fling one's kit in the filth of their 'midden'. It is, of course, only the wretched peasantry who behave in so unseemly a manner and I doubt not but that our own lower classes would do the some or worse to a French army fighting in England. It is not the true French, no more than it would be the real English, who behave like this. Pig blood will always come out, runs it in the veins of English, French, Spaniard or Basuto. It is Fritz's great fault that pig blood runs throughout his social system.

13th April '16

The attack scheme has been altered today. The main thing is that we have been given a much further and more difficult objective. Also the Staffords, Queen's and ourselves are in the front line with the 21st in Brigade reserve. It means a wider front and a lessening of men on it but the Staff appear very confident of our superiority in guns and all we can hope is that their confidence may be justified.

Parson Wood[i] came in to tea. He is a somewhat dolorous person but means well, works harder and is I fully believe a most Christian man. He thinks us a sad lot of rogues and I have no doubt is justified according to his lights.

I have had two sweet letters from you today, my own, together with a most scrumptious parcel of all sorts of goodies. We have had quite a beano for tea and will continue to do so till the stock runs out and we fall again on to the lean days.

Our late irascible landlady and her *père* are to be evacuated tomorrow. It is rather rough on them but the authorities are very down on anything which might lead to friction.

i Padre Clifford Wood.

Chapter 9
'God bless the fool who made that shell'

14 April–9 May 1916

14th April '16

We move tomorrow back to Corbie. A lot to be done there is there. We are to practise attacks, bayonet work, consolidation of trenches etc. and all the hundred and one little things the omission of which from the general scheme just makes all the difference in the world. This is to be the greatest battle in history and we all pray it may result in victory to our arms. It is all quite exciting, everyone being in more or less a state of expectancy. Troops keep moving in, guns seem everywhere, field guns, heavy guns, giant guns and howitzers of all weights and calibres. There should be some hair flying when they get the order to loose off. I wonder how Fritz is preparing for it all. Pretty thoroughly I expect if we know him at all. However, I think he is up against it this time. And we shall see what the next month will bring forth.

15th April '16

It was most interesting this morning up in the new Durham trench on the top of the hill past Bronfay farm. From it the locality of our attack lies spread out like a map – a most absorbing one at the moment. For long enough we gazed at it through our glasses. There was nothing to say – nothing. You get your orders and you prepare to go. It is all wonderfully simple, like most big things. It will simply be a scrambled repetition of the hundred and one other attacks we have performed during training, scrambled because of the men who will be knocked out on the way. Either we will get there or we will be shot. Yet it causes no excitement. It is really quite wonderful and altogether different to what one expected. If we attain our objective and hold it the world will ring and English hearts will leap for joy at news of a great victory. But it is hard indeed to realise here that we stand on such a threshold. One so soon becomes accustomed to the life, to expecting danger that one accepts it as part of the daily routine, even though one never gets to like it or even to cease to regard it with interest. That, I doubt not, is too much to ask of human nature.

16th April '16

Corbie again. And a welcome change indeed. To walk a clean street, to see shops and decent civilians, to sit in a furnished room and eat off china plates and drink from glasses is quite a joy in itself. It is pleasant, pleasant indeed.

Major Merriman and I rode over together first thing this morning. It was a lovely morning and the ride an according happiness. We came to take over the practise battle grounds from the Staffords. We came with high expectations. That was foolish of us. We should know the Army better by now. What we found was no Staffords and only a water-logged field by the canal with some odd twine tied about it and some trenches scored out of the surface. However, it will do well enough. The CO and I walked over it this evening and planned and talked for an hour. The scheme has been settled more or less and tomorrow I am to take the company and set to work.

17th April '16

All day on marking out and planning the trench system on our sodden *campagne*. It has been a long job and a tiring [one] but it begins to [take] shape and by tomorrow noon should be finished and ready for use. It is very interesting and I earnestly hope will serve its purpose well.

This evening I have been working out the Sports for next Saturday with Wicks and young Harrison. They should be a success and we all look forward to them.

Earlier your sweet letter arrived and then the Easter Egg. What a truly characteristic thought of yours to send it me from Baby. It has pleased me mightily. Lord, how I long for a sight of your dear faces again.

18th April '16

Another day on the trenches. It still rains and the men were wet through but stuck to the job well. They know, I feel sure, all about our preparations and what they are for and I think it is greatly due to the subdued excitement thus imbued that they work so well on this job.

The afternoon I gave them off, partly on account of their damp state and mainly because of the way they had worked.

19th April '16

We hear today that the Borders[i] have had rather a thin time in their sector just on the left of our line. They were heavily bombarded and the front line blown in but they held on and did, we hear, very well. Thirty-nine dead and seventy casualties in all we are told is the total damage. It is rather unsatisfactory and must have upset them considerably. I hope they will get a chance at Fritz when the time comes for us all to go for him. A pounding like that requires some wiping out and a battalion remembers it a long, long time. There must be many such scores to be wiped out.

i 2nd Bn, Border Regt.

20th April '16

The battn concert came off tonight and was a top-hole affair. All sorts of people rolled up to give us a turn and some really first class talent was displayed. The hall was packed and the men as excited as schoolboys, yelling the choruses and whooping to the band. I hope their stay in Corbie will do them the good intended.

We cannot hear the guns here but the flashes at night can be plainly seen and tonight the sky is flickering with them. Grimwood was over to recite to us and he rang up the general for permission to stay. The general told him a repetition of last night's bombardment was taking place, and that the unfortunate Borders were getting it again. It is rather sickening and one cannot help wondering why we don't loose our guns in reply and thump Fritz till he quits. As an Army I'm afraid we are inclined to take things too easily. In this case, however, I trust the Borders have not suffered casualties.

21st April '16

Two letters from you today and both telling me that my letters had not arrived. What a petty irritation it is. You say one letter you received was half blotted out and the news I told you about Verdun blotted out. What utter piffle! What empty-headed asses there must be in that safe job of censor? What possible harm could lie in the sending of good news? I ask you. What evil would it do our cause to record the fact that Fritz has taken a licking? Presumably he already knows it himself.

Some of these Base people should be tarred and feathered. I can just see a fatuous ass with weak eyes and spectacles, puffing a pipe or even a cigar as he sits in his warm office in some town by the coast and shudders that we here should even desire to say 'Boo' to the enemy or attempt to cheer up those at home when we have done it. I'd like to take all Base people and toe them into the trenches when it has been raining for a week or so and leave 'em there for an eight day tour to learn sense. Perhaps when they came out some of the fatuosity would have been washed off them.

22nd April '16

The Sports today in spite of the rain were a success and especially so for B Coy. We had men in one place or other for nearly every event, pulled off the Relay (mile) and had 1st and 2nd in the 'Best and Smartest Turn-Out'. I feel most braced about it and know the men will be jolly well bucked about it. The CO was pleased about it. He told Townsend that to have both first and second in such an event showed keenness and reflected considerable credit on me. Good old B they always rise to the occasion and I feel quite certain always will.

Gomersall, I hear, has quite a little joke. Going to Courses, Assistant Adjutants, etc., he has been practically the only duty officer in his company for over a month now. Of course OC Coys and 2nds-in-Command alternate their tours. Gomersall says, 'I take a different Captain in with me each time to assist me with the work.'

Newdigate[i] of the Borders was in this evening. They came in today after a trying tour in the line. Fritz tried two 'cut-outs' on them. The first was successful in that he killed thirty and wounded sixty of them with shell fire. The second failed utterly, partly because of the effective measures adopted by the Borders and partly because of the artillery fire our guns brought to bear on him. Newdigate says we pounded him to blazes. And tonight our guns are strafing like the very deuce. There is a bombardment of the first order going on up there. I trust the Hun is getting a thorough pasting.

23rd April '16

Bowly's result is out. He was sentenced to dismissal but this was reduced by the C in C to forfeiture of seniority to the date of sentence. A let-off indeed. Yet Bowly has taken it badly. Has a grievance against the world in general. It is a pity. I am afraid the suspense has soured him. He is to be transferred, and leaves tomorrow. On the whole I am glad. I never

---

i Capt. Richard Francis Newdigate.

could thoroughly trust him now, one never can a person who drinks. However, it is over, let it pass.

The general was over today and took us in a march past. The men looked and went past well. He was very pleased with them and said there was a great improvement.

He was very nearly put out by a shell the other day as was Grant. Grant is awfully bored about it. He says he was never so frightened in his whole life before.

24th April '16

Don is back. I am awfully glad and thoroughly happy to see the old boy again. He is a good chap, a good soldier and a good man.

We tried the attack as a battalion this morning and the general saw it this afternoon. He also spoke to the men, told 'em they'd done well, that their record already was a good one and that the battalion was all right. We all agree with him. Also we feel we'll do all right when the show comes off. The Manchesters have a record second to none and I pray to heaven the 22nd may be able to add to its lustre. It will be a great thing to have done.

Bowly is gone.[i] I am ashamed to say that I am almost relieved that this is really a fact.

25th April '16

A topping little company route march this morning, through Bonnay, La Houssoy and back via La Neuville. The road runs round the valley slopes with the little Ancre sparkling among the trees in the bottom.

It is pretty country, very peaceful and lazy-looking, not at all like war, not at all. It is too full of the springtime for that and it seems hateful that here the world should be so sweet a place and, only ten miles off,

i Lt Reginald Walter Bowly was transferred to the 20th Manchesters.

man, to whom it was given, should be using all his ingenuity to turn it into a hell, a terrain wherein he may slay his fellows.

This afternoon the officers played C Coy in the battn final.[i] Unfortunately I played. It is the first game of soccer I have ever indulged in and I am afraid I made but a sorry showing. However, my conscience is clear because I did my best and it was no fault of mine that I was played. My body, though, is weary unto death. I ache in every joint and limb. Woe, indeed, is me!

26th April '16

I have had an easy day indeed. A topping ride to Heilly, for the battalion's money, along the river road which runs with the stream on one side and fields of sprouting corn on the other. The entrance to the village is in keeping. The ground rises to the left and where the skyline is cut by the château wall a great cliff of red, moss-grown, creeper-clad or crumbling bricks replaces the natural chalk and supports the château orchard, the cherry, apple and pear blossoms of which one can just catch a glimpse of above it from the road.

At the bottom of this cliff is the kitchen garden, snugly tucked in where it will catch the sun and no chill draughts can get at it. It is a riot of rhubarb, cabbage, lettuce and all other sorts of delicious things jumbled up in motley order among clumps of forcing domes. Along the cliff wall are perhaps a dozen straw hives, the drone of whose busy occupants comes soothingly to the wayfarer in the dust of the roadway, mingles pleasantly with the babble of the stream and makes him think of the loveliness of life and the sweetness of the maid he loves. I would that the war was over and that we might walk together into Heilly on this, the Bonnay road.

i 'I played Outside Left in the great final match of the Battalion Cup Tie!! This afternoon!! – the first time since I was 10 that I have ventured on Association Footer except to play once in goal in Salisbury' (Bland, 26.4.16).

27th April '16

Here we are in old Bray again.[i] The same old Bray, hot, bare, grubby and battered. Yet, strange to say, we find we have quite an attachment for it – it seems almost like being at home to return here. I scarcely mean that, of course, but one experiences a modification of that sort of feeling in getting back here.

The march was rather trying. The day was scorching hot and men fell out rather badly. I had six go, and feel very annoyed about it. One always finds the men with guts on these occasions. They stand out clearly from the ruck of the neurotic. It is of the latter that the majority of those who fall out are composed. They dwell on their own troubles till these swell enormously and the man who is only suffering normally believes he is in martyrdom and drops down groaning. One feels inclined to kick them where they lie.

I shall strafe my faint-hearts in the morning.

28th April '16

The battalion has gone in to the line today and I am one of the derelicts left out. Merriman, Lloyd and Cowan accompany me but already I am sick of it. One feels like a childless wife without the battalion. It is positively hateful. John Cotton is back with us to lend a hand and the air is full of jumpiness, everyone expecting to raid or be raided. Raids seem all the go at the moment though what benefit they hold for the cost of them I, for one, do not see at all. Fritz started them, of course. He always does do damn silly things like that. And now we have butted in in retaliation. And we have gone one better by raiding not only at night but in broad daylight. The net result so far as I can see is to render Coy Commanders' lives in the line an absolute burden to them. One will live in a continuous state of strained expectation.

Would that the big scrap would come off! But that now appears

---

i Grovetown Camp, Bray.

161

further removed than ever. What a game this is. They now talk of us going back for a rest. And only a fortnight ago we believed we would have been in Mametz before this!

29th April '16

A day spent in soaking in the baths, strolling along the river bank – easing limbs which still remind me that I played football – and in writing both letters and the commencement of a short story.[i] A thoroughly lazy day and one for which Cowan, Lloyd and myself are thankful. The Major[ii] I have not talked with about it but I expect his sentiments are similar. He and Lloyd have talked books the whole evening. Both are well-read, clever men and their conversation is pleasurable to listen to. Lloyd is a cynic, a clever one so that even his bitterest sallies have the saving grace of wit. To a victim they would be the more stinging because of that. In ordinary times he writes weighty articles on social questions for the *New Statesman*.[iii]

This Army of ours is really very wonderful. Merriman is one of the best-known and cleverest barristers on the Northern Circuit. Yet here we are thrown together, I as the ignoramus of the party, in a way nothing else than this war could have brought about. In ordinary life our callings are divergent as the Poles, we would never have met, never have come to really know each other presuming we had. Yet I am sure all three of us are glad that we have done. War is not all uselessness.

i The short story, *Beyond the Line: A Tale of 'No Man's Land'*, would be published in the *Weekly Telegraph*, coincidentally on the day that May was killed.
ii Maj. Frank Merriman.
iii 'A day or two ago, I walked down to the river with Lloyd, who is also out of the trenches, and had a chat with him. He is not at all reconciled to the army. The unanimity with which absolutely everyone simply loathes military life is almost comic. We never speak of the war, except to say, "When will it be over?" Everyone, except myself (and Lloyd) seems to bet on August or September, but of course none of us know anything' (Tawney, 2.5.16).

The Major quoted a phrase this evening. I don't know where he got it from but it is good. 'This war,' he said, 'Is one long boredom, punctuated by moments of extreme terror.'

30th April '16

Grim[i] came in to see us this morning from the Brigade. He wants to get back to the battalion. And greatly should we be glad to have him, if only for purely selfish reasons. We are eleven subalterns short at the moment, all being engaged on various outside jobs where their services could quite well be dispensed with. However I suppose the Big Men like to have a spruce entourage even though they may not be strictly entitled to one, and he but stirs a wasps' nest who tries to interfere. It is, I suppose, a malicious crank of mine, but I do enjoy hearing of the little weaknesses, the little human touches regarding the Big Men whom one is so liable to forget are of the same clay as the rest of humanity.

The General's, I hear, is a tendency to fussiness. He becomes excited if the corps invites itself to tea with him. He frets and fusses, gives orders again and again. 'The watercress, is it clean? The tea, is it not too strong? And the patties, are they not rather rich, the cake rather damp? About the watercress, what was it you said? The corps are coming to tea. Didn't I tell you? Ah, yes, of course I did. Do see to it that the tea is not too strong, nor over-stewed. The general likes it just so.'

And so on at odd intervals, which recur with greater frequency as the hour for the visit draws nearer, till by the time the illustrious ones actually arrive the Staff is reduced to a state of perspiring nervousness and feels totally incapable of entertaining the two very charming fellows who have come to see it with no other idea than that of having an enjoyable afternoon free from the constraint of their own exalted mess.

i 2nd Lt Herbert Grimwood had left to join the Brigade Headquarters on 26.11.15.

We hear today that the Kut has fallen.[i] What a pity. What a sadness for Townshend. Poor man and his poor army. We feel very sorry for them. But gallant fellows all, they did their utmost, no men can do more and their capitulation can therefore hold no disgrace for them. It will be bitter news for Lake, however, and for all with him.

1st May '16

A ride to Heilly today with Lloyd. We went with a twofold object, Lloyd being desirous of trying the much talked of restaurant there and I my new horse. For I have parted with my old Lizzie to Tom Worthington and have taken in exchange his much more flighty Marcel. Marcel was a trifle too much for Tom and I must say I found her something of a handful but she is a good mare and worth riding. When we started to come home it was dark. I only know the way across country but, the night being too black for that route, we were compelled to seek a passage by road. The inevitable happened. We became lost, mainly owing to the stupidity and utter ignorance of those portions of the army which we met and from whom we asked advice. Eventually we arrived in Bray at midnight, two jaded revellers indeed.

i It seems that at this date, officers on the Western Front in France were not aware of the true events in Mesopotamia. When Turkey entered the war on the side of Germany, a new front was opened in Mesopotamia in the Ottoman Empire. An early engagement was the siege, from December 1915 to April 1916, of the Allied garrison at Kut Al Amara, 100 miles south of Baghdad, which was commanded by Maj. Gen. Sir Charles Townshend. Despite efforts to relieve the town, the besieged British and Indian troops finally surrendered. Captured soldiers were brutally treated on their forced march to a POW camp at Aleppo. By contrast, Townshend's luxurious surroundings on an island on the Sea of Marmara was regarded in London as notorious. Sir Percival Lake, who replaced the sick Sir John Nixon as CinC, British forces, was immediately ordered to break the Siege at Kut. After two failed attempts, he was summoned to London to testify before the newly established Mesopotamia Commission which was investigating the military setbacks in the region.

2nd May '16

Two new officers arrived last night – Nanson and Cook.[i] They both seem decent stuff. I have the former and 'Ram' the other.

I write this in the Rat Hole. I am in a day before I expected but, coming up with the new fellows, the CO seized upon me and told me to remain. There is a big lot to be done, pressure has to be put on. The general is not at all satisfied with progress and has been strafing people so now all hands and the cook are on and, for B [Company], if he is not satisfied with the night's progress tomorrow I'll eat my hat.

Fritz has been quiet since I have been in but it is the first time I believe. He is rather great on sudden strafes now, and we all live in expectation of being next to share his little flutters.

3rd May '16

Up all last night messing about on top with Nanson – who, by the way, took it very well for the first time under fire – looking after the men digging a new trench. They worked like trojans and were through by this morning deep enough for the general to walk along so be it he wished to.

Today we have carried on with various [working] parties everywhere and Don and myself were shelled with one whilst having a look at its progress. Fritz put over about half dozen whiz-bangs all round us. It was quite exciting for the moment.

This evening we have taken over from D Coy and are now in the firing line for five days. There is a tremendous amount of work to do and I cannot think that we will be able to complete it.

Quite an exciting little patrol tonight. Hadfield[ii] got across to Fritz's wire with a [working] party just in time to see one of their working parties put to a disordered rout by a lucky rifle grenade of ours. Our party was then seen and a large patrol of Fritz came out and tried to cut it off so that Hadfield had to retire to a flank and spend an hour

i 2nd Lts Joseph Nanson and Henry Rodham Cook.
ii Sgt Herbert Hadfield.

getting his people back to us. This, however, he achieved without mishap.

One of the men, Dooley, a most unpromising specimen in Prince's platoon, I heard a good story of today. Dooley was sitting on the Paradise[i] one night when our batteries opened on Fritz. One of the shells pitched short and entered the ground with a fierce thud right under the spot where the man was sitting. It was a dud. 'God bless the fool who made that shell,' said Dooley, and never troubled to change his position.

4th May '16

Another day of work in the trenches and a night off work out of them. The Coy is doing well and making a good show.

Fritz has shelled us a bit and put grenades and canisters over quite freely. Such things are fast becoming a usual feature of the daily round, a feature of the general enlivenment of the line.

Lloyd was wounded tonight with a shell splinter in the leg and Murray was taken away at a moment's notice to take charge of C.[ii] I do not think Lloyd is seriously hurt but of course it is rotten for him and for us. It means the battn has to go minus a valuable officer.

Hadfield was out patrolling again tonight but this time there was nothing exciting, Fritz keeping to his trenches.

5th May '16[iii]

More work and more progress, more trench-mortaring and rifle grenades on both sides all the afternoon and night.

i Pte Henry Dooley. 'Paradise' was slang for latrine.
ii Capt. Gordon Ramsbottom, OC, C Coy, was on leave.
iii 'I have managed to borrow various novels in different quarters & with a bit of their aid have spent a time in complete idleness. It is lovely spring weather. From the little window in the slanting roof of the loft where I sleep I can look down on the valley of the [Somme], a wonderful confusion of greens & pinks & browns, all the trees rushing out in the last few days of sunshine' (Tawney, 5.5.16).

The Company continues to do well. We wired the whole of the support line tonight, got some more out in front of the fire trench and have made first rate progress with the traverses in both trenches. Our wiring was mentioned in Brigade Trench Orders today and I earnestly trust we may get a special mention before we are finished.

I had to go down to the Second Line this afternoon, leaving young Nanson in charge and, whilst I was away, Fritz opened a hurricane fire on poor old Mansell Copse sector. I hurried back thinking the young fellow might be a bit nervous but found him quite calm and cool. I think he will turn out all right.

Sgt Whitehead had a real good patrol 'stunt' tonight. He got over with six men inside the German wire and threw bombs into their trench. They were challenged and a sentry called out 'English soldiers'. Rapid fire was opened on them from all round and bombs thrown but the whole lot got back safely. It is good going.

6th May '16

Another day of work and strafing. I think our patrol of last night is the main cause of the latter. It has upset Fritz. He put over today and tonight about 100 rifle grenades and forty canisters. It makes things pretty lively and one is always in an unpleasant state of expectancy. I expect, however, that he is in precisely the same frame of mind seeing that we dropped 80 grenades upon him, about 20 Stokes bombs[i] and 10 or a dozen sixty-pound mortars. The night was an intermittent flash and bang, both of varying intensities and one was continually subjected to most unpleasant jars and shocks. It is a great game. Shelmerdine and Oldham have been amusing themselves collecting dud Fritz grenades and extracting the detonators. Shelmerdine nearly blew himself up. I call it a most unhealthy lust for souvenirs. Personally when such things fail to explode I am only thankful. So is Murray. We are not fire-eating soldiers, Don and I. We

---

i The Stokes trench mortar was a 3-inch, smooth bore, muzzle-loading weapon designed for high angles of fire.

should prefer to kill the Hun from the safe seclusion of a bomb-proof dug-out and I feel we have something of a grievance that such a desirable state is denied us.[i]

7th May '16

Nothing much to record today. It has just been a usual day of work and sunshine, very pleasant and not at all warlike. Fritz has been quiet as have we. Quite a change from yesterday. Prince is not well which makes us rather shorthanded but I hope he will be all right after a full night's rest and able to take on tomorrow again.

I had two ripping letters from you tonight in one of which you mention having seen Garside and how the meeting pleased you. I am very glad, my own, because I know he will have assured you of how safe I really am. It was fortunate for me that he saw Baby because now I will be able to hear first hand how the sweet mite looks and is. What a picture of peace and comfort and all that is sweet and clean in life thought of her brings before me. And how I simply long for leave and the sight of you both again.[ii]

i 'The Battalion, which comes out of the trenches tomorrow, will have been in for 10 days, and I have had a complete rest and feel much stronger. I have done nothing but sitting still & read, except for some long talks with Bland and Lloyd. The latter, by the way, has been wounded, at least it counts as a wound, though it was the merest scratch on his leg and hardly drew blood, caused by a small piece of canister. He has not gone to bed and can walk quite well . . . Lloyd, like me, is fed up with the war and the army. Bland, to me, maintains an heroic equanimity, which makes me feel a miserable grumbler, but Lloyd tells me he is a creature of mood & and on occasion is as bored as we are. I don't think Lloyd altogether likes him . . . But he, Bland – is a good soul' (Tawney, 7.5.16).

ii After a period during which all leave had been stopped because of enemy submarine action in the English Channel, Gomersall wrote, 'Leave has started again, but I cannot say for how long, as it may be stopped at any moment.

A really splendid little affair has just taken place. A patrol of mine under Sergeant Hadfield – six men – went out from F 12.3 at 8.30. Nanson was in the line but I went up too, as, being a bit of an old woman, I like to be there when there are many of the men over the top. One never knows what may happen. About 9 o'clock Nanson sent for me and, hurrying up, I found young Fortune,[i] one of the patrol, on the parapet asking for me. It appeared our patrol had bumped a German one about thirty strong and Hadfield wanted the Lewis gun on them. There was a wiring party out but Nanson had already told them to lie down. It was a bit risky but I told the gun to fire which it did, keeping high and strafing the Hun parapet. I fired for morale effect only and hope this was achieved. We put in two magazines and then Fortune came back, under fire from the German line, to say some of the Fritz patrol had been pushed forward and asking for further orders. I sent word to Hadfield to bomb them and then withdraw. On receipt of this he pushed his bombers forward, and Clarke,[ii] one of them, shot and killed a Hun. All three then stood up and threw their bombs among the main German party where they exploded. Fritz at once bombed back and opened fire not only from his patrol but from all along his parapet. We therefore did the same and the fun became fast and furious – a regular private battle. Under cover of it our patrol came back, Fortune first crawling painfully and calling out, 'Oh, sir. Oh, sir.' He had been hit twice, poor boy, and was suffering from shock. Then Hadfield brought the rest in. Five had been hit, Hadfield twice also, but he had stuck to his job, helped Fortune through the wire under a stinging fire and then seen the remainder in. He has done well, as have they all.

Another thing from my point of view is that all leave to Manchester and District is stopped, owing to an outbreak of small-pox' (5.5.16).

i Pte James Fortune.
ii Pte John Albert Clarke.

8th May '16

We came out tonight after a fairly quiet day. The Staffords[i] took over from us and the relief was quick and easy. It was a lovely moonlight night and the walk down to Bray top hole accordingly. Rather, I should say, the ride down, for Murray and I jumped an ammunition wagon whose driver gave us a lift. It was a swift ride though somewhat bumpy, the road being rough, the cart unsprung and the horses fresh. However it was quite enjoyable and another little experience. One cannot have too many. [ii]

i 1st Bn, South Staffordshire Regt.

ii 'I have not been in the trenches for nearly a month, and the battalion, which came out last night, will not be in again for a week. Moreover when we came in, though of course accidents do occur, the danger is not great. My company has not a single man dead, and only 5 or 6 slight wounds, during a period of nearly 4 months that we have been in & out of the trenches. So you see – on a cold view – the danger is not great. Don't be misled by casualty lists. I have read *Victory* again. The power of Conrad is a perpetual amazement. He has the gift of creating an enchanted world in which emotions & thoughts seem to revolve within a vast and mysterious yet harmless universe, and in which whispers of encouragement and despair seem to come from inanimate things. I have lent him to our Quarter-Master Sgt [Garside]. He is in private life a Manchester cotton broker, a keen and extremely acute businessman, and with humanity, which endears him to me in the rather arid relationships of our little world. But the army discourages reflection, and he may find Conrad's sombre imagination too great a strain. You would be amused to hear men here talk of the war. How shocked our patriots would be. "Never again" is the usual sentiment – and I believe most of them mean it. The few who read the journalists' account of K[itchener]'s army – "with the glint of battle in their eyes" – as one put it – explode with laughter. Their feelings don't make any difference to their conduct here, but I think and hope they may provide a rude shock for militant politicians, when all is over' (Tawney, 9.5.16).

9th May '16

The usual slack day of rest. A bath this morning in the Divisional tubs and a stroll round in the afternoon with Worthy and Don Murray. In the evening we called in at the Brigade Bombers where I was introduced to the *First Seven Divisions* and found it so absorbing as to entirely captivate me and take me out of the conversation until my rudeness was impressed upon me and I was forced to put it down.[i]

It reminded me of the great fight of the Buffs[ii] and Yorks and Lancs, Richebourg way, against a German Army corps. They struggled there for three days supported by two puny batteries of 18 pounders, and held the assaulting mass till the evening of the third when sheer weight of numbers forced them back. The Buffs had four and the Yorks and Lancs six hundred casualties but morally and in point of casualties the victory was theirs. It was a soldiers' fight, clubbed rifles in a wood – *mêlée* with the shells to separate the sides and those only – and all that sort of thing. Hats off to those old Regular battalions. Tough and hard and efficient they were, trained to a turn, plucky to the bone and led by the pick of the nation. Neither their memory nor their deeds will ever fade and the latter, though emulated, will never be excelled.

i Ernest W. Hamilton, *The First Seven Divisions, being an Account of the Fighting from Mons to Ypres* (Hurst Blackett, 1916).

ii The East Kent Regiment. This battle was part of the campaign for the 'race to the sea'. During this battle the BEF successfully held the line in its sector against repeated German assaults.

Chapter 10
'The flickering, angry light
of a burning village'

10 May–3 June 1916

10th May '16

A ride with Worthy today round the battery over the back of the hill and back along the river from Etinehem. My favourite little ride that is.

There is now to be a 'stunt'. We are going to raid Fritz and capture or kill some portion of him. That is good, and I pray it may be a great success. Young Shelmerdine is to be in charge with Street and Cansino[i] to help him. It will be a regular slap-up affair – tons of artillery and all that. The line is livening up with a vengeance.

Had grub at HQ tonight and quite enjoyed the change. Tawney is back and in great form. He is a regular Benedict now. One of us. Good luck to him and his wife. He tells me they saw you in London. I envy him. But I look forward confidently to the time when I will be in the same fortunate position.[ii]

---

i 2nd Lt Edmund Alger Street joined the battalion on 19.2.16. 2nd Lt Joshua Hain Cansino did so on 19.4.16.
ii While on leave, Tawney and Jeanette had visited Maude. During 1916, Tawney's

11th May '16

I was talking with John Cotton this afternoon, up on the top, where he was superintending the digging of the trenches for the 'stunt'. John dearly loves the Top Men. He is the best fellow in the world. That is his only weakness, if, in his case, weakness it be, for he is so artless about it all that one is only conscious of humour in regard to him. His latest acquisition is a friend he has unearthed who commands a battery near here. The younger, irrepressible element of the battalion call him the 'Jamp', which, being interpreted, means 'John's Artillery Major Pal'. 'Jamp' is a nice man, though, at the moment, rather a disgusted one. It appears that the man who had the battery before him was quite incapable and was bundled home in a hurry. And no sooner was he home than he was promoted colonel, mainly in view of his invaluable experience of the front. 'What a game it is.' I veritably believe that if half of us here got home and played to the gallery a bit we'd be colonels in a month with fresh battalions to mould.

It would be quite easy. Yet nobody does it. Which speaks well for the high-mindedness of the majority of British officers. Few are self-seeking. Honour is undoubtedly our national standard of value. A man would greatly prefer a small lift where the lift would really mean to him that he had earned it than a big lift where his conscience might not be so clear. I think it our greatest national asset – this desire for justified honour. It is the secret of England's greatness. Her heart is clear and true and lucre does not really matter to it.

12th May '16

The Staff have started a new game. It is called 'Programmes of Work'. And it goes like this. OC Companies, Battalion Commanders and others whom

---

wife Jeanette had been unwell and, with his absence, their relationship was strained, but when he had returned to France, May must have heard via Maude some happier news and compared him to Benedick, Shakespeare's mischievous knave in *Much Ado About Nothing*.

it may concern have to work out when in the trenches a schedule of how they are going to occupy the time they are out of the line with training. Accordingly this is done, in neat, tabulated form on sheets of flimsy, and duly submitted for approval. The Staff, I take it, is awfully bucked with it. One can imagine them looking at it, rubbing their hands and saying, 'Splendid, splendid, every hour occupied – and most profitably. It will indeed do the men good.' And so everyone is happy with the exception, perhaps, of the aforesaid OC Company or Battalion Commander. Those belonging to this series who still have any conscience left maybe worry a little. A conscientious man would when, knowing his company is down for company drill, he finds himself with three cooks and four light duty men as the total of the unit under his command. The Staff have taken all the rest for mining parties, digging parties, demolition parties and a hundred and one other parties all graced with high-faluting names. A conscientious man wants to tell people. An ordinary one just says, 'My poor devils never get a minute's rest,' gets on his horse and goes off for a ride, knowing full well that the Staff will be quite happy with their 'Programme of Work'. What a game it is! What a deadly game for a man who takes life seriously! His sort get invalided home. The best way is to seek for the humour of the situation. Which reminds me that we'll find amusement in the grouses and grumbles of those who still soldier at home. If they only knew it, what a bed of roses are they on. They do not yet know that they're alive. There a man does one eight hour day, has eight hours' sleep and eight hours to himself. And then he grouses. The poor fool. Here, in addition to being under fire all and every day, in the line and out, he does hard manual slogging for about 14 hours out of the 24 and averages about five hours' sleep *per diem*. I am afraid there will be a bitter awakening for some of the lads at home. No, I am not afraid, I am glad. It will make men of them – or they will go under. And the sort that go under are better there.[i]

---

i 'We wish a thousand times a day that the peevish folk who grouse and quarrel and wash dirty linen across the water could be flung into the front line and just behind it for a week, and see what war really is, what it means to the nation whose soil it is fought on, how marvellously they bear themselves, with what

We had another company concert last night – a really splendid show. So good that we give it again tonight for the men who couldn't get in last night. These things are the goods.

13th May '16

There was a strafe on our right last night, on the front of our old division. It appears the 18th caught it pretty severely but gave as good as they got and did very well. The King's were also in it, doing good work. They are fine battalions and it is a good division, the old 30th.

We gave the second concert tonight. Hundreds of men were turned away. It would be worthwhile to run a show every night only, if we did, the Hun would most likely get to hear about it and shell us out of our theatre. Therefore here it can only be an occasional treat.

I have started on a map and data for a lecture on Townshend's doings in Mesopotamia.[i] It will, I think, be good hearing for the men, since, though that force is now lost to us, its example of gallantry and endurance still remain to help us over any bad patch in the unfailing way heroic examples do. Preparations are about complete for our raid on the next tour in. I wish I was in charge of it. It will be a good thing and should bring credit on the battn and aid in killing some more Bosche, the end we are all here to attain.

---

quiet optimism and cheerful patience; if they could but see a battalion returning to billets – and <u>such</u> billets – after 4 days struggle with slush and cold – <u>singing</u>, by God, <u>singing</u>; if they could see the enormous machinery working in such ways that every man in and out of the trenches gets bread and butter and jam and hot tea and hot bacon every morning of his life, if they could see the equanimity with which the normal risks are faced, the jest when a shell drops at your feet and fails to burst, the quip at the perpetual bullet which snaps near the entrance to every officer's dug-out day and night, and the genial profanity of everybody, oh! I would love to put the whole damned lot of them in the line and push 'em over the parapet, and have done with 'em' (Bland, 13.3.16).
i An accurate account of the Siege of Kut had presumably now reached May.

14th May '16

The CO has come back from Flixecourt today, full of beans and fierce anti-Bosche ideas. I am glad he is with us again.

The news of the loss of 500 yards of trenches at Givenchy is to hand this morning and now no doubt we only have to await the paeans of victory in the German press. There is no doubt that the Hun works his army to political ends very successfully. We do not. We prefer to hold our toll of life till we pay it for something big. No doubt we are right in the end. It is an English characteristic to be slow. The victory in the Great Battle is what, after all, will be the only thing that matters. When we do strike it will be with a most mighty blow.

The Hun method is to concentrate every piece of artillery on a small front, pound it out of recognition and then advance on the remains, making prisoners of those few unfortunate men whom it was not possible to evacuate during the bombardment. These little successes are and can only be temporary but they look well in the papers and our press does little to show them in their true proportion. It enlarges upon any such minor success of our own and is thereby compelled to give equal prominence to what the Hun does in reply. It is a pity, since it puts us perilously near the same ridiculous position in which the German press now finds itself through its over-indulgence in roseate prognostications of what its U-boats were going to do to the 'hated English'. We are, by the way, only four days off our extermination now. Leaflets dropped in Corbie have promised that we shall be wiped off the face of the earth on the 18th inst., though precisely how it is to be done is not stated. That is rather inconsiderate of our chivalrous foe. To complete his little act of gallantry he should have certainly told us how.

15th May '16

Sunday – and I am afraid we took advantage of it, lounging in bed till 8.30, reading and smoking. It is the first time we have been able to indulge in such a luxury for months – and we appreciate it to the full. As you were, today is not Sunday but Monday. It was yesterday we lay abed. This morning we were up betimes. It is wonderful how one gets mixed with the days here and how one can forget by the evening exactly what occurred of a morning.

This evening we have been up to Durham Trench and Peronne Avenue, practising manning them in case of attack. It was almost as light as day but the line was abnormally quiet, so that we were able to do all we desired with as much ease as if it had been day. The moon was really extraordinary in its brilliance.

Ram is back from leave and not looking at all well. He was ill whilst at home, unable to sleep and that sort of thing. I am told that it is nerve trouble but I trust it may pass off. We can't afford to lose Ram from our list of officers. I always thought him so strong and brave too, one of the last fellows this game would affect. However, we shall see! Perhaps his furlough has been a trifle strenuous.

16th May '16

Grim, whom I saw today, tells me he thinks he will now be put permanently on the Brigade Staff. I hope he is. He deserves it. He is a worker, an optimist and a most conscientious man. A born humorist, a splendid companion and the possessor of a fund of common sense.

We have been to see the Stokes gun this afternoon. It is really a splendid weapon for trench warfare and I devoutly hope we may be able to move forward before the Hun gets a quantity of any similar engine of destruction.

All the Hooks[i] were there. Colonels Norman, Longbourne and our own CO, Duke from the brigade, Morris (2nd-in-Command) of the Staffords and majors and captains to burn. Quite a turn-out. Harris

---

i Hooks, possibly slang for 'hangers on' (to power). Lt Col. William Wilding Norman of 21 Manchesters; Lt Col. F. C. Longbourne, of 2nd Queen's Royal West Surreys; Lt Col. Paul W. Whetham of 22nd Manchesters; Capt. J. P. Duke; Maj. Robert John Morris of 1st South Staffordshires.

– little 'Bum' Harris[i] – the gun officer, was quite nervously damp by the time he'd finished talking and I don't blame him.

17th May '16

The battn has gone in again and to my surprise I have been left out with three other 'derelicts' Merriman, Lloyd and Cowan. We had all taken this scheme as over, but evidently it is not. We are quite in the air, however, as all the other elements have gone to the Bois des Tailles, whither we adjourn tomorrow.

Cowan has been exceedingly funny, telling stories to beat the band. 'Somebody says something about "Stand to" is one I must remember. Also, I want to go to Manchester'. You mean you – …… well have to go. The major also coined a good joke relative to situation reports, our daily bug-bear in the line: "Wind-up. Situation: bloody."

18th May '16

Life is full of changes. Last evening we were all settled in Bray, settled as though we had never been anywhere else. We all [have] become quite attached to dirty, dilapidated Bray. And now tonight I write in a roomy – old airy – apartment situated on the top of a tree-clad hill in the Bois des Tailles. Two hours ago there was virgin brushwood where we have now just finished [constructing a] mess, but quick work, keen men and a rustle round and here we are in a mess room, 12' by 12', by 10' 6" high, waterproof-roofed and canvas-sided with our beds round the walls and our lamp burning cheerily on the table. The owls hoot outside, the traffic rumbles busily on the Corbie road, the guns rumble angrily on the other flank and away in our rear is the flickering, angry light of a burning village. But overhead the evening breeze plays, rustling through the trees, the moon is aloft in a perfect sky and down in the valley below a

i Harris was also nicknamed 'Bottom' (see fn 30.3.16).

nightingale is singing. It is all quite pleasant and charming, even the odd fires flickering among the trees where odd men are frying ration steaks or bacon, prodigal of tomorrow's rations. It is a complete change from Bray – quite a pleasant one up to now.

19th May '16

There is little to record except that a perfect day has been marred by the receipt of continual reports of casualties from the battn.[i] They have only been in two days and the casualties already total seventeen. It is swift going – for a 'quiet' part of the line such as ours is supposed to be, though we no longer believe that tale.

I had a sweet letter from you today, full of sweetness and love and the breath of the springtime. It was ripping to have it here in peace and the witching surroundings the Bois furnishes. I hear today that we go for a rest after this tour, and to the Bois de Treux. It is not far away but if it is anything like this the battalion should have a happy time there and one which should do the men an awful lot of good, provided the weather holds.

The trenches will reek vilely after this sun. It always brings the smells out, the nauseating smells of decaying bodies and of the manifold foulnesses which men have trodden into their floors for months gone.

One curses the trenches in winter and one curses them in summer, in fact one curses them always and in all weathers. One can think of no good word to say for them. Where then does their undoubted fascination lie? I am conscious that it is there but reason for it I never

i 'More excitement yesterday, I'm sorry to say. As a result I lost another NCO (a Corporal of mine and also 5 men) . . . They sent a huge number of rifle grenades over, and I had some very exciting experiences at times. I was 10 yards from one man who was wounded, and my servant had two very near escapes, being behind a traverse only a yard away. We are having a very unfortunate time, and my Platoon has caught it more than any other Platoon in the Battalion, as out of 62 men I have lost 13 including 8 NCOs' (Gomersall, 19.5.16).

can lay my finger on. The nearest I can get is that the very presence of danger is a fascination. And yet it is not – danger has no fascination for me, not consciously anyway. Yet I own the trenches attract me. Perhaps it is that when one is in them one feels that, more or less, one is doing one's job. It may be that. In fault of any better explanation I will let it stand.

This afternoon I perpetrated a vile sketch of our camp showing our quarters, Maiden's tent, the Quarter-Master's Stores and the officers' cook-house in the rear. Its only excuse for existence is that it will serve as a slight record of four happy days.

20th May '16

Went across to Billon Wood this morning to see some mining experiments by the RE [Royal Engineers]. They were very interesting and bid fair to have good uses. I noticed a shell was dropping on Bray as we passed, and later we heard that four Staff officers, the BSM [Brigade Sergeant Majors] and two CSMs [Company Sergeant Majors] had been all badly wounded by an unlucky shot which landed in the yard of BHQ whilst the CO's orders were in progress. One feels quite glad to be out of Bray. I trust we plastered some of Fritz's villages in reply.

Merriman and Lloyd have gone in today and Cowan and I follow tomorrow. Casualties keep coming in. There are over twenty in the battalion already. Two of my lads have been killed. The toll seems too high for just holding on, but then the line is not the same as when we came in.

Cowan told an amusing tale this afternoon. When on leave, he met Ram in London – they happened to have two seats together in the Alhambra.[i] After the show they sought for supper and a drink but, of course, under our new regime, everything was closed. In desperation they sought the advice of a belated cabby. 'Where can we get a drink?' 'There's

i The Alhambra Theatre on Leicester Square (on the site now occupied by the Odeon Cinema).

only one place I know of, sirs. That's the "Junior Turf". You go first to the right, second to the left' etc. They were deeply grateful and set off hurriedly. But alas! the "Junior Turf" was a cabman's shelter. Evidently someone's leg had been pulled.[i]

Cowan saw a Bosche prisoner in Corbie today. He was a decent-looking young fellow of 21, and had been in the war from the start and twice to the Russian front. He was a Saxon and belonged to the 63rd Regiment, opposite us. He said he was fed up with the war as were many others in his Regiment and that many would desert but for fear of being shot by us when coming over. He said that lately their rations had been dry, rye bread and coffee three times per day. Often the coffee was cold. He asked for cake, was given ration bread and jam and wolfed it. 'But this is cake,' he said when told we had none. His story is apparently true and, if so, it is certainly encouraging because continued shortage of food can only result in reduced morale. Certainly this man was wan and white and in marked contrast to our own ruddy-faced, healthy-looking men.

21st May '16

The Rat Hole again and, I find, a day before we were expected. The battalion is in for ten days, not eight. Had we only known there would have been but little chance of rooting Cowan and I out of the Bois.

There is nothing fresh to record. It is just the same old story here, 'This must be deepened and that must be dug whilst, as to the other thing, undoubtedly that should be revetted *tout suite.*' It is like coming back to some old job you have known all your life. Personally I feel quite fed up with it, so what the others think goes without saying, for, without any boosting spirit at all, I'm sure I am as keen as any of them. The fact is we are stale. We want a change and a rest. And yet we are not to have it, not after this tour anyway. Howsoever, 'Carry on' is the order of the day.

i Certain cabman's shelters were, in fact, notorious for selling liquor after hours.

22nd May '16

I write in *Werfer* Villa in the full blaze of the morning sun. We moved up here last night and there has been no sleep since. We may not sleep in dug-outs at night and the conditions of a trench board on the trench floor are not conducive to slumber. Therefore we do not sleep at night – or at any rate I do not, but prowl around dodging rifle grenades. These have become simply chronic here and have claimed nine men in two days already. They are beastly little things which come whizzing at you at an awful lick and detonate on striking. Last evening we shut them up with retaliation but at present we are not meeting with quite the same success.

We cannot always have it our own way however.

23rd May '16

Another day of rifle grenades. They killed one and wounded two of my men at lunchtime but we quietened them down before evening by severe retaliation.

We had a little strafe tonight against some large Hun working parties which my patrol discovered. As however it took us over an hour to get the guns to fire at them I am not too optimistic about results. The delay was atrocious and there is now a tour on to enquire reasons.

Don came in again this evening, having been sent for by BHQ. I am glad to have him, though sorry he should have been denied his tour out.

24th May '16

Young Prince returned [from a hospital in Rouen][i] tonight fit and well and full of the Anthem of leave. This will let Murray get out, for which

i Almost all of the military hospitals at Rouen remained operational throughout the war. They included eight general, five stationary, one British Red Cross, one labour hospital and two convalescent depots.

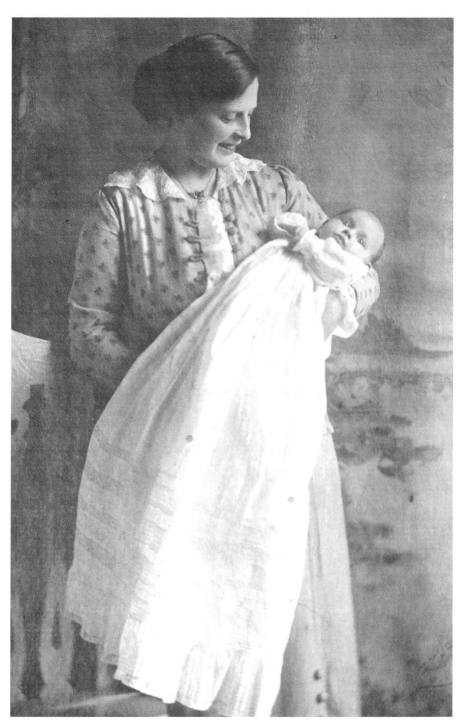

Maude with Pauline after her christening in Didsbury Parish Church, Manchester, 1914.

Photographs of Maude and Pauline in a leather-bound case, which Maude had posted to Charlie, referred to by him on 24 March 1916.

Maude, Pauline and Charlie, who is perhaps at home on leave in February 1915. During the war Maude moved from Manchester back to Essex.

'My dear, dear girlie … what joyous times have been ours in other summers.' Maude.

Pauline, aged about four, with her teddy bear, c.1918.

Three of Charlie May's seven pocket books, in which his diaries were meticulously written each day.

'Our camp in the Bois', a 'vile' sketch by Charlie May. 'Its only excuse for existence is that it will serve as a slight record of four happy days.' (19 May 1916)

In the 1st Army of the New Zealand Expeditionary Force, Captain Charles Edward May,
seated, at camp at the Imperial School of Instruction at Zeitoun, Egypt, 1915.

Designed by Sir Herbert Baker, Dantzig Alley British Cemetery is on the road between the villages of Mametz and Montauban.

Charlie May's headstone, at Dantzig Alley British Cemetery, where 220 men of the Manchester Regiment are buried. May was killed near by at Bucket Trench.

Frank Earles in the early 1920s, the horrors of war now behind him. While in hospital he met Thomas Lipton, a merchant and champion yachtsman, who offered him a job.

Pauline, a family friend and Maude in the forest of Fontainebleau, to the south of Paris, where Frank was working in 1922 for Lipton's Tea.

After Pauline's wedding to Harry Karet in London, 1950, the bride and groom depart for their honeymoon near Calais, France.

I am glad. He has sat up with me tonight and we have yarned the hours away with tales about our old days, soldiering in the Scottish and King Edward's Horse. It is wonderful how quickly a night passes and also how one learns to do without sleep.

Unfortunately it has rained. The mud is already up to our ankles. It is quite like old times – but none the more pleasant because of that.

Our raid was to have come off tonight – but has been indefinitely postponed. Oldham now has charge of it and I hope he will get a chance of doing the little job some other time.

Fritz has turned off today considerably. We have never let him alone and I think that is the reason. Every grenade he has sent over he has had two back for till he has become sick of it and chucked it up.

25th May '16

Wilson, 21st,[i] was up this morning for a look round. They take over from us tomorrow.

The rain has come again and we gradually became bogged once more. However, it cannot last and tomorrow no doubt will bring the sun. It has been a mixed day, a little shelling, plenty of grenade fighting and some trench mortar work. Also our snipers tell me tonight that they have hit six Huns. We have easily had the best of today's essays all round and I think Fritz must begin to wish he had not started this rifle grenade touring.

Gee,[ii] my bombing corporal, has given me one of Fritz's latest pattern grenades tonight. It was a 'dud' and is a perfect specimen, I am very pleased with it. Gee picked it up on top just in front of London Road. The man who fired it had forgotten to remove the striking arrangement. Fritz must have some poorly trained fellows even as have we.

i 2nd Lt George Frederick Wilson.
ii Cpl William Gee.

26th May '16

We came out this afternoon – a daylight relief, and very easy and pleasant it was even though Fritz put shrapnel over whilst the relief was taking place and gave us a few anxious moments. He got none of our men, however, though the Berks[i] unfortunately stopped some. One of their poor fellows was an awful mess. He was killed and about four others more or less badly mauled.

Our present resting place, Grovetown Camp, is a queer collection of tents, huts, shelters and bivouacs. It has all the joyful disarray of a Bedouin encampment and nearly as varied a population. From what one can see it is a place which has just 'happened'. It is laid out with no attempt at order, the engineers in tents being jumbled down in the midst of MGC [Machine Gun Corps] dug-outs, infantry officers' tents and huts and alongside infantry shelters and infantry bivouacs. At one end the Indians are in shelters of tarpaulin and canvas, with a Pioneer Battalion cheek by jowl with them in sand-bag huts.[ii] It is all a jumble, it all smells fresh and clean but it is very like war. What it will develop into if the rain comes the Lord only knows, and He, for the good of mankind, is inscrutable.

27th May '16

Went in to Bray for a bath this afternoon and met Strode there, of the Borders, and Brocklehurst of the Queen's.[iii] The former desired to see Ram and the latter Murray. Strode came back to tea and Brocklehurst later. The latter is only really content when gibing at the Army. He told a tale yesterday of what happened to the Festubert way.[iv] Their Divl

i 6th Bn, Royal Berkshire Regt.
ii The 20th Deccan Horse of the British India Army participated in the last cavalry charge of the war at High Wood.
iii Lt Edward Randall Chetham-Strode; Capt. Thomas Pownall Brocklehurst.
iv The Battle of Festubert, in the Pas de Calais, took place in May 1915. By its

General suddenly decided that a certain communication trench must be fire-stepped to allow of flanking fire. The trench was about a mile long and every day and night for weeks the devoted soldiers laboured at the work, losing many of their numbers in doing so. But at last it was finished. Then the brigade went out for a month's rest. They were proud of their work and they talked about it often. Judge their surprise then on returning to find all their handiwork broken down and the trench restored to its original indefensible state.

The reason was this. The incoming general was a testy martinet. His first visit up, he tripped over a sand-bag and fell. 'Remove all of them .... things at once. Remove them all,' he said. And it was even so. And a stout defensive work ceased to be because a gouty general bumped a corn-afflicted foot upon an infinitesimal part of it.

No wonder Brocklehurst finds the Army amusing!

28th May '16

Up to the brigade today, where I saw Duke and Grimwood and touched the latter for a very welcome whiskey and soda. It was a scorching afternoon. Afterwards I met Day of the Trench Mortars and rode with him to see the 'Bangalore torpedo'[i] experiments at Bray where they were being given for the benefit of our 'stunt' team. It was quite interesting and very successful results were achieved.

---

end, one kilometre of territory had been gained with 16,000 casualties on both sides. The divisional generals included Maj. Gen. Sir Hubert de la Poer Gough of 7th Div, within which served the 2nd Queen's.

i Devised in 1912 by Capt. McClintock of the Bengal, Bombay and Madras Sappers and Miners of the British Indian Army, the 'Bangalore torpedo' was a series of pipes screwed together to form a longer pipe, at one end of which lay the explosive charge. This extended barrel was then inserted through a hole in the parapet before firing. Originally designed to clear booby-traps and mines, it was very inaccurate, and so was usually used to clear barbed wire defences before an attack.

Coming back we saw a strange sight. Nothing less than some hundred men, stripped to the buff digging in a trench. It was like an artist's effort of 'Labour'. Big muscles and supple joints swelling and swinging with the rhythm of the pick whilst the perspiration stood out in beads on the white flesh. It was a gladsome sight.

Merriman tells me he is likely to go to the Judge Advocate's Department, so leaving the battalion. I hope it is true. It would suit him so much better than his present job and would let him use his undoubted talents in the sphere all his training has suited him most for.[i]

29th May '16

Rode over to the Bois des Tailles today to see the model trenches of the Mametz system laid out by the 21st. It is a topping little piece of work and most instructive. Afterwards I went over to the top of the hill above Albert and watched the lines – on both sides – being shelled. There was some big stuff flying about and I found myself taking quite a sporting interest in the shooting.

I found my attitude rather cynical when it occurred to me how little of the sporting element I would have seen in it had I been in the line. There is all the difference in the world between the feelings of the sheller and the shelled.

The Italians have fallen back and Fritz still pounds at Verdun.[ii] In the meantime we sit still. But the guns keep coming up, more and more of them and no doubt our push will come when the time for it is ripe. But the waiting is long. And life in the Army for an officer is a lazy one. In peacetime I should think it must bore a fellow stiff except during manoeuvres. Here we have much more to do when we are back away from the line than when we are in it as we are at present.

i 'Merriman is on his way to a cushy job. His name has gone forward to [the] 4th Army Judge Advocate. I hope he will get it because he will fit the part so wonderfully well – "Lord Paramount of Court Martial"' (Bland, 4.6.16).
ii Verdun is some 150 miles south-east of the Somme region.

30th May '16

Fritz has blown in Wellington Redoubt and we have smashed one of his villages to bits and set it on fire in retaliation. So the game goes on. And I wish the order would come that would loose all our guns and let us strafe him as he should be strafed. Next week we do the 'stunt' – the little cutting-out affair of which Oldham is now in command in place of Shelmerdine. I hope it will be a success and the boys do well in it. We are a trifle sick about it, the Brigade having more or less taken it out of the CO's hands. It is a pity and a mistake. But, I suppose, it is one of the things we have to put up with for having a young and ambitious brigadier.[i] He wants to run everything himself, a youthful fault because youth is the same in its action whether it refer to the young in years or to the young in position.

The major[ii] has gone to his court-martial affair. I hope he makes a big success of it.

Wood has come back to us, after a joyous month in hospital at Rouen, cured of his wound and in great form.

31st May '16

We played the Borders tonight at footer and beat 'em 2–nil. It was a good game and was rendered a trifle more exciting than some other matches I have been to by the fact that Fritz commenced shelling the wood whilst the game was in progress, the shells passing over our heads and exploding on the slope above.

1st June '16

Ascension Day. Also the first day of the Midsummer month. It is hard to realise that the winter seems so close behind us still and the year so little spent. Yet one cannot alter dates. They are unassailable facts.

i Brig. Gen. Sir John Randle Minshull-Ford had been appointed CO 91st Bde, 1916. (One of the forenames he gave his daughter was Mametz.)
ii Maj. Charles Allfrey.

Tom [Worthington] and I got leave and rode to Corbie. It was a welcome change indeed. We stuck to the fields the whole way and the breath of the breeze coming bowling over the clover, the rye and the grasses was a thing to remember.

We had lunch at the *Poste*, tea at a café and an interesting talk with a young French Lieutenant from Chipilly. The 20th French Division has come up there, the crack division of our Allies' Army. It is to push on the right with us when this comes off. When? For all we know it is as far off as when the subject was first broached months back.

But our own little show is close at hand now. It takes place tomorrow night.[i]

2nd June '16

We have been up and manned the Intermediate Line today. It is a good line, quite scientific with ample opportunities for cross and enfilade fire.[ii] Quite one of the best bits of trench work I have yet seen. The brigadier was there and Grant, the former as brimful of ideas as ever. I expect we will receive a ream or two of fresh literature on this subject now. That is the one fault one finds with energy in this war. It oozes out into yards of stodgy literature, facetiously known as 'bumph'.

The 'stunt' comes off tonight and the team has left, cheered by the battalion and full of hope with our good wishes behind them.

3rd June '16

I wrote the above about 8 p.m. It is now 10 a.m. of the 3rd. Last night was one of the most anxious most of us have ever spent. The first word

i This is a raid on Bulgar Point, an enemy listening post, at 11 p.m., with Lt Eric Oldham and forty other ranks, with cover from a unit led by 2nd Lt Joshua Cansino. Rehearsals at a facsimile of the German trench had taken place in fields south of Bronfay Farm.
ii Gunfire, often sweeping, directed along the length of a target.

came at 12 midnight, after the most terrific bombardment: 'Most men returned, Lieutenants Oldham and Cansino wounded'. The next was half an hour later: 'Sergeant Burchill killed, Oldham wounded, Street and Cansino and 14 men missing. Two prisoners.'[i]

Nothing else. We could get no word through. It was horrid. The poor boys up there dying and we down here helpless to do anything. Poor lads. Burchill had no right to be there but he went out getting the wounded in and was shot in the stomach doing it. Men say they would never have got in but for him. He was a gallant boy. So was Street. He was hit twice and got caught on the German wire. A sergeant tried to help him but was twice wounded in the attempt. 'I'm done. Go back now, sergeant,' said old 'Stuggins' [Street] – and that's the last we've heard of him. He had killed two Germans with his revolver a few minutes previously, but they got him in the end.

Oldham found the Bosche wire uncut and he pulled it apart with his own hands. He was hit in the shoulder and the leg but stuck it till weakness compelled him to go back. He helped a worse-wounded man along.

Sgt Bradley was hit twice, killed a Bosche, bound up Burchill in No Man's Land, came into our line with all his men to report and then went out again with a patrol to search for the missing.[ii]

i The raiding party of Lts Eric Oldham and Edmund Street and forty other ranks assembled at Minden Post, where the men were split into five sections and directed to various points, while the covering party, led by Lt Joshua Cansino and twenty men spread out in no-man's land to prevent flanking attacks. A preliminary bombardment of about forty minutes was laid down by artillery, but when the raiding party reached the enemy wire it was found to be insufficiently destroyed. In spite of this, a point of entry was made and five enemy dug-outs bombed with about fifteen Germans killed. Four prisoners of the 2nd Silesian Regt were taken, but only two survived the journey back after the others had been shot when offering resistance. The despatch was in error: it was Lt (not Sgt) Vivian Burchill who was killed. 2nd Lt Street and Lt Cansino also died.
ii Sgt J. Bradley.

One of the missing returned this morning. He had been lost in No Man's Land. We are therefore six men and one officer (Cansino) unaccounted for. No one seems to know anything of poor Cansino. Dransfield, one of my men, captured three Germans, shot one who tried to escape but brought in the other two.[i] He also helped Oldham over the last bit in.

We have thirty men hit, two officers killed, one wounded and one missing. It is a heavy price, but no doubt it is the fortune of war. It has cast a shadow over us all. Poor foolish, gallant Burchill. He had no right there at all. He was out against orders. But he died like an officer should.

3rd June '16

We are in the line again. But it is a sad incoming.

Poor Street, Cansino and one other unidentified can be plainly seen tangled in a heap among the German wire, right under their parapet. A Bosche sentry is mounted over them and keeps popping his head up every now and then to have a look at them. I saw him first through the telescope and the sudden apparition of his great face caused me to think him a fiend of hell gloating over his victims.

The poor fellows are quite dead. It is evident now that Cansino, hearing Street was in difficulties, went to help him and was killed in the attempt. It is one more case of the Supreme Sacrifice. The boy did well.[ii]

i Pte Allen Dransfield.
ii 'It's extraordinary. All the original A Coy officers are gone, and I alone am left. Yes, at one blow we have lost 4 officers, three killed and Oldham wounded. Street, Burchill and Cansino are dead. Oldham, Street and Cansino with 60 NCOs and men raided the German trenches opposite on Friday last night. They had been practising the show for three weeks and all was arranged, every man to his task, perfect in every detail. As a show it was a success. They did considerable damage, secured two prisoners and dealt destruction to a great many more. The only hitch was the enemy wire, which had not been cut by the Artillery preparation. Street, as last to leave the Bosche trench, ran greatest risks, and got fast in the wire. Burchill went across to help him and received a

190

It is pitiful to see them lying there but it is not possible for us to get them in, they lying too close to the enemy. No doubt he will save us the trouble tonight.

Poor Street was a married man with three children and Cansino was also married. It is a sad business.

Routine Orders by Brigadier No. 566 General J. R. Minshull-Ford,
Special Commanding 91st Brigade Order – 3rd June 1916
The Brigadier General Commanding wishes to express his admiration for the
gallant manner in which the Officers, NCOs and men of the 22nd Battalion the
Manchester Regiment, carried out their attack on BULGAR POINT last night.
The task allotted to this party was carried out exactly as had been ordered.
Considerable losses to the enemy were inflicted, and valuable information obtained.
The Brigadier General Commanding deeply regrets the losses which the
battalion suffered during the operation and is confident that when the day comes
all ranks of the 22nd Battalion the Manchester Regiment will avenge their fallen
comrades, and display the same courage and devotion to duty.
(sgd) A. K. Grant, Major
Brigade Major [i]

---

fatal stomach wound, and Cansino did likewise and, so far as we know, was killed in attempting to save Street. The latter two have not been recovered. Oldham is all right, with a "blighty" in the shoulder. 6 men are missing. The Officer losses are appallingly heavy, but the task attempted was magnificently accomplished. We mourn our three beyond speech' (Bland, 14.6.16).

i May copied the full text of this order into his diary. The CO later said that Cansino 'died in the act of performing a splendid deed in the face of almost certain death'. Lt Eric Oldham was wounded, as were twenty-two other ranks and six missing. Oldham was awarded the Military Cross and Sgt Frederick Kewley the Distinguished Conduct Medal. Oldham was also later awarded the Military Medal, as were Ptes Allen Dransfield and H. Edward Wolstencroft.

Chapter 11
'The greatest battle in the world is on the eve of breaking'

4–26 June 1916

4th June '16

Today Greenlees[i] took me through his now completed Advanced Dressing Station at Minden Post. It is a splendid affair, twenty feet below ground, lofty, well-aired and lighted with acetylene lamps. It is painted white throughout, has accommodation for forty stretcher cases and is fitted with an operating room and every other necessity for speedily helping the wounded. The RAMC built it themselves and it is a job they may well be proud of.

We had an accident this morning. One of our trench mortar bombs exploded in the gun and set off eighty others in the ammunition dug-out. It has blown a hole 15 feet deep and about 15 yards across. One man was buried and three others wounded. Considering the largeness of the explosion, a light total indeed.

During the evening a lot of heavy stuff dropped in the line, completely filling up one end of Lancaster Street East and part of the fire trench.

i Capt. Dr James Campbell Greenlees.

In all four men were killed and three injured and these again by being buried.

No doubt we are being retaliated on for our raid the night before last.

Walking round this morning I was struck by the two distinct types of trench we own, they are the clay and the chalk ones. The clay are always deep – one feels very safe in them – but they hold the wet and cave in badly when shelled. The chalk ones keep dry but they have an uncomfortable habit of getting shallower day by day. The reason is that the sides crumble and fall in. This is trodden down and so gradually fills up the trench. They detonate shells much more quickly than the clay, however, and do not succumb to the explosion to anything like the same extent.

On the whole I think I prefer chalk trenches.

5th June '16

A patrol brought in a funny thing tonight. It had crawled over to the Bosche wire and found, about ten yards out from this, a row of papers – about five yards between each paper – like this:

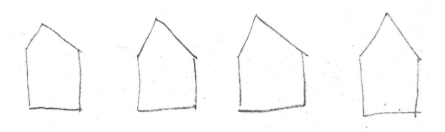

All the papers were folded the same way and all pointed to Fritz's wire. They were quite new and freshly folded though they bore the date Dec 14th, 1915.

They were all copies of the *Gazette des Ardennes*, the sheet in which

Fritz endeavours to curry favour with the French inhabitants of the occupied territory. As yet we do not understand it. One of the prisoners taken the other night has now been examined. He is a Silesian Pole, 37 years old, has only come from the recruit depot at a fortnight or so ago and had only been in the trenches eight days. It seems to me he got out of the war very lightly. He says rations are ample, a direct contradiction of the evidence of our last prisoner.[i]

One never knows what to believe with these fellows.

6th June '16

In [trench] 66 Street there is a tiny little nook carved in the wall. In this is a clip of five rounds and over the top, engraved in chalk, the notice, 'Do not touch. Brigade S. A. A. [Small Arms Ammunition] reserve'.[ii]

We have been shelled on and off all day yet we have only had three casualties. Narrow escapes however have been plenty but, once over, these are rather nice. They give people interesting conversational items, with which to inflict their friends at a later date. Fritz made good practice on us, knocking in the front line in six places, the supports and communication trenches in four and breaking two dug-outs. We are, however, well traversed now and the line should stand as good a pounding as any. *A propos* of this is a little artillery story. Our ammunition, be it whispered, is not all that it should be. Sometimes it does not go off, at others it goes off when it shouldn't and often it only half explodes. After we had been shelled one day C Company, who had suffered somewhat and were correspondingly annoyed, asked for 'retaliation' of all guns. This was promised and the men told. They immediately sought points of vantage and at last our guns commenced. They put over twelve, eight of which were 'duds'.

The men immediately commenced to sing 'Thank God we have a Navy'.

i Captured on 20.5.16.

ii This is a joke, suggesting that five rounds in a clip is all they had in reserve.

Townsend, in a thoughtless moment, retailed this to the battery commander at mess one night. There is now a certain frigidity between them.

7th June '16

The naval battle now seems clear and apparently we have done all right. It is an awful pity the Fleet could not get up in time. I bet poor Jellicoe is sick about it.[i]

And now comes news of the loss of Kitchener.[ii] What rough luck on him to end up so, the victim of a stinking submarine. It is a great pity. But the country is fortunate in that he was spared to it until his work was done. I wonder who will get his job. I do not envy him it. It is not easy to succeed a great man, at least I should not think so.

It has rained like the deuce tonight and Bunting and I got quite wet on our tour of duty. The sentries, however, were all quite happy and the line quiet.

The general told me this morning that we will be relieved tomorrow, go to Grovetown for a few days and then back near Amiens for at least a fortnight's rest. Cheer – O! It is good news. But alas, to temper it, comes word that leave is cut down to 7 days and an officer can only go every eight days instead of every fourth. This is just putrid and most awfully rough on the poor beggars who have had no leave at all yet. Personally it jumps me from June 18th to July 16th in one swoop. It is simply rotten. I had so counted on seeing you two on the 19th. However, one must not grouse.

i The Battle of Jutland was fought off the coast of Denmark between 31.5.16 and 1.6.16. It was the largest naval battle of the war, with a full-scale clash of battleships. Both sides claimed victory, but for the Allies it resulted in an effective blockade of the German ports, which could only be breached by submarines.
ii Lord Herbert Kitchener was killed when HMS *Hampshire*, the armoured cruiser taking him to negotiations in Russia, was sunk by a German mine on 5.6.1916.

The battalion has received the following from the corps and the division today:

7th Division

The Corps Commander will be glad if you will be kind enough to convey the Brigadier-General Minshull-Ford and all concerned his appreciation of the forethought and skill displayed in the preparations for the raid on BULGAR POINT in the night of 2/3rd June, and of the determined and soldier-like manner in which it was carried out by the officers, NCOs and men of the 22nd Battalion Manchester Regiment.

The fact that the air photo does not reveal the existence of the trench described as R.S.[i] in the report is most unfortunate. Had it not been for this, the raid would have been conducted with but little loss.

The Corps Commander sympathises with the 22nd Manchesters on the loss of the gallant officers and men.

J. R. Major

HQ XV Corps for Brigadier-General General Staff

5.6.16

91st Infantry Brigade

The Divisional Commander has directed me to request that you will add to the above remarks of the Corps Commander an expression of his own appreciation of the fine conduct of the officers, NCOs, and men of the 22nd Manchester Regiment.

C. Bonham-Carter, Lt Colonel

HQ 7th Division, General Staff, 7th Division,

6.6.16

i Following this raid, with such loss of life, the 7th Division staff tried to shift blame from the inability of the artillery to destroy the German fortifications and the Corps Commander tried to identify an 'R.S.' trench as the main cause of the problems. The air recce did not show an enemy trench, but in the report a staff officer identified the trench as 'Reserve Supply'. The soldiers who survived might have, on their return, described it as a German Reserve Supply trench.

They are good letters and we value them highly. Only one point can be quibbled. It was not the trench R. S. which caused our losses but the complete failure of our artillery to cut the German wire at the right place.

8th June '16

We have come out today again and are now in Grovetown once more all among the mud and the wet and the rain.

However we have word that we are going out for a rest so any little inconvenience like that fades into insignificance. The CO goes on leave tomorrow and I am to be left in charge of the battalion until he returns or until one of the majors comes back.[i]

It is rather a responsibility and I trust I may be given strength to rise to it successfully.

Word has just come in that we move tomorrow to the Bois des Tailles. It is good news. If only we have it fine we shall have a happy time there.

9th June '16

We have moved. The men are all in little canvas shelters on the ground and the officers in tents. I, now being a 'bleed',[ii] have one to myself, one in which Bunting, rising to the occasion, has erected various tables and seats and wash-stands. They are contrived out of biscuit boxes and odd stakes but they do well and give an air of comfort.

The colonel has gone, excited as a schoolboy and I am left. Word has

i It was unusual for an OC to take leave at the same time as his two majors. This is the second time that May has been given temporary Powers of Command, for disciplinary purposes, with possibly a small addition to his pay.
ii Meaning that May had higher status, though one slang meaning of this word is 'extortioner'.

come that Major Allfrey will not come back so I am indeed in charge.[i] It is a big thing at 27, but, so long as nothing very unforeseen arises, I think I will manage all right.

I feel very sorry for Major Allfrey. It will, I think, be a blow to him but I am afraid, kind, good-hearted man though he was, he was little help to the CO or to the battalion. In his place I trust we may get a real, live, energetic soldier, one upon whose judgement we may rely and who will be a help all round.

10th June '16

After orders this morning we went up to the Intermediate Line and settled dispositions in this for the four companies. It rained like the deuce and rather caught some of us out, Don Murray, Bland and myself being soaked to the skin.

On the way back Fritz shelled the Happy Valley fairly heavily and we had perforce to walk along at a respectful distance and watch it. It was a fine sight but rather too dangerous to be absolutely enjoyable. He did good shooting, but then he always does. His gunners must be clever fellows. He also shells our wood with heavies – six- or eight-inch stuff. He did so this morning but fortunately hit no one. The fact that he does, however, renders the present not quite such a place of rest as one might desire.

Tomorrow, though, we move further on and, I trust, into a haven a little less liable to have large, hot, noisy missiles dropped upon it.

Troops are moving up again in numbers. This district is fast filling to its utmost capacity. It makes one think that the push is near. I trust it is and, also, that the army is not weakening the Ypres salient in our favour. That, it seems to me, is one of the chief dangers in this type of warfare.[ii]

i Maj. Charles Allfrey was court-martialled. During the remainder of June, twelve officers and fifty-three other ranks were added to the battalion's strength.
ii 'I have just returned after being out working for 10 hours with a 100 men and 50 Royal Engineers making a railway & it has been some job' (Gomersall, 10.6.16).

11th June '16

We have moved and are now installed in decent huts in the west end of the Bois [des Tailles]. They are long, low, peak-roofed hutments daubed all over with fantastic, variegated colourings. The camp looks for all the world like the 'whares' of a Movie.[i] They are dropped down anywhere among the trees.

It would be an ideal existence but for the rain. That has come again and persistently. It is a great pity since it absolutely spoils our stay, putting us ankle-deep in mud. Tawney, the Doc, Maiden and I mess in the one hut. I sleep in one of my very own being still a bit of a 'bleed'. That honour will I am afraid be but short-lived now.[ii] It is however very enjoyable while it lasts and I make the most of it.

We have got out a Programme of Work – the usual Round, Game One – but see no hope of adhering to it, working parties absolutely bleeding us for men. However, these are urgently necessary and are not so bad whilst the weather holds. When it is bad, though, as it is now, they are hard indeed on the men who get muddy and wet to their middles with no chance of drying off.

12th June '16

A tour round this morning on the old gee [Marcel, May's horse] to look at the country allotted to us for manoeuvres, provided, that is, we ever get any men to manoeuvre with. It is a decent piece of ground laden with clover and dog-daisies and sweet-smelling grasses but oh, so wet. The rain pours persistently. And the working parties go on.

Tonight we hear that a new Second-in-Command has been detailed to

i 'Whare' in Maori means some sort of 'hut' or 'building'. In rural New Zealand at that time films were screened publicly in temporary or portable huts or shelters.
ii Capt. Paul Victor Davidson, 2nd Royal Warwickshires, was appointed three days later.

us. Captain Davidson of the 2nd Warwicks is the man. We do not know him but we have all heard of his regiment and we trust he will turn out to be a good soldier and an experienced one. If he is we can do with him. We all now anxiously await his advent which, I expect, will take place tomorrow.

The officers are all pretty sick about it. They want me to have the job. It is good of them but, personally, I am glad that things should be as they are. I can do with a deal more experience before taking on such a job. At any rate I feel that I could much better fill such a post after being through one general action.

I trust Davidson may have seen Loos.

13th June '16

Over to the division today in the pouring rain to see Colonel Bonham-Carter and Major Webster[i] about their working parties. They were very nice and went fully into the question and for the first time for weeks we have got down to really satisfactory arrangements.

We are all very pleased about it. A business-like understanding is what we have all been wanting.

The colonel told me that all work was most urgent. That everything was to be pushed to the utmost, the C-in-C being anxious to have all ready for the push at the earliest date possible.

Lloyd was told a good tale at the brigade yesterday about one Parker,[ii] an old 21st captain who has dropped into a Staff job although he has never yet been in the trenches. His case is one of the minor scandals of the Army.

It was the night the Borders were so badly strafed. The Staff were sitting on tenterhooks listening to the bombardment when Parker came into the room and up to Grant and said: 'The Borders haven't sent in their daily Summary Report.' 'Good God, man,' said Grant, 'They're being blown to hell.' 'Yes, I know,' persisted the stickler, 'But the Report should have been in by six and the bombardment didn't start till 6.20.'

i Lt Col. Charles Bonham-Carter; Maj. Webster (unidentified).
ii Capt. Reginald Frank Parker.

Thank heaven that some of our Staff know from personal experience what it is like to have hot iron flying about their ears.

Every man has been detailed now for one party or the other and every subaltern also. This means that the captains are the only people about – and they are at a loose end. The subalterns who are in [from the line] the day time are in bed, they having been up all night. This afternoon was typical. I went into the hut which B and D share. Roy Mellor was awake and I sat on his bed yarning. Then Cowan woke up and Tom Worthington and Murray and we started the gramophone. It was like some scene from the backwoods, everybody lolling about on old valises in the low wooden hut lit only by a single candle. Outside it rained persistently. We played *The Gondoliers, The Little Green Gown, Ailsa Mine, The Perfect Day* and all the old songs, till we made ourselves thoroughly sentimental and home-sick. I am afraid we are a pretty soft-hearted lot and I begin to understand why sailors are notoriously so.

14th June '16

A quiet day. Nothing at all happened. Just the usual working parties and the consequent necessity for killing time on the part of senior officers. It has rained and we have sat and talked or read, discussing the Russian offensive and speculating on how many more prisoners our Allies will capture before they are through with it. The Austrians seem to have crumpled badly.[i] No doubt they are utterly fed up.

i On the Eastern Front, the Allied Russian Army had begun an offensive. Commanded by General Brusilov, a considerable advance was made in 6.1916 against the Austro-Hungarian line on its south-western front, which succeeded in capturing several hundred thousand of the enemy. However the success was short-lived when German reinforcements were pulled back from the west, and by September any further Russian advance was stopped. These enemy reinforcements, the defeat of Russia's Romanian allies and the lack of forward progress on the Western Front had halted the Russian advance. A year later, under Bolshevik control, Russia withdrew from the war.

15th June '16

Something in the nature of a *contretemps* has occurred today. Two competitors for the position of Second-in-Command have arrived and we therefore do not quite know where we are. Davidson, the younger, a captain from the 2nd Warwicks, came first and Major Woodward[i] from the L.N.L. [Loyal North Lancashire Regt] next. The former is a very nice fellow, quite young and with about the same experience as myself. But he is a Regular. That is the fetish here. Personally I think it rather unfair on the New Army. The new Major is straight from ten years' Egyptian service and has never seen a trench. Also he is elderly and unsmart. Of the two I prefer Davidson and I think we are all of this opinion.

Definite orders for the big offensive have now come in. It is to be quite soon, within a fortnight I believe. It is the largest thing yet attempted and if it means our success, I think it will be the beginning of the end.[ii]

16th June '16

This afternoon Davidson and I rode up to Durham trench to reconnoitre the ground of our advance. The face of the earth is changed up there, has changed within the last seven days. It is now honeycombed with gun emplacements. Guns are everywhere. Guns of all calibres. Some 9.2s were registering on Mametz whilst we were watching. They are terrible shells and simply knocked lumps out of the village. 9.2s, eight inch, six inch, 4.7s, 4.5s, eighteen pounders, thirteen pounders, all sorts and conditions there all bristling out of the ground ready to belch forth a regular tornado of fire. As Worthy said when he saw it, 'Fritz, you're for it!' It is a sentiment I quite agree with.

Ammunition is pouring up, that for the heavies by motor transport,

i Maj. Francis Willoughby Woodward.
ii 'In the long run, an advance – should it take place – might be more economical of life than trench warfare, with its constant dribble of casualties' (Tawney, 20.6.15).

that for the lighter fry by wagon and limber. Two convoys of the latter, each of them fully 500 yards in length passed the Bois at sundown. It was a great sight.

It is marvellous, this marshalling of power. This concentrated effort of our great nation put forward to the end of destroying our foe. The greatest battle in the world is on the eve of breaking. Please God it may terminate successfully for us.

Fritz I think knows all about it. At any rate a day or two ago he put the following notice on his wire opposite the 4th Division.

'When your bombardment starts we are going to bugger back five miles. Kitchener is b.....d. Asquith is b.....d. You're b.....ds. We're b.....ds. Let's all b.....r off home.'

It is vulgar, as his humour invariably is, but the sentiments are so imminently [sic] those of Tommy Atkins that it must certainly have been a man with a good knowledge of England and the English who wrote the message.

17th June '16

We have moved to Bonnay today and are once more back in billets. It feels quite strange to see oneself in a mirror. Personally, I have not done so since I saw you on leave, four long months ago. It was a fine day for marching and the change is very welcome here. We stay, I believe, about four days and then go back and into the line ready for the assault.

I must not allow myself to dwell on the personal – there is no room for it here. Also it is demoralising. But I do not want to die. Not that I mind for myself. If it be that I am to go, I am ready. But the thought that I may never see you or our darling baby again turns my bowels to water. I cannot think of it with even the semblance of equanimity.

My one consolation is the happiness that has been ours. Also my conscience is clear that I have always tried to make life a joy for you. I know at least that if I go you will not want.[i] That is something. But it

---

i At the time of his death, May's estate was valued at a healthy £852.

is the thought that we may be cut off from each other which is so terrible and that our Babe may grow up without my knowing her and without her knowing me. It is difficult to face. And I know your life without me would be a dull blank. Yet you must never let it become wholly so. For to you will be left the greatest charge in all the world; the upbringing of our baby. God bless that child, she is the hope of life to me. My darling, *au revoir*. It may well be that you will only have to read these lines as ones of passing interest. On the other hand, they may well be my last message to you. If they are, know through all your life that I loved you and baby with all my heart and soul, that you two sweet things were just all the world to me.

I pray God I may do my duty, for I know, whatever that may entail, you would not have it otherwise.

18th June '16

We have done nothing today but clean up and rest – and well needed it was. The CO is back so we should soon now have our definite orders. As it is we have the men all patched in pink – the Divisional colours and many others daubed about with sloshes of yellow or white or red. These to signify carriers or runners or what not. They are awfully braced about it.[i]

Had tea with C Coy on their river frontage. They have tents under the trees on a patch where the hay has been cut. It is very pleasant there with the tiny rustic bridge and the stream gurgling along beneath it.

i For the assault, troops wore either coloured patches sewn into the back of their battledress or bright paint was daubed onto the back of their uniforms to distinguish them from the enemy. Sometimes shiny metal tags were worn at the back of their necks so that, when the sun shone, gunners could see them glinting and avoid aiming towards their positions.

19th June '16

This afternoon we went out en masse to practise attack with aeroplane control. It was quite interesting and worked without a hitch. It rained however and wet us after a hot climb and has resulted in a bad chill *pour moi*. I now lie in bed full of aspirin and ache in the eyes, head and back, feeling thoroughly miserable and a trial to my friends. By tomorrow I trust the fit will have passed and that I will be myself again. One cannot afford to be ill at this time.

20th June '16

We have moved back to Morlancourt today quite unexpectedly and I expect we'll stay here till the battle comes off. The place is full of troops, the 21st Yorks and [the 6th] Dorsets being here with the Lord knows how many machine gunners, artillery etc.

The Staff has wind up that we will be shelled. I hope not, not yet anyway. A night or two more sleep will be very acceptable. I have two more new officers now, Jones and Brunt.[i] They seem two good fellows and the latter has seen previous service as a platoon sergeant. I think I have struck two very likely men.

Donald has been told today that he is not to go in. He is dreadfully upset about it, poor old boy. The four Seconds-in-Command[ii] are being left out and they have all gone and got drunk tonight as a protest. It is a pity, but one cannot blame them. Under similar circumstances I think it more than likely that I should do the same.

21st June '16

A day full of orders, reams and reams of them till one's head is in a

i 2nd Lts H. F. Jones and William Edward Brunt.
ii A Coy, Lt Eric Oldham; B Coy, Capt. Donald Murray; C Coy, Capt. Tom Worthington; D Coy, Lt William Gomersall.

whirl and one hardly knows where one is or what this or that or the other fellow is going to do. It requires quiet and seclusion to digest the detail – essentials not too easily obtained but a walk up on to the open ground with Donald in the evening and a quiet talk over it all brought clarity of thought and an ability to write my own orders for the company.

This has now been done and relieved indeed I am. I think l have done all that lies in my power to make all clear to everyone and with reasonable good fortune we should get to our objective and capture it.

I pray to God we may be victorious and break the Hun line thoroughly. The battalion has a great honour thrust upon it. It is the right of the immortal 7th Division and my old company is right of the line. Little did I dream in those far off old Morecambe days that I should rise to command a company, which occupies a position envied by every battalion in the Army. It is up to us to justify the trust and, if I know my men, we will.

22nd June '16

Up on the top with the company [command] telling them their jobs and practising various formations. The men are as keen as mustard and fit for anything.

This evening the officers met together and talked o'er. Worthy has a pretty tricky job on, but he'll do it well.

John Cotton was very humorous. He says that it is probable that he'll meet his old pal Moses within a week. He is, however, most keen on seeing Noah. He says he wants to tell him that he really knew nothing at all about shipbuilding. John says, 'What I shall say to him is, what about the *Lusitania*?[i] That was some ship. Your old Ark wouldn't have made a decent life-boat for it!'

He is a good fellow – one of the very best and, personally, I hope it may be a long time before he meets his old friend.

i The RMS *Lusitania*, torpedoed and sunk by a German U-boat in May the previous year, was clearly still a topic of discussion.

23rd June '16

Everything is speeding up no end. Ammunition by the hundred wagon-load [is] pouring up. The village is alive with transport and artillery and the Bray-Corbie road one incessant stream of heavy-laden motor-lorries.[i]

It should certainly not be for lack of ammunition if this time we do not make a huge success of the venture. Yet one cannot help feeling a little anxious and worried. So much depends on this great throw and, for us, it is our first venture into anything really big. I doubt not, however, but that it is a much more anxious time for Fritz. His higher commands cannot but fail to be somewhat nervous with so much on their hands at once, what with the Russian advance and now this.

This time, at long last, should really see a heavy blow delivered to Prussian prestige. If that is accomplished little else matters.

24th June '16

Tonight we had a little reunion of all the old boys. There was the doctor, Murray, Worthy, Bill Bland, 'Gommy', Mellor and myself and we sat round a table and sang all the old mess-songs of Morecambe, Grantham and Salisbury.[ii] It was top-hole, and we all loved each other.

There are so many new faces with us now and so many old ones missing that the battalion hardly seems the same – and one cannot let oneself go with the new like one loves to with the old boys. I would that the battalion was going over with all its original contingent. How certain we would have all felt then. Not that the new stuff isn't good. Some of it is excellent. But we knew all the others so well. However, I

---

i 'The country behind the line here is crammed with troops, English and French, and vast guns pass through, dragged by caterpillars. The men say the Staff send us the same guns round & round here like a circus to keep up our spirits by the illusion of overwhelming artillery support!' (Tawney, undated).

ii Just seven days later, four out of these seven men – who had trained together at Morecambe, Grantham and Lark Hill – were dead and two seriously wounded.

have no doubt that this is no new experience at any rate for those who have soldiered long in this war.

More orders today. Still they come. The foolscap is piling up into most formidable piles. One almost begins to feel that if any mistake is made in the fight it will be from over-organisation. The bombardment has commenced. It is quite gentle as yet but it will speed up in intensity with each succeeding day. Up to now Fritz is quiet. I've no doubt he is saving up ammunition for a real good burst when he does start.

I am told that he has little more than 150,000 troops on the whole British front at the moment and that it will take him nearly a week to bring up another 100,000. How much truth to attach to it of course I do not know but I believe it to be fairly authentic.

In conjunction with the French, our front is to be forty miles in extent and we have any amount of both troops and guns to cover this. The unforeseen alone excepted then, it looks as though we should break through somewhere. At any rate friend Hun is likely to have all his work cut out to stop us.

25th June '16

Up on the top with Donald and the doctor this morning watching the bombardment over La Boiselle, Fricourt and Mametz. The speeding up has commenced. The hillsides over there are under a haze of smoke already. Shells which, bursting, throw up clouds bulkier than the 'Cecil',[i] white puffs, black puffs, brown puffs and grey. Puffs which start as small downy balls and spread sideways and upwards till they dwarf the woods. Darts of flame and smoke – black smoke these last – which shoots high and then into the air like giant poplar trees. These are the h.e.s.[ii] The shooting was magnificent. Time and time again the explosions occurred right in the Hun trenches. By Mametz Wood an ammunition dump must

i 'Cecil' gun: possibly named after the battalion's former and elderly CO, Lt Col. Cecil de C. Etheridge.
ii High explosives.

have been struck. The resultant smoke column was enormous. Mametz itself one cannot see. It is shrouded in a multi-coloured pall of smoke all its own. It must be awfully rotten for the Huns holding the line, yet one feels no sympathy for them. Too long they have been able to strafe our devoted infantry like this, and without hindrance or answer from us. What is sauce for the English goose is surely sauce for the German gander – and may his stomach relish it.[i]

26th June '16

We are now back in the Bois [des Tailles], tucked up in old tents and shelters, whilst the rain pours down and we are leaked upon. However that is a minor detail now. The bombardment is intense, one continuous boom and rumble. Fritz has retaliated, shelling our wood, among other things, slightly. But up to now his reply has been feeble indeed in comparison to what he is getting.

According to latest information the Hun is pushing hard again at Verdun. No doubt he hopes to draw troops from here. I am afraid, Fritz, that this time you are too late.

In three days from now we should be through you and threatening your final line.[ii] I bet the French go with a hearty good will. I think they look to this as their greatest chance since the war began.

i 'Don't be anxious if you get no letters for a week or a fortnight or even more, as it is rumoured that the post is to be suspended for 14 days. On a long view, the present situation is not encouraging. The "Gers" seem to be reaching the point where they are uncertain how to use their reserves . . . I do hope France may be delivered of the Bosches this year. When I was in the last village a woman told me that she had not seen her husband for 4 years. It is heartbreaking for them' (Tawney, 25.6.16).
ii 'The whole of the German line has been named by us – every blessed trench – and is as familiar to us, each in our own sector, on the map, as is our own system . . . Our Manchester lads are in good form today, burnt brown, eager and keen. I love 'em' (Bland, 26.6.16).

Chapter 12
'We are all agog with expectancy'

27th June '16

The Battle of Mametz, I suppose, may really be taken as having now commenced. True, it has been working up, so far as artillery activity is concerned, for the last three days but as no infantry have yet come in I take it that I give no offence to anyone if I call the period ending today as the 'Preliminary Proceedings'.

From today, however, the battle should begin to show definite shape. Infantry are now moving up. Small parties as yet it is true, but still the infantry. Runners and wire cutters, signallers and dump guards have already gone. The assaulting troops follow tomorrow. The mass of detail we have waded through to reach this point has been enormous but at last we have mastered it and the army is ready to strike.

The guns are never silent, sometimes their detonating is one reverberating roar which fills the whole air and causes even the ground to tremble. At others they dwindle down a little until you can distinguish the notes of different guns but always they fire and fire and fire. The Bosche must be having a regular thin time of it all round.

28th June '16

We were to move up tonight to take up our positions, were all ready and anxious to get away, to get up and moving and done with the waiting.[i] Waiting is rotten. I think it tries the nerves more than the actual moment of assault. Then one has action, movement, a hundred things to strive for and to occupy one's attention. But, in waiting, there is nothing but anxiety and fruitless speculation on every phase conceivable.

But we have not moved. At the last moment came an order 'Stand by'.[ii]

And so here we are still, the artillery pounding on as ever and we left, with speculation rife, and rumours bright and rumours grave, flying about on all sides, to twiddle our thumbs and wonder.

Cowan has come out of the line this afternoon. He has been in charge of the wire-cutting party and Donald has gone in to take his place. The old boy was pleased as 'Punch' about it. He feels quite sure that he'll be in the show yet.

The news from everywhere today is excellent. The moment seems very auspicious for us to strike. Perhaps we will on Friday?[iii]

i The 22nd Manchesters had been allocated a position on the right of the line, next to the Sixth Army of France. B and D Coys were to be in the first wave, followed by A and C Coys. Their first objective was Dantzig Alley on the right flank of the village of Mametz. Fearing the worst, May asked a fellow officer, Capt. Frank Earles, OC of D Coy, that if anything should happen to him, he hoped that Earles would visit his wife, Maude.

ii Because of a forecast of inclement weather, a delay was announced at 11 a.m. This meant that the battalion remained in the Bois, 'tucked up in old tents and shelters'. The original day for the assault had been named Z Day, with its preceding days named U, V, W, X and Y – as codes for a progressive artillery bombardment. After this announcement, 28.6.1916 was renamed Y1 Day, with Z Day scheduled two days later.

iii 'What does it feel like to be on the edge of what might prove to be the mightiest battle waged in the history of the world? . . . Like all romance, it is most unromantic to the participation at the time of participation. The spirit cannot grasp either the facts or the issues, the imagination is at work with the

29th June '16

A long day of waiting. The time seems interminable and one simply hates the thought of the long hours before us before the dawn comes. However, no doubt we'll get through it all right.

We move from here at 10 p.m. and should be in position about 1 a.m.

The bombardment still goes on. Mametz, they tell us, has ceased to be. The Hun should be getting pretty well fed up. Indeed from the statements of various prisoners and deserters it would appear certain that he is. Nearly six days of the most appalling bombardment he has had now – a thing calculated to shake the morale of the finest troops in the world. It destroys sleep and interferes with rationing. Lack of either of these always affects a soldier. If his old machine-gunners have only suffered in proportion to his other ranks we should not be too seriously hurt doing our job.

We are all agog with expectancy, all quietly excited and strung to a pitch but unhesitatingly I record that our only anxiety is that we will do our job well. That is but natural. This is the greatest thing the battalion or any of us have ever been in.[i]

[There is no entry for 30 June. Charlie obviously had no time to write in his diary, but on this day all COs received a Special Order from Brigade Headquarters to the men waiting anxiously in the trenches: 'The use of

---

practical difficulties, and the brain is busy with the overload of detail, immediate or prospective. We are all like ants, as they appear to a disturber of their nests, terrifically busy in an apparently purposeless orgy of chaos' (Bland, 28.6.16).
i 'If letters don't arrive for a day or two be brave & don't worry, I shall be alright & remember I am now very very happy and have a very light heart. I am also very proud to be able to take a hand in dealing a smashing blow to the hated Hun,' wrote Gomersall (29.6.16). 'Give my lads such a lot of hugs and thank them for their dear letters which are beautifully written and spelt. God bless you,' Bland wrote home (29.6.16), and to his wife he sent a pressed Forget-Me-Not and a note with the words: 'My darling . . . All my love for ever . . . Alfred.'

the word retire is absolutely forbidden, and if heard can only be a ruse of the enemy and must be ignored.']

1st July '16, 5.45 a.m.

We marched up [to the assembly trench at 9.30 p.m.] last night. The most exciting march imaginable. Guns all round us crashed and roared till sometimes it was quite impossible to hear oneself speak. It was, however, a fine sight and one realised from it what gun power really means. Fritz, of course, strafed back in reply causing us some uneasiness and a few casualties before ever we reached the line.

The night passed noisily and with a few more casualties. The Hun puts a barrage on us every now and then and generally claims one or two victims.

It is a glorious morning and is now broad daylight. We go over in two hours' time. It seems a long time to wait and I think, whatever happens, we shall all feel relieved once the line is launched. No Man's Land is a tangled desert. Unless one could see it one cannot imagine what a terrible state of disorder it is in. Our gunnery has wrecked that and his front line trenches all right. But we do not yet seem to have stopped his machine-guns. These are pooping off all along our parapet as I write. I trust they will not claim too many of our lads before the day is over.

Now I close this old diary down for the next few days, since I may not take it into the line. I will, however, keep a record of how things go and enter it up later. The diary of the Battle of Mametz should be interesting reading . . .

At this point, Pocket Book 7 ends abruptly.

★   ★   ★

Days before this last entry, Charlie had written to Maude, thanking her for sending two Alexandra Roses,[i] and telling her of the position that the battalion would take in the assault:

France

Monday 26.6.16

My Darling Maudie,

Just one last little note for some days, since after tonight I will have no chance of writing for the best part of a week.

The biggest show of the war is now on, the greatest bombardment the world has ever seen is banging and booming away in the valley and on the hill over yonder. No-one has whispered it before but you'll know all about it and what we have achieved by the time you receive this. At present we are lying behind the line waiting to go up for the assault . . . In the assault the battn has the position of honour, the right of the Division and B has been chosen as right of the battn, in the leading line. Lloyd supports me. Worthy has his company in the front line on my left and Bill Bland is in support of him.

I little thought in those far-off days in Morecambe that I should ever rise to have such a trust given to me. The Coy is the envy of the battn, and the battn is of the whole Division. To be the right of the finest Division of the British Army is no small honor, dearest, and I know you will be as proud of it as we are.

For myself, Maudie, I pray [to] God in all humility that I may do my job well, achieve my objectives, hold them and generally carry out our orders correctly and successfully. For the men I have no doubts. They, I know, will be splendid. They are as keen as mustard and fit to a turn . . .

All the love and devotion of my heart and soul to you, my dear wife and to our darling Baby. Know that I will think of you all the time.

Au revoir, my love,

---

i The Alexandra Rose was the symbol of a charity founded in 1912 by Queen Alexandra, the consort of King Edward VII, and marked the fiftieth anniversary of her arrival from Denmark onto British soil. The sale of these roses raised funds for charitable institutions.

Your loving hubby

Charlie

P.S. I am wearing one of your Alexandra Roses into action. Worthy is wearing the other. I gave it to him because he liked the idea.

Maude's anxious reply was dated 30 June. Charlie never saw this letter.

2 Grove Mansions
Wanstead, Essex

My Darling Charlie,

Your letter of the 26th reached me this morning – & my darling darling husband what can I say to you in answer to it? For sometime past I have been dreading such news as you have given me in your letter – somehow I felt that the time was drawing near for the big move – but I have always tried to put it out of my mind & to think that perhaps you might be spared taking part. That your company – the battn & the division would hold such an important position in the assault I never dreamed of – & my darling husband when I think of all the danger you are encountering – at the present time – my heart thumps with fear. My dearest – I am trusting in God & praying – Baby with me – that you will be spared to come through these terrible days of fighting safe & well & return to us my darling man.

I shall not expect a letter from you for at least a week – it was good of you to warn me my Charlie – somehow I feel that God will look after you.

Of your great responsibilities – & the great trust that those higher in command have placed in you – I can't write about. I feel very proud – & I know that those men who are under your care & orders will do well & that they are safer in your hands than those of any other living man.

You know dear love that in you I have absolute trust – & I am confident you will bring B Company through with honour & as few casualties as is possible. Oh! My darling husband how thankful I am that at this time I can look back on our few years of married life & know that they were perfectly happy & to know that we have always been since we first learnt to love – absolutely all in all to each other. How glad I am that Babs &

I sent you our Alexandra Roses – I like to think that you are wearing one dear & that you gave one to Worthy. When I sent the roses Charl dear – I never realized that you would be going into action yet. Well! The time we have all waited for has come – the papers are full of accounts of raids – artillery work etc etc: – but so far no news of a big infantry assault.

My darling darling boy God be with you – I can only pray & shall only wait with what patience I can . . .

Would it be possible to give my best wishes to your men? If at all poss: try to do so. & tell any who come to or near London to let me know their whereabouts. My whole soul goes out to you my heart's dearest tonight – in love & trust & longing. God will be good to us – he will keep little Pauline's Daddy safe. Send me a field postcard if you have not time for more. My own – my love.

Yr wife, Maude

Epilogue
'My dear one could not have died more honourably or gloriously . . .'

The Allied artillery began its bombardment of enemy trenches, shortly after Charlie put away his pocket book and pencil on the morning of 1 July, at 06.30 hours. 'The bewildering tumult seemed to grow more insistent with the growing brilliance of the atmosphere and the intenser blue of the July sky,' Tawney remembered later. 'The sound was different, not only in magnitude, but in quality, from anything known to me. It was not a succession of explosions or a continuous roar; I, at least, never heard either a gun or a bursting shell. It was not a noise; it was a symphony. It did not move; it hung over us. It was as though the air were full of a vast and agonized passion, bursting now into groans and sighs, now into shrill screams and pitiful whimpers, shuddering beneath terrible blows, torn by unearthly whips, vibrating with the solemn pulse of enormous wings.'

At 7.15, on Charlie's part of the line, gas was released by the Allies. At 7.22 the Stokes mortars opened up and at 7.26 smoke canisters were discharged to obscure the assault. With three minutes to go, mines buried underneath the German trenches were detonated. At 7.30 the artillery barrage lifted, and the first wave of officers blew their whistles and led their men up ladders and over the top.

And the supernatural tumult did not pass in this direction or that. It did not begin, intensify, decline, and end. It was poised in the air, a stationary panorama of sound, a condition of the atmosphere, not the creation of man. It seemed that one had only to lift one's eyes to be appalled by the writhing of the tormented element above one, that a hand raised ever so little above the level of the trench would be sucked away into a whirlpool revolving with cruel and incredible velocity over infinite depths. And this feeling, while it filled one with awe, filled one also with triumphant exultation, the exultation of struggling against a storm in mountains, or watching the irresistible course of a swift and destructive river. Yet at the same time one was intent on practical details, wiping the trench dirt off the bolt of one's rifle, reminding the men of what each was to do, and when the message went round, 'five minutes to go', seeing that all bayonets were fixed. My captain, a brave man and a good officer, came along and borrowed a spare watch off me. It was the last time I saw him.

At 7.30 we went up the ladders, doubled through the gaps in the wire, and lay down, waiting for the line to form up on each side of us. When it was ready we went forward, not doubling, but at a walk. For we had nine hundred yards of rough ground to the trench which was our first objective, and about fifteen hundred to a further trench where we were to wait for orders. There was a bright light in the air, and the tufts of coarse grass were grey with dew.[i]

As he climbed into enemy view Charlie May was proudly wearing his Alexandra Rose. His loyal batman, Private Arthur Bunting, was following closely behind him as they made their way forward, each struggling across no-man's land, through sheets of rifle and machine-gun fire with approximately seventy-two pounds in weight of kit and munitions on their backs. Within ten minutes, just as they reached the German lines at Bucket Trench, Charlie was hit by shell fire. The Manchester Regiment official report reads:

i The watch had been borrowed by Tawney's friend, Capt. Bill Bland. Tawney's description, entitled 'The Attack', was published in the *Westminster Gazette*, 8.8.16.

The Battn was on the right of the 91st Bde assaulting line. The Battn was formed up in our own trenches at 7.30 a.m. moved forward to the assault in 4 lines, B and D Coys forming the first 2 lines (B on the right and D on the left) and C and A the second 2 lines (C on the right and A on the left). Each company occupied a 2 platoon frontage. Bombers, Lewis Guns etc. went forward in the positions allotted to them in the various lines. The leading companies reached the 1st objective – line BUCKET TRENCH – DANTZIG ALLEY – with heavy casualties and the supporting companies with the remainder of the leading companies then pushed on towards the final objective (FRITZ TRENCH) but owing to still heavier casualties (principally from M.G. and shell fire) were unable to reach it . . .

'I was with Len & all the other boys in the German trenches but when the Captain got hit,' wrote Private Bunting afterwards to his wife Effie. 'He had just given me a message to pass down the lines & I wasn't three yards from him, only I had just turned the corner of the trench, when I heard the shell burst & Captain called to me, I nursed him best I could & tied his limbs together with my puttees, poor fellow, and while I was with him, Dear, I said my prayers over & over again for it looked a thousand to one on us both being blown to pieces & no cover to get under, it was just a case of awaiting your turn next please.'[i]

Bunting remained with the body of Charlie May for three hours, under heavy fire, trying to effect rudimentary first-aid by bandaging his legs together, before dragging him back to the British trenches. There, and later in the billet, he gathered his possessions, including Charlie's wedding ring, his unopened and unposted correspondence, and the pocket books in which these pages were so meticulously written.

i The fellow soldiers Bunting mentions would have been known to Effie. As was common in the Pals battalions, it is likely that young men from the same neighbourhoods or workplaces had enlisted together. Undated letter, with permission from Adrian Bunting.

In Wanstead, Maude had been nervously waiting to hear any news. Unfortunately Bunting's letter to her has not survived, but she replied:

Tuesday, July 11th 1916

My Dear Bunting,

With a heart full of sorrow & anguish I write to thank you for your letter & for your words of comfort & most of all for your faithfulness & the loving care that you gave my beloved husband.

I know that you did all that it was humanly possible to do under the sad circumstances. It is a crushing blow – but I am praying for strength to bear it bravely as he would have had me do & for the sake of our little daughter who is as yet too young to realize her great loss. I have had many letters of sympathy & all the details from Colonel Whetham & officers & also from the Doctor – but I am trying to write to you today – because you were with him during his last hours & I turn to you in this time of poignant grief.

I know that my dear one could not have died more honourably or gloriously – he gave his life as you say – for his King & his country – & he would not have had it otherwise. You too will feel a great sense of loss – you have done so much for him – but I want you to know how much he loved his work & all the brave men who it was his fortune to command. In his last letter to me he wrote of you all – & the trust and confidence he had in B Company.

I want you to write to me again as soon as you are able & to tell me just one or two more things that I feel I must know & only you can tell me.

During those three hours that you sat by my husband did he suffer? Was he conscious? Where were his wounds? Did he say any words at all that you could distinguish? Tell me everything – my heart aches to know.

Will you let me know your permanent address – and promise me that when you are next on leave you will wire to me – then I could either meet you in London or visit you in Manchester.

For the sake of my dear husband I want you to promise never to let me lose sight of you – you did all a devoted servant & friend could do for him in his last extremity. 'He gave his Utmost to the highest'.

In the first great shock of my bereavement my thoughts turned to Captain Murray & to you & I prayed that his wife and yours might be spared the suffering of my stricken heart. God be with you – & comfort all those who are desolated by this terrible war. Believe me ever Bunting.

Yours most thankfully,

Maude May

I ask you not to show this letter to anyone.

Arthur Bunting wrote again to Maude, explaining what belongings he had gathered and how they would be shipped to her. Her reply to him, later in the month, was kind but also beseeching:

I should so much like to visit some of the B Company men if they are near here – but so far I have not been able to find any of them – although I have made many enquiries. I trust you are keeping well. Tell me all you can remember about the dear Captain – you can understand how much I long to hear every detail – even to what he said and I don't know how I am able to possess myself in patience until I see you when you are home on leave.

About the ring – when you send it – please register it – I should be so distressed if it were lost and I am longing to have it in my possession. It never left my dear one's finger during his lifetime – from the day I placed it there – and it will ever be one of my greatest treasures.[i]

Thank you for seeing to the Captain's packing – everything has reached me quite in order – the heart-breaking task of unpacking the Valise and touching his clothes etc. seemed to bring home to me more than ever this dreadful calamity. I don't know how I shall go through life without him – the loving care and devotion he showered upon baby and me was greater than I can ever put into words. Can there be anything in life for me again?

The photographs in the leather case of baby and me and the Captain's pocket book [his final diary] – was he carrying those with him when he

i Maude received at least two packages: the second of which was registered and would have contained Charlie's wedding ring.

was struck? Was he carrying his haversack? And the cap that came home – was that the one he was wearing at the time?

I shall worry you with all these questions but these details mean so much to me. When I see you I want to hear every detail from you about my beloved – from the time the attack started until the time he passed away. You are to spare me nothing Bunting! Oh! How I long for a talk with you!

The first news of the assault along the whole front had been keenly awaited, and was published in the national press with some optimism of its outcome, but by the end of the first week of July, the horrific number of casualties was beginning to be disclosed at home, and when the names of the dead were learned they were remembered at commemorations, on street corners and in pubs, and their obituaries published in newspapers, factory and office newsletters and parish magazines. The *Manchester Guardian* published the following, twelve days after the assault:

Captain Charles Campbell May, Manchester Regiment, aged 28 [sic] only son of Captain Charles Edward May, New Zealand Forces, whose death has already been announced, was killed by shell-fire on July 1, after his Company had penetrated into the enemy's trenches. 'Though mortally wounded,' his Colonel writes, 'He gallantly continued to give orders and encourage his men to the last. Had he lived, I would have recommended him for a DSO.' Born in Dunedin, New Zealand, he obtained his commission in January, 1916, and was promoted a Captain a month later. Previously he had served six years with King Edward's Horse, and at the outbreak of war founded and commanded the Legion of Volunteers in Manchester. Captain May was well known in Manchester business quarters,[i] and leaves a widow and one little daughter.[ii]

i The 'Manchester business quarters' may be a coded reference to the fact that May was a Freemason, having joined the King's Colonials' Lodge (No. 3386) attached to the King Edward's Horse in London.

Also in Essex, Lillie, Charlie's sister, received a letter from her father, Captain Charles Edward May, who was serving with the New Zealand forces in northern France.

Rouen, France
5 July 1916

My dearest Lily . . .

Our noble Charlie was killed on Saturday last leading his company into action. My heart bleeds with yours my sweetheart. We can be comforted in the knowledge that he died as he lived – honourably. God has his soul in keeping for us. I cannot write much dearest. Leave is stopped – but I think my appeal will be granted so that I can come to you with mother. I have written dear mother – poor soul – suggesting she should come to you so that we can be near Maudie, and in fact all be together for a time. I thought I would wire Fred[i] as I did not want you to be alone when you heard the sad news.

 With my heartfelt grief I am your fond and affectionate

 Dad

 P. S. God bless you and give you strength to bear this greatest of blows. Bless you all.

Two days later he wrote a second letter:

My dearest sweet Lily . . .

I went to the Hospital [in Rouen] yesterday and there found two wounded Officers of dear son's Regiment. One was too bad for me to see, the other gave way when I told him the sad news. After a time he came round and wished me stay with him. The following is what he said of our dear son. He was a keen and well-loved Officer. When the Regiment was without a Colonel, Charles acted in that capacity, so he must have been well up in his work.

 The young fellow's name is Ryall – a 2nd Lieut.[ii] He, poor fellow, saw

---

i Frederick John Worledge, Lily's husband.

ii 2nd Lt George Ryall, who had joined the battalion 6.1916.

nothing of the attack, as he was hit badly immediately he left cover, and knew nothing until he was brought here. He also said that Charlie would not change places with anybody in that awful battle of Saturday last. Take comfort, therefore dearest in the knowledge that our glorious son took with him that grand and noble character which was his always. I am now going to the Hospital again and hope to see the other poor chap a little better so that he may perhaps give me some account of our dear one. Will continue this on my return.

Bless you dear Lily.

4 p.m. I have just returned from the Hospital and was able to have a chat with Lt Woodhouse,[i] another of Charlie's chums. Both are to be put out of service. Woodhouse was in the same mess as Charlie and he speaks of him with tears in his eyes as an officer they were all proud of, a cheery soul! You will be glad to know that Charles spoke so lovingly of us all so much that he, Woodhouse, quite knew us well dearie. I will do all I can [to] lighten your sorrow. You like all of us are proud of our darling boy. I hope to send a wire at any time saying I am coming home. I have written dear mother and Maudie a similar letter to this . . .

Dad

★   ★   ★

Charlie May is buried alongside several hundred others in the Dantzig Alley British Cemetery,[ii] just east of Mametz, on the road which leads to Montauban. It is very near to the site of Dantzig Alley trench, captured by the 2nd Queens and 22nd Manchesters on 1 July.

By the end of the first day of July, 22nd Battalion of the Manchesters had suffered ten officers and 120 other ranks killed, eight officers and 241 men wounded, with another 111 men missing.[12] Among those killed

i Lt Marcus Loftus Woodhouse was also wounded 1.7.16.
ii Plot 2, B 3. May is also commemorated on the war memorial outside the former St Luke's Church, on the corner of Northern Grove and Burton Road, West Didsbury, South Manchester.

included Captain Bill Bland, a promising scholar who had, before the war, turned down the offer of a professorship at Melbourne University to enlist; Lieutenant 'Gommy' Gomersall, a former grammar school boy and chartered accountant; keen scientist and Captain Frank Earles's former school mate, Lieutenant Roy Mellor; Lieutenant William Brunt, the journalist who had recently been promoted from the ranks; Second Lieutenant Joseph Nanson, a fine all-round athlete and former quarry worker; Sergeant Frederick Knowles, and Corporal William Gee.

Captain 'Worthy' Worthington was wounded, but survived the war to return to the cotton trade in Manchester. Captain Earles also survived, and joined the 18th Manchesters. After receiving serious wounds to his lung at Bapaume in October 1916, he was shipped back to hospital in England. In a hospital at Rouen, Charlie's father, Captain Charles Edward May, had met the wounded Second Lieutenants George Ryall and Marcus Woodhouse. Others included Second Lieutenant John Wood, older than most but who had already served in the Dominions, Second Lieutenant 'John' Cotton, who had been a railwayman, and the former civil servant Lieutenant John Prince. Dr 'Doc' McGregor lived to 1965, Second Lieutenant 'Frankie' Harrison played cricket for Cheshire and Major Frank Boyd Merriman continued his distinguished legal career, was elected to the House of Commons in 1924 and elevated to the peerage in 1941. Another who was wounded was the political journalist Captain Charles Mostyn Lloyd, who later covered the Versailles Peace Conference and became editor of the *New Statesman*.

Charlie's batman, Arthur Bunting, survived the Somme and after May's death was transferred to the service of Captain H. F. Jones. In April 1917, Bunting was captured at Vimy Ridge and taken as POW to Dulmen Camp in Germany and then to Melmes in East Prussia (now Lithuania). While a prisoner, he was grateful for food and cigarettes sent from England, and recorded that Maude was particularly generous. He lived to see the Armistice in November 1918, but became a victim to the Spanish influenza pandemic that was sweeping across Europe in December. To mark her thanks for his devotion to duty, Maude gave Effie, his wife, a carriage clock inscribed with the words, 'To Private A. Bunting in recognition of his devotion to Capt C. C. May, 22nd

Battalion, Manchester Regiment, Killed in Action, July 1st 1916 near Mametz, France.'

Sergeant Richard Tawney also survived, having lain severely wounded in no-man's land for thirty hours, but he managed to drag himself back to safety. In 1917 he was medically discharged from the Army and returned to England where he taught economics. In 1924 he was appointed the economic adviser to the first Labour government.

The total count for British and Commonwealth troops on 1 July 1916 was 19,240 dead and 35,493 wounded.[13] On the evening of the second day, when General Sir Douglas Haig entered these events in his own diary, he wrote, 'the total casualties are estimated at over 40,000 to date. This cannot be considered severe in view of the numbers engaged, and the length of the front attacked.'[14] By November 1916, the end of the Battle of the Somme, these figures had climbed dramatically: it is recorded that the total casualties of British and Commonwealth troops was 419,654, of whom 95,675 were killed or missing. Total French losses were 204,253. The estimate for Germans lost was 465,000.[15]

Although it had been Bunting who after his captain's death had collected Charlie's belongings, including these diaries, it was Captain Earles who very probably arranged for them to be shipped back to England. Just before the first big assault, Charlie had asked Earles, who he had known before 1914 and who was now alongside him, whether, if he died, he would visit Maude at home in Essex and take care of their daughter. Frank fulfilled his promise, and more. Three years later, on 19 May 1919, he married Maude, with four-year-old Pauline in attendance, and proved to be a loving husband and stepfather.

In July 1920 a ceremony watched by hundreds took place in the centre of Manchester, when the King's Colours were presented to the 16th, 17th, 18th, 19th, 20th, 21st and 22nd Battalions of the Manchester Regiment. It is not known how many survivors of the original Pals were able to take part in this parade.

The desire to consecrate a chapel in memory of the regiment was such that, in 1936, Lord Derby agreed that the Derby Chapel in Manchester Cathedral should be re-dedicated to the regiment. A committee was formed to raise funds and, in memory of the fallen, donations of furniture and other gifts were received from the regiment and the public.[i] The Cathedral Honorary Architect was Hubert Worthington of the 16th Battalion, and brother of Tom Worthington, or 'Worthy', of the 22nd Battalion. The chapel, where the Regimental Colours now hang beneath its elaborately carved timber roof, was inaugurated the following year.

---

i A number of oak chairs were presented to the chapel, one of which, in memory of Captain Charles Campbell May, was given by Maude and his comrade from the trenches, Frank Earles.

. . . No braver or more determined men ever faced an enemy than these sons of the British Empire who 'went over the top' on the 1st July 1916. Never before had the ranks of the British Army on the field of battle contained the finest of all classes of the nation in physique, brains and education. And they were volunteers, not conscripts. If ever a decisive victory was to be won it was to be expected now.

Captain Wilfred Miles, *The Official History of the Great War*, 1925

Acknowledgements

In 1950, my cousin Pauline May, who had been a civil servant, became engaged to Harris or 'Harry' Wolfe Karet. After their Jewish wedding, which caused some division in both families, they moved into a flat in Notting Hill Gate, where a suitcase containing some of Charlie's possessions was placed in the attic. Many years later Pauline died, and when Harry planned to move the case was opened. He found it contained not only Charlie's war diaries, but also drafts of his stories, poems and journalism, scrapbooks of newspaper cuttings and photographs. He asked a friend, Joyce Weiner, to type a transcript of the diaries, a task she commenced in 1980.

It was not easy: on a manual typewriter, she worked with a magnifying-glass trying to decipher Charlie's neat but tiny handwriting, leaving only one hand free to type. Where words were unreadable she left gaps. Some names she misspelt, but Charlie was guilty of this, and she only copied him. He himself offers little help, sometimes not identifying a name or place, or using a nickname not seen before, or spelling his French mistakenly, or including a word in Maori. Or adding mysterious acronyms known only to himself. I later read Joyce's transcripts with a fresh mind, but returned to the source in order to scrutinise them.

From a young age I had been close to Pauline and Harry, so his cousin Georgina Jay, who had inherited a quantity of personal possessions from Harry after his death in 1999, passed the suitcase to me. I inspected its contents, but their significance did not hit me until some months later. I now thank her again. With the help of my sister, Mavora Roberts, I deposited the documents at the Manchester Regimental Archives at Ashton-under-Lyne so that they could be preserved and also made available to future researchers. In 2012, the historian Anthony Fletcher suggested that I was 'sitting on a treasure', and that I should edit the diaries myself and have them published. I thank Anthony, and my friend Brian Harding, for their encouragement. I should also not forget Robin Cross, John Ingram, Brenda May, Colin Parr, Anthony Rudolf and Allen Steel.

I had been contacted by Adrian Bunting, a retired Army officer, and grandson of Arthur Bunting, who had seen a television drama in 2005 called *The Somme* which featured Charlie, and had obtained my contact details. He gave me copies of Bunting's letters home to his wife and also those between my great-aunt, Maude May, and his grandfather. His military experience, access to further sources and hawk-eyed proof-reading of the manuscript have assisted me greatly. I also thank him for permission to include the correspondence of his grandfather.

A second retired officer and military historian, Robert Bonner of the Manchester Regiment, read the manuscript and introduced me to the Manchester Regiment Group Forum, a flourishing on-line information exchange. I have known nothing like this before and am impressed by the huge range of knowledge that its stalwarts are willing to share. This book would be nothing without Robert himself, Wendyg, Mack (Bernard McIlwaine), The Mons Star (Roy Sellstrom), Harribobs, Tim Bell, Timberman and many more. In Manchester I thank Mike Berrell for his local research. The chief archivist of the Manchester Regimental Archives at Tameside Local Studies, Larysa Bolton, and her colleagues have been extremely helpful to me in the compiling of this book, far beyond the call of duty, whether I have been present or at the end of a telephone line or email. The seven pocket books of diaries are catalogued as MR4/17/295/1/1 to 1/7. Charlie's other writings, listed in the appendix, and photographs are catalogued as MR4/17/295/2/1, then through MR4/17/295/3/2, 3/3, 3/4 and 3/5. Copies of the diaries are also available in the Imperial War Museum, London.

I am indebted to Naomi Rudolf in Dunedin, New Zealand, for her careful research. The discovery of Susan Worledge, a remote relative, has also been extremely helpful. Susan has kindly provided letters and photographs. My second sister, Rosie Gutteridge, also supplied a family photograph. I am grateful to Anthony Richards, Head of the Documents and Sound Archive of the Imperial War Museum, and his colleague Simon Offord, who have enabled me to access the letters of Captain Alfred Bland, referenced IWM:194038. I also thank Bland's great-grandson Daniel Mace for his permission to use these letters. For permission to use extracts from the letters of Lieutenant William Gomersall, I thank Victor Gomersall, his nephew in Australia.

The letters of Richard Tawney are deposited at the London School of Economics, where, after the First World War, Tawney became a distinguished professor. They were deposited by Major General Sir Charles Vyvyan, to whom I am grateful, and to Sue Donnelly, head of archives, and her colleagues at the library of the London School of Economics and Political Science. They are not yet fully catalogued, but are listed under TAWNEY/ADD, TAWNEY/II and TAWNEY/VYVYAN. The photograph is referenced at LSE/Tawney/27/11.

At the Library of the National Army Museum I was fascinated to learn something of the history of King Edward's Horse and thank Kate Swann, a curator here, for her help.

There are also certain authors whose books have been useful. These are Alastair Cowan who wrote *The 22nd Battalion Manchester Regiment* (Fleur de Lys Publishers, 2011); Michael Stedman who gives a vivid account of the Service Battalions in *Manchester Pals* (Leo Cooper, 1994); Robin Cross who wrote the wider history, *In Memoriam* (Ebury Press, 2008); Malcolm Brown's widely respected *Book of the Somme* (Sidgwick and Jackson, 1997); and Lawrence Goldman, whose impressive *The Life of R. H. Tawney: Socialism and History* (Bloomsbury, 2013) has been helpful in providing answers to my questions about his subject. And finally Anthony Fletcher's *Life, Death and Growing Up on the Western Front* (Yale University Press, 2013).

For the use of images I am grateful to the following: Kate Murphy of the Museum of New Zealand Te Papa Tongarewa, Wellington, for references O.034194 and O.011756; Emma Lefley of the National Maritime Museum, Greenwich, for the photograph, ref. GO1952; also

Steven Bailey, Derek Taylor and the Dunedin Fire Brigade Restoration Society Inc.

For the Index of Names I am indebted to Robert Bonner, Adrian Bunting, Alastair Cowan and the Manchester Regiment Group Forum already mentioned. First World War Army Service Records are now kept at the National Archives in Kew (File Nos WO 363 and WO 364). Medal Roll Index Cards are No. WO 372. Officers' records survived a raid in the Second World War, but bomb and water damage to a warehouse in Arnside Street in Peckham, London, in September 1940, where the MOD records of many privates and NCOs were kept, are known as 'burnt' documents. The records of other privates and NCOs which were being examined for Claims at the Ministry of Pensions and so survived, are known as 'unburnt' records. While the greatest possible care has been taken to ensure this Index is accurate, I apologise for any errors that have been made.

I should not forget my agent, Andrew Lownie, for his continued patience, and of course the very helpful team at HarperCollins, including Arabella Pike, Kate Tolley, Essie Cousins, Kate Johnson and John Gilkes, without whom you would not be reading this.

Finally I must thank Chris Primo and Sally Vince for answering my cries for help whenever I met a computer problem, Cecilia for being such unforgettable company, and Ellie, who has been sharing our household with strangers on pages who tend to become, over months and years, intensely familiar and almost alive.

Gerry Harrison, 2014

Charlie May: Other Writings

May's short stories, written between 1912 and 1916, are typical of their time – mostly charming whimsical tales of lost love, chivalry and derring-do. Some are set in New Zealand, and a few later ones were written in France. His poems are lyrical, with a romantic, Edwardian feel.

Short Stories

All for the Love of a Lady
The Awakening of Archibald
Better Man than her Lover
Beyond the Line: A Tale of 'No Man's Land'
The Blacksmith of Broken Cross
At Buddacombe
By the Lake Track
Captain Latimer
Commandant of the Passes
A Deal in the Calico
The Den of the Katipo
The Edge of the Precipice
Fireman's Jealousy: A Real Life Romance
General Knowledge
Home Tales from the Antipodes
In the Train

The Intruder

Jimmy: A Tale of a Young Lieutenant who did his Duty on the Outpost of Empire

The Little 'Pilot'

The Luck of the Sandemans

A Meeting of Fortune

The North Sea Lights

The Old House

The Other Side

Paradise, a New Zealand Love Story

The Poem: A Story of the Trenches

The Reaper

The Repayment

Sawney

Miss Simplicity

On the Skipper's Road

The Southerly 'Buster'

Steam Strategy

Stepping Stones: A True Tale of Macclesfield and Australia

The Story of the 'Vittoria Affair'

The Vincible Bower

The Whaler

When Dalgleish Came to Canvey: A Stirring, Smuggling Yarn in which a Maid Proves to Be

The Wooing of a Grenfell

Poems:

White Cloud: a poem of New Zealand

The Tale of Hiram Carord

To the Unenlisted

TO THE UNENLISTED....................

Masters,have ye heard the call,
"England needs us,one and all?"
Then,must England longer plead
Us to aid her in her need?
Can we refuse her her behest,
We she suckled at her breast,
Can we skulk in infamy
When for her 'tis life to die?
Masters,ye have heard her need,
Must she longer vainly plead?

Ye have heard of Prussia's heel,
Steeped in blood and shod with steel,
Ye have heard her vaunting boast -
That steel-shod heel shall foul our coast.
But,could we brook the Weald of Kent
Seared with flame and ravagement,
Could we brook our children slain
By swxxk the swine who sacked Louvain?
Ye have HEARD of Prussia's heel,
Have ye thought how it would FEEL?

Is the blood of Devon Drake
No longer present in our make?
Are xkx we men of England curs
Unfitted for our Empire spurs?
Is our Empire,hardly won,
To fall,in bondage,to the Hun?
Is our loyalty to our King
But a lip-served,empty thing?
Oh,are the sons of England curs
Who will not give their lives for hers?

Dare we meet our valiant dead,
Who died to keep us safe abed,
Dare we tell we would not go
When our England asked us to?
Dare we lift our eyes again
To the mothers of the slain?
Dare we pay the widows' doles -
Who saved our lives,and lost our souls?
Dare we plead,'I cannot go,'
When our land requires us so?

Men,how long must England plead
Us to help her in her need?
Will we wait till,in despair,
She forces us her coat to wear?
Or will we rally to her call
And fight her battles,freemen all?
Listen,she speaks the English-bred,
"Is England's spirit with England's dead?
Wilt living die,or dying live?" -
The answer,reader,is thine to give.

                              C.C.M.

Index of Names

Abbreviations used

2iC	Second-in-Command
CB	Companion of the Bath
CIGS	Chief of the Imperial General Staff
CO	Commanding Officer
Comm.	Commissioned
CQMS	Company Quarter Master Sergeant
DSO	Distinguished Service Order
HQ	Headquarters
KC	King's Counsel
KCB	Knight Commander of the Bath
KCMG	Knight Commander of the Most Distinguished Order of St Michael and St George
MC	Military Cross
MiD	Mentioned in Dispatches
MM	Military Medal
MSM	Meritorious Service Medal
OC	Officer Commanding
OTC	Officers' Training Corps
POW	Prisoner of War
RAMC	Royal Army Medical Corps
RFA	Royal Field Artillery
RFC	Royal Flying Corps
RMC	Royal Military College

General Officer Commanding, 7th Division of XIII Corps

Sir Herbert Edward WATTS   5.1   (1858–1934). Lt General. Took command of division, 9.1915. Comm. 1880. Previously with 2nd Prince of Wales Own or West Yorkshires. KCB, CMG, KCMG, MiD.

Commanding Officers of the 91st Infantry Brigade
(formerly 30th Div but transferred to the 7th Div on 20.12.1915)

Until 3.2.1916
Francis James KEMPSTER   (1855–?). Brig. General. Comm. 3.1875. Had served in 2nd Afghan War, 1880; in Bechuanaland, 1884; in Sudan, 1887. Col. in 1896. In northern India, 1897. From 1902 on retirement list, until recall in 1914. DSO.

Until 20.11.1916
Sir John Randle
MINSHULL-FORD   (1881–1948). Maj. General. From Windlesham, Surrey. Comm. 1900, Royal Welch Fusiliers; became CO of 1st Bn. Wounded at Neuve Chapelle, 1915. Appointed Brig. Gen. with Home Forces and then again in France. Retired 1938. CB, DSO, MC.

| Cyril John DEVERELL | 8.4 | (1874–1947). Brig. General. Born Guernsey. Educated at Bedford School. Comm. 1895, Prince of Wales West Yorkshires. Served in Anglo-Ashanti War, 1896. Lt, 1898. Maj. 1915. CO of 4th Bn, East Yorkshires. CO of 20th Infantry Bde, 1915. CIGS, 1936. Retired, 1937. KCGB, KC, OBE. |

(in alphabetical order)

Sir Charles BONHAM-CARTER	13.6	(1876–1955). Lt Col. Educated at Clifton and RMC Sandhurst. Had served in 2nd Boer War. Queen's Own Royal West Kents. Staff Officer. KCBG, CMG, DSO, Légion d'honneur. MiD.
DILLON	18.1	Maj. Royal Field Artillery. General Staff Officer 1.
Jesse Pevensey ('Jake') DUKE	23.3.	Bde Capt. until 3.6.16. 2nd Royal Warwicks. Also served in Second World War. DSO, MC, MiD.
Arthur Kenneth GRANT	17.1	(1881–1964). From Colchester. Comm. 1900. Bde Maj. 2nd Queen's Royal West Surreys.
Reginald John KENTISH	17.1	(1876–1956). Bde Capt. until 12.2.16. Previously with Royal Irish Fusiliers and then CO of 1st East Lancs. Head of 3rd Army School of Instruction, Fléxicourt. Later, Brig. General. CMG, DSO.

Francis Cecil LONGBOURNE	16.5.	(1888–1963). Brevet Maj. From Guildford. Served with Mounted Infantry in South Africa, 1900. Joined Queen's Royal West Surreys, 1902. CO of 2nd Queen's. CMG, DSO, Légion d'honneur, MiD.
Robert John MORRIS	16.5	Maj. From Horsham, West Sussex. CO, 1st South Staffordshires from 31.6.1916. Previously, Maj. with Notts and Derbys. Later, temporary CO of bn with Devonshires.
William Wilding NORMAN	16.5.	(1860–?). Educated at Oxford Military College. Had served in Tirah Campaign. Lt Col. 21.12.1905. CO of 21st Manchesters, 21.12.1908. Had retired from British Army in India, 23.10.1912. DSO, MiD.
Reginald Frank PARKER	13.6	Bde Capt. From Woldingham, Surrey. On General List, but previously 2iC of 21st Manchesters. MC, MiD, OBE.
WEBSTER	13.6	Maj. General. Staff Officer.
Paul W. WHETHAM	1.1	Lt Col. Had served with 21st and 23rd Manchesters; appointed temporary Lt Col., 22nd Manchesters in 1915, after taking over command from Lt Col. Cecil de C. Etheridge while training at Grantham. Later commanded bn of Royal West Kents. Retired, 2.1919. DSO.
Clifford WOOD	13.4	(1884–1961). Padre. Born Bridgwater, Somerset. Worked on Great Western Railway. Later ordained as Baptist Minister. Attached as temporary

Chaplain to Manchester Regiment
4.6.1915. Served as padre on Home
Front during Second World War. Last
ministry at Winchmore Hill, north
London, in 1934. Retired, 1950.

22nd BATTALION, MANCHESTER REGIMENT

Charles Moubray ALLFREY   25.1   (1874–1943). Maj. From Boughton
Monchelsea, Kent. Previously Capt. in
3rd Royal West Kents. Court-
martialled, 7.6.1916.

21308 James Herbert BECK   16.1   (c.1877–?). Pte (Colonel's messenger), 6
Platoon, B Coy. From Harpurhey,
central Manchester. Previously a mill
warper. Severely injured 21.9.1918 and
invalided home.

20902 George J. BENSON   6.4   Sgt. Admitted to hospital with severe
shell-shock.

M.M. BETHMANN   14.11   Interpreter in November 1915.

Albert Edward ('Bill')   21.11   (1881–1916). Capt., OC of B Coy. From
BLAND   Kidderminster. Educated at Queen's,
Oxford, to which he had gained a
classical scholarship. In 1904 became
historian in Public Record Office.
Lecturer with Workers' Education
Association in London. Co-editor,
*English Economic History: Select
Documents* with Richard Tawney (see
below) and Philip Brown, in 1914.
Refused to accept professorship at
Melbourne University to enlist in Inns

of Court OTC; in 1.1915 transferred to 22nd Manchesters. Later 2iC of bn. Killed in Action 1.7.1916. Buried in Dantzig Alley British Cemetery.

Reginald Walter ('Bubbles') BOWLY   11.11   (c.1875–1918). Capt., 2iC of A Coy. After court martial on 8.4.1916, then transferred to 20th Manchesters, from which attached to 1st Cheshires. While attached to 20th Cheshires, Killed in Action, 29.5.1918. Buried in Tannay British Cemetery, Thiennes.

20413 J. BRADLEY   2.6   (1886–?). From Rusholme, Manchester. Sgt, 7 Platoon, B Coy.

William Edward BRUNT   20.6   (1893–1916). 2nd Lt, B Coy. From Buxton, Derbyshire, reporter for *Buxton Herald*. Promoted from Sgt in Oxford and Bucks Light Infantry to a comm. in B Coy, 22nd Manchesters, 20.6.1916. Killed in Action, 1.7.1916. Buried in Dantzig Alley British Cemetery.

20277 William BULL   22.2   Pte (runner), 5 Platoon, B Coy. From Stockport. Put on report by Tawney (see below), then punished for his conduct by Bland and May (see below). Wounded, 1.7.1916. In hospital in Rouen, then sent home. Discharged, 3.7.1917.

21090 Arthur BUNTING   28.11   (1885–1918). Pte, 1 Platoon, A Coy. From Ardwick. Previously coach-builder. Took on 'extra duties' as orderly, first with A Coy and then as his batman with B Coy when May took command. After May's death, Bunting transferred as batman to Capt. H. F. Jones (see below). In 3.1917, captured at Vimy Ridge; POW to Dulmen Camp in Germany and then to Melmes in East Prussia. Died 12.1918 of Spanish Influenza. Buried at Vittener Cemetery. Commemorated on Russian War Memorial at Brookwood Cemetery, Surrey.

Vivian BURCHILL   9.1   (?–1916). 2nd Lt, B Coy. From West Kirby, Liverpool; son of Managing Editor, *Liverpool Courier*. A sportsman, attended Liverpool Institute. Comm. 1.2.1915. Died of Wounds, 2.6.1916. Buried in Bronfay Farm Military Cemetery.

Joshua Hain CANSINO   10.5   (1890–1916). 2nd Lt. Born in Casablanca, Morocco. From Broughton Park, near Salford. Educated at Cheetham Higher Grade School and Manchester School of Technology. Gained an MSc. Later studied in Berlin and Paris. Enlisted as Pte with 4th Royal Sussex in 9.1914. Comm. with 22nd Manchesters in 9.1915. Killed in Action, 2.6.1916. Commemorated at Thiepval and on Manchester University Memorial.

20743 George CARR   25.3   Pte, 12 Platoon, C Coy. Right-half with bn football team. Discharged 16.11.1917.

20748 John Albert CLARKE	25.3	(*c.*1890–1918). Pte, 6 Platoon, B Coy. From Altrincham, Manchester. Invalided home to hospital in Sheffield. Later transferred to 10th East Yorks. Killed in Action, 28.10.1918.
Henry Rodham COOK	2.5	(*c.*1883–1917). 2nd Lt, C Coy. From Altrincham. Educated at Merchiston Castle School, Edinburgh. Comm. 18.6.1915. Joined 22nd Manchesters 1.5.1916. Killed in Action, 7.9.1917. Buried in Sunken Road Cemetery, Fampoux. Commemorated on Altrincham War Memorial.
Hugh Stapleton ('John') COTTON	11.11	(1886–?). 2nd Lt. From Audlem, near Nantwich, Cheshire. Previously foreman for London & North West Railway. Comm. 25.1.1915. Transferred to Railway Operating Section, Royal Engineers. Wounded, 1.7.1916.
William James ('Pat') COWAN	18.2	(1886–1969). 2nd Lt, 2iC of D Coy. Born in Liverpool. In 1914 went to Belgium with Legion of Frontiersmen, and fought at Battle of Yser. Comm. with 22nd Manchesters 1915. Wounded 1916, but returned to bn in 1917. Appointed Adjutant at Catterick. Later Advertisement Director for *Illustrated London News*.
William Boston CUSHION	8.1	(1891–?). Lt, CO of 9 Platoon, C Coy. Previously an electrical engineer. Transferred to RFC as temporary Maj. Later worked with 5th Distribution Stores in Edgbaston.

20980 Charles(?) DALEY	1.3	Pte. Althouth there were many Daleys in the bn, this is possibly Charles Daley of D Coy, who replaced Smith (see below) as cook.
Paul Victor DAVIDSON	12.6.	(1886–1946). Maj. Born in Appleby, Westmoreland. Educated at Haileybury. Had served in 1910 with Southern Nigerian Regt. Later with 2nd Royal Warwicks to which he afterwards returned as Lt Col. In 1923 posted to Baghdad, HQ Mesopotamia, as CO, Iraq Levies. After military service obtained a job with the Rover Car Company. DSO, MiD.
21477 Henry DOOLEY	5.5	Pte, B Coy.
Albert Victor DOWLING	15.3	(?–1923). 2nd Lt, 19 Platoon, D Coy. From Dalkey, Dublin. Previously at Ministry of Labour.
20487 Allen DRANSFIELD	2.6	Pte, 8 Platoon, B Coy. Later, a Cpl with Labour Corps. MM.
Francis John ('Frank') EARLES	25.11	(1887–1972). Capt., OC of D Coy. Born in Macclesfield. Educated at Modern School, and from 1905 at Grammar School (with Harrison and Mellor below) as a pupil-teacher. After Borough Road College, London, attended Emmanuel College, Cambridge, and joined OTC. By 1914 teaching in Liverpool. Comm. 12.1914. Adjutant. Temporary Capt., 2.1915. Severely wounded, 10.1916, and on 'light duties' until end of war. Married

Charlie May's widow, Bessie Maude on 19.5.1919. Moved, with stepdaughter Pauline, to Paris where he was general manager of Lipton's Tea; returned to London and then to Birmingham where he obtained employment with Alfred Bird & Sons (Bird's Eye). Died in Shorncliffe, Kent, and buried in Macclesfield. Commemorated on War Memorial now in King's School, Macclesfield.

Cecil de C. ETHERIDGE

Lt Col. From Reserve Officers List. Served with East Yorks and Royal Warwickshires. First CO of 22nd Manchesters in 1914. While in training at Grantham, relinquished command to Lt Col. Paul Whetham (see above). DSO.

EWALD 18.3

Interpreter. From Alsace. DCM.

Henry Lander FAULKNER 15.3

(?–1933). 2nd Lt. From Shirebrook, near Mansfield. Previously Yorks and Lancasters. Transferred to Royal Engineers. After war was inspector of mines.

21146 Harold Cecil FINCH 8.1

(1887–1920). Pte, 2 Platoon, A Coy. From Chorlton-on-Medlock, Manchester. Previously a tram driver for Manchester City Corporation. A stableman by profession, became groom for bn horses. Suffered attack of myalgia, and was admitted to 10th Casualty Clearing Station. Later lived in Longsight, Manchester.

21395 James FORTUNE	7.5	Pte, 7 Platoon, B Coy. Previously a turner. Wounded 1.7.1916. Sent to Edinburgh War Hospital. Later transferred to 17th Manchester. POW from 30.4.1918.
20920 Thomas Moreton GANDY	6.4	Cpl. Killed in Action, 14.3.1917. Buried in New Cemetery, Foncquevillers.
11551 Robert Taylor GARSIDE	29.12	(c.1890–1947). CQMS. Sgt, B Coy. Born in USA. From Lower Broughton, Salford. Previously a clerk. Enlisted 2.9.1914. Posted to 22nd Manchesters 9.1.1915, and promoted on same day. First-class shot. Admitted to Endell Street Hospital, London, 18.9.1917, after groin injury. Convalescence at King's Lancashire Hospital, 15.1918. Posted to 3rd Manchesters, 19.2.1918. Discharged to Class Z from 8th Reserve Bn, 17.2.19. Later a cotton broker. Died in Fylde, Lancashire.
20291 William GEE	25.5	(c.1888–1916). Cpl (bombing). From Levenshulme and Old Trafford. Killed in Action, 1.7.1916. Commemorated at Thiepval.
William Ellis ('Gommy') GOMERSALL	22.4	(1894–1916). Lt, CO of 15 Platoon, D Coy. Originally from Yorkshire but family moved to Urmston, near Manchester. Educated at Manchester Grammar School until 1911. Accountant until 8.1914 when enlisted as Pte. Comm., 5.5.1915. Killed in Action, 1.7.1916. Commemorated on Thiepval Memorial.

20356 Frederick GRADY	28.3	Cpl (cook), 6 Platoon, B Coy. Transferred to 365 Coy, Labour Corps.
20427 George Kinsey GRESTY	6.4	(c.1891–1916). Sgt, 7 Platoon, B Coy, but transferred to D Coy. From Stockport, manager of a dairy in Longsight. Killed in Action, 6.4.1916, with L/Cpls Heathcote and Helliwell (see below). Buried in Bronfay Farm Military Cemetery.
Herbert ('Grim') GRIMWOOD	26.11	2nd Lt, CO, 17 Platoon, E Coy. Reported missing, 14.3.1917, but was taken prisoner. Seems to have had pre-war experience as actor.
20498 Herbert HADFIELD	3.5	Cpl, 8 Platoon, B Coy. From Chadderton, Oldham. Previously, cotton spinner at Malta Mill, Middleton. Wounded, 7.5.1916, but remained on duty. Admitted to Hospital in Rouen with shell shock; then to Edinburgh War Hospital. MiD.
Frank Arthur ('Frankie') HARRISON	27.2	(1895–1958). 2nd Lt, CO of 4 Platoon, A Coy. Born in Leek, Staffordshire. Educated at Modern School and Grammar School in Macclesfield, then articled as chartered surveyor. Played for Cheshire County Cricket Club.
20294 Alfred HEATHCOTE	6.4	(c.1893–1916). L/Cpl, D Coy. From Lower Broughton, Salford. Died of Wounds, 6.4.1916. Buried in Citadel Cemetery, Fricourt.

20928 John Edmund HELLIWELL	6.4	(*c.*1889–1916). Pte, 15 Platoon, D Coy. From Todmorden, Yorkshire. Killed in Action, 6.4.1916. Buried in Bronfay Farm Military Cemetery.
21128 Henry ('Harry') HINSLEY	7.3	(1884–?). Sgt, 14 Platoon, D Coy. From Stockport. Previously a clerk. Later gassed and wounded, and discharged to Z Class Reserve. MM.
20934 William JARVIS	10.3	Pte, 19 Platoon, E Coy. Transferred to Labour Corps. MM.
H. F. JONES	20.6	2nd Lt, B Coy. Mattress-maker. Joined 22nd Manchesters 20.6.1916. After 1.7.1916 some surviving officers were swiftly promoted. After May's death, he requested Pte Bunting as batman. Within eight months, as Capt. transferred to the RFC.
21042 Frederick KEWLEY	3.6	(1890–1959). Sgt, 6 Platoon, D Coy. From Barrow-in-Furness, where he worked in shipyards. Then moved to Oldham Road, Manchester. Joined 22nd Manchesters, 12.1914. DCM, MM.
Frederick Charles KNOWLES	10.1	Sgt and Coy Sgt Maj, B Coy. From Nottingham. Had served in South African campaign. Court-martialled on 31.3.1916, and reduced to rank of Sgt. Killed in Action, 1.7.1916.
Orric Joures KNUDSEN	8.11	(1892–1974). 2nd Lt, CO of 11 Platoon, C Coy. From Lytham. Previously steamship agent in Manchester. Joined Manchester University OTC, 1914. In 11.1914 joined 3rd Bn, Public Schools

and University Men's Force. Comm.
12.1914. Staff appointment in late 1916
as Railway Traffic Officer in military
transportation. Later, Honorary Vice-
Consul of Denmark in Liverpool and
Manchester. OBE, DSO, MSM, MiD.
Croix de Guerre, Belgium, Légion
d'honneur, France.

Charles Mostyn LLOYD	8.1	(1878–1946). Capt. From Surbiton. Later 2iC of 22nd Manchesters. Wounded, 1.7.1916. From its founding in 1913, wrote articles for the *New Statesman*. After war returned to paper as sub-editor. In 1919 covered Peace Conference at Versailles for *Manchester Guardian*. Took over editorship of *New Statesman* in 1926. In 1922 had been appointed head of department of Social Administration at London School of Economics and Political Science, where he remained until retirement in 1944.
George Barbour ('Doc') MCGREGOR	12.11	(1882–1965). From Didsbury. Educated at George Watson's College and Edinburgh University. Lt, attached as MO of bn from RAMC. Wounded, 1916, and again 1.1917 at Bertrancourt. Gassed, 1918. MC, MiD.
Earl Langford MAIDEN	2.2	(1881–1958). Lt and Quarter-Master. Previously heating and ventilation engineer. Transferred to Labour Corps, 1918.

Charles Campbell MAY

(1888–1916) Capt. Born in New Zealand. Killed in Action, 1.7.1916. Buried in Dantzig Alley British Cemetery. Commemorated on War Memorial in West Didsbury, Manchester. MiD.

Roy MELLOR   9.3

(1895–1916). Lt, OC of D Coy. Born in Macclesfield; attended Modern School and Grammar School with Earles (see above). A keen sportsman, he played football and cricket. Won Science Scholarship to Manchester University. Joined OTC. In 1914 enlisted in Royal Fusiliers Public Schools Bn (see Knudsen above). Transferred to 22nd Manchesters. Musketry Officer, Acting Adjutant and Intelligence Officer. Killed in Action, 1.7.1916. Commemorated at Thiepval Memorial.

Frank Boyd MERRIMAN   8.11

(1880–1962). Maj. on General List. Educated at Winchester College. Called to bar at Inner Temple in 1904, became barrister in 1914 and KC in 1919. Enlisted with 20th Bn Manchesters in 1914 and transferred to 22nd Bn in 1915 in which at first OC of A Coy. Later became Judge Advocate, 4th Army. In 1918 appointed to Staff Reserve of Officers as Lt Col. Recorder of Wigan 1920–28; elected MP for Manchester Rusholme from 1924; became Solicitor-General. Knighted in 1928; elevated to peerage in 1941 as 1st Baron Merriman. Commemorated by plaque in Knutsford parish church. PC, KC, GCVO, MiD, OBE.

David Stanley MURRAY	10.11	(1882–?). Lt, CO of 8 Platoon, B Coy. From City of London. Later transferred to 2nd Bn, West Indian Regt and served in Palestine. Later, lived in South Africa. MC and bar.
Donald ('Don') MURRAY	10.11	(1880–?). Capt., OC of B Coy, from Reserve of Officers. From Hampstead, north London. Export merchant. Previously, Pte with 23rd Royal Fusiliers (Sportsmen's Bn), then 21st Manchesters as temporary Capt. DSO.
Joseph NANSON	2.5	(1895–1916). 2nd Lt, B Coy. Transferred from 25th Bn. From Llangollen in north Wales. Educated at Park Gate and at St Bees, Cumberland. Athlete. Worked for father in slate industry and then in building construction. Joined 22nd Manchesters 1.5.1916. Killed in Action, 1.7.1916. Buried in Dantzig Alley British Cemetery.
20806 James NUTTALL	28.1	Sgt, 13 Platoon, D Coy. Bn chief clerk, orderly room. L/Cpl. in 1914. Rapid promotion, probably because of sudden vacancies and pre-war clerical experience.
Eric OLDHAM	25.12	Lt, CO of 1 Platoon, A Coy. Son of Mayor of Hyde. Previous experience in hat-making at Oldham & Fogg. Obtained MSc at Manchester University and joined OTC. Attended

bomb-throwing course in Suffolk. After a month in France was attached as Liaison with French Army because of language skill. Wounded, 3.6.1916. MC.

John Franklin PRINCE	13.11	Lt, 6 Platoon, B Coy. Born in Pilkington, near Bury, Lancashire. Previously with Ministry of Labour. Wounded, 1.7.1916.
Gordon Openshaw ('Ram') RAMSBOTTOM	14.12	(1886–1929). Capt. OC of C Coy. Comm. 1914. From 7.9.16 with 2nd Borders. From 11.2.17 to Armistice returned as CO of 22nd Manchesters. Later became cotton merchant. DSO and bar. Italian medal for Military Valour.
20461 William George RODMAN	30.11	L/Cpl, 7 Platoon, B Coy. From Pendlebury, Salford. Severely wounded, 7.1916. Sent to 3rd General Hospital, Wandsworth, London, 20.7.1916. Discharged, 9.1916.
Harold Williamson ROYLE	16.2	(1889–1986). 2nd Lt. From Wilmslow, Cheshire. Previously worked for Peel, Watson & Co. Evacuated to England because he had gone 'stone deaf'. Later transferred to Russian Military Mission as Liaison Officer.
George RYALL	7.2	(c.1883–?). 2nd Lt. Born Tipperary, Ireland. Previously a schoolmaster. Joined 7th Bn, Royal Dublin Fusiliers, 1915. A month later, comm. and transferred to 22nd Manchesters 6.1916.

Wounded, 1.7.1916. In 1918 joined RAF (formerly RFC). Retired to Southampton.

Joseph Armitage SHELMERDINE — 13.11 — 2nd Lt, CO of 5 Platoon, B Coy. From Pendleton, Manchester. Educated at Cheltenham College. Previously cotton manufacturer.

20057 Richard SMITH — 23.12 — Pte. Originally with 1 Platoon, A Coy, but transferred to B Coy as cook with Bunting (see above) when May took command of B Coy.

Edmund Alger ('Stuggins') STREET — 10.5 — 2nd Lt. Former Lloyd's underwriter. Previously a Pte with 28th London Regiment. Killed in Action, 2.6.1916. Commemorated at Thiepval.

20328 Richard Henry TAWNEY — 25.11 — (1880–1962). Pte, 5 Platoon, B Coy. Noted economic historian, educator and political activist. Born in Calcutta, son of a Sanskrit scholar; educated at Rugby School where he formed a lasting friendship with William Temple (later Archbishop of Canterbury). At Balliol, deepened support for social moralism and joined Christian Social Union. Enlisted as Pte and refused comm. As Sgt, seriously wounded on 1.7.1916. Recovered in England before transfer to 71st Training Reserve Bn. Medically discharged, 1917, and never collected his medals. Academic at LSE, where brother-in-law, William Beveridge, was director. Advocate of Adult

Education. Advisor to PM Ramsay MacDonald's first government in 1924. Had previously co-edited *Economic History: Select Documents*, with Bland (see above) and Philip Brown in 1914.

20122 William Robert THOMPSON	18.3	Sgt. As a result of dissatisfaction in Merriman's Coy, was transferred into May's C Coy. Killed in Action, 2.6.1916.
John Edward ('Towny') TOWNSEND	11.11	(*c.*1887–*c.*1920). Capt. and Adjutant, 1915. From West Didsbury. Previously a warehouse salesman.
20825 W. Henry WHITEHEAD	10.4	(*c.*1887–1917). L/Cpl, 13 Platoon, D Coy. Killed in Action, 12.1.1917. Buried in Varennes Military Cemetery.
Frank Cowlin WICKS	19.1	(1892–1965). 2nd Lt, CO, 14 Platoon, D Coy. From Bristol. In 1912 wicket-keeper for Gloucestershire County Cricket Club.
21070 H. Edward WOLSTENCROFT	3.6.	(*c.*1896–1917). Pte, A Coy. From Bradford, Manchester. Died, 14.3.1917. MM. Buried in Gommecourt British Cemetery No. 2.
John Patrick Hamilton WOOD	26.11.	(*c.*1871–1916). 2nd Lt, CO of 10 Platoon, C Coy. From Winchester. Had served with Paget's Horse in South Africa, and in 1911 as Acting Sgt in 4th Bn, Rifle Bde in Cairo. Wounded, 1.7.1916. Died of Wounds, 11.7.1916. Buried in Frankfurt Trench, British Cemetery, Beaumont Hamel.

Marcus Loftus WOODHOUSE	7.7	(*c.*1888–1950). 2nd Lt. From Levenshulme. Trained at Bede College, Durham. Previously elementary school teacher. Joined 22nd Manchesters 6.1916. Wounded, 1.7.1916. Later worked for Manchester Education Committee.
Francis Willoughby WOODWARD	15.6	Maj., Loyal North Lancashire Regiment. From 7.11.16 to 20.12.16, CO of 22nd Manchesters. Previously Governor and Commandant of Troops, Nile Province. DSO.
Thomas Ryland ('Worthy') WORTHINGTON	20.11	(1880–1949). Capt. of C Coy. Comm. 6th Bn, 8.1915. Wounded, 1.7.1916. Later managing director of export merchants in Manchester. MC.

21st BATTALION, MANCHESTER REGIMENT

Charles James Mottram HOBSON	26.2	Capt. From Edgbaston, Birmingham. OC of B Coy. Wounded, 15.7.1916.
Francis Frederick OMMANNEY	12.3	(*c.*1869–1949). From Sheen, Richmond. With 3rd Volunteer Bn Territorial Force Reserve and 6th East Surreys. Temporary OC as Maj. in 21st from 6.1.1915. General List, No. 76, POW Company 5.1917. Ministry of Munitions 12.1917. Returned to Territorial Force 12.1917. Later in Treasury Solicitor's Office.

Frederick Thomas TAYLOR   14.1   Capt. From Newport Pagnell. MC.

George Frederick WILSON   25.5   (*c.*1889–?) 2nd Lt. From Anerley, Manchester. 'Embodied' into 5th Bn, City of London Regt. (Rifles). Comm. 30.8.1916 with 21st Manchesters. Killed in Action, 1.7.1916. Buried in Dantzig Alley British Cemetery.

23rd BATTALION, MANCHESTER REGIMENT

T. H. BARNARD   2.3   2nd Lt, CO of 18 Platoon, E Coy. Transferred from 22nd Bn.

William Morrison REID   2.3   (*c.*1887–1916). Temporary 2nd Lt, transferred from 22nd Bn. From Edinburgh. Wounded, 25.2.1916. Was bn's first wartime casualty. Died of Wounds, 26.2.1916. Buried in Merville Communal Cemetery.

2nd BATTALION, BORDER REGIMENT

Edward Randall CHETHAM-STRODE   27.5   (1891–1917). 2nd Lt. From central London. Educated at St Paul's School. Previously a stockbreeder. Attached from 3rd Bn. Wounded, 3.1915 and 6.1917. Transferred back as Capt. to 3rd Bn. Killed in Action, 1.10.17. Buried in Tyne Cot Cemetery, Belgium.

Richard Francis NEWDIGATE   22.4   (1894–1916). Capt. and temporary Maj. From Dorchester, Dorset. Educated at Wellington

College. Wounded, 6.1915. Killed in
Action, 4.9.1916 at Longueval. Buried
at Menin Gate.

1st BATTALION, EAST LANCASHIRE REGIMENT

Thomas Stanton LAMBERT   29.11   (?–1921) Col. Had served in India. In
9.1914 assumed command of 1st East
Lancs after CO was killed on the
Aisne. He was wounded a fortnight
later, causing loss of his right lung.
CB, CMG.

Wilfred Austin SALT   28.11   (1894–1962). Lt. From Gorton,
Manchester. Student of chemistry.
Enlisted 1914. Later Staff Capt. in XVII
Corps, then Maj. on General Staff.

Edward WOODGATE   1.12   Capt. and 2iC.

EAST YORKSHIRE REGIMENT

MANSFIELD   3.1   Maj.

1st BATTALION, NORFOLK REGIMENT

George Philip BURLTON   1.2   (1896–1916). Capt., 1st Norfolks. Born
in Murree, India. From Ealing,
London. Educated at Wellington
College and joined OTC. Comm.
9.1914. Died of Wounds from

exploding mine after having been taken prisoner, 5.6.16. Commemorated at Arras Memorial. MC.

| HICKEY | 4.2 | Lt. |

2nd BATTALION, QUEEN'S ROYAL WEST SURREY REGIMENT

Thomas Pownall BROCKLEHURST — 27.5 — Capt. From Reigate. Previously a Pte in London Regt. Comm.. 2.5.15 in Queen's Royal West Surreys. Killed in Action, 1.7.1916. Buried in Dantzig Alley British Cemetery.

THORNTON — 11.4

Edward Charles THORNYCROFT — 12.4 — (1887–1952). Lt. From Bishop's Stortford, Herts. From 3rd Bn, Queen's Royal West Surrey Regt (Special Reserve). Wounded, 1.7.1916.

ROYAL ARMY MEDICAL CORPS

James Campbell GREENLEES — 4.6 — Capt. and Dr, 22nd Field Ambulance, RAMC. Educated at Kelvinside Academy and Cambridge. Practised as doctor. Headmaster at Loretto, his alma mater. International rugby player for Scotland. DSO, MiD, Légion d'honneur.

ARMY SERVICE CORPS

| Henry Miles STAPYLTON-SMITH | 4.2 | Driver-Mechanic. Comm. 24.4.17. |

91st BRIGADE TRENCH MORTAR BATTERY

| DAY | 28.5 | |

XXII BRIGADE ROYAL FIELD ARTILLERY

Aubrey ('Bottom' or 'Bum') 30.3 (1893–1916). Lt, 106th Bty. From
HARRIS Wrexham, Wales. Previously a senior language master at Merchiston Castle School, Edinburgh. Transferred to RFA from 21st Manchesters. Killed in Action, 4.9.16. Commemorated at Thiepval Memorial.

Alexander Winton 23.3 Maj. 104th Bty, XXII Bde.
ROBERTSON From Westcliffe-on-Sea. MBE.

William Charles Samuel 18.1 (1888–1916). Capt., 106th Bty.
WARR Joined Army in 1903. Eleven years in ranks; Sgt in 1914. Comm. 12.4.1915 with RFA. Killed in Action, 1.7.1916. Buried in Dantzig Alley British Cemetery. DCM.

WHITHAM 30.3 104th Bty.

91st BRIGADE BOMBING COMPANY

Richard Standeford PULLEN	14.1	(1882–1917). Lt. From Wolverhampton. Previously a brewer. Pte with 6th South Staffs until Comm. Killed in Action in Belgium, 26.10.1917. Buried in Hooge Crater Cemetery, Ieper.
F. G. ROSS	14.1	Lt. From Medstead, Hampshire. Had served in 20th Manchesters as CO of C Coy. MC.

Notes

Foreword

1 *Cyclopaedia of New Zealand* (Otago and Southland Provincial Districts), 1902.
2 *Papers Past*, National Library of New Zealand. *Otago Witness*, 12 June 1901.
3 Ibid.
4 *Daily Mail*, 1911, MR4/ 17/295/3/1, Manchester Regiment Archive at Tameside Local Studies and Archives, Central Library, Old Street, Ashton-under-Lyne (hereafter MRA).
5 CM entry for 7 December 1915.
6 *Fireman's Jealousy: A Real Life Romance, Glasgow Weekly Herald*, 7 December 1912; MR4/17/295/3/1, MRA.
7 CM entry for 19 November 1915.
8 Letter to Jeanette, 17 December 1914, Tawney Papers, London School of Economics and Political Science, Houghton Street, London.
9 Private correspondence with Adrian Bunting, 25 June 2013.
10 Michael Stedman, *Manchester Pals*, Leo Cooper, 1994, p. 62.

Epilogue

11 Lt Col. Paul W. Whetham, *Manchester Guardian*, 13 July 1916.
12 Alastair Cowan, *The 22nd Battalion Manchester Regiment*, Fleur de Lys, 2011, p. 17.

13 Malcolm Brown, *The Imperial War Museum Book of the Somme*, Sidgwick and Jackson, 1996, p. 92.

14 Andrew Robertshaw, *Somme 1 July 1916*, Osprey 2006, p. 78.

15 Wilfred Miles, *Official History of the Great War*, Macmillan, 1938.

Index

Bowly, Capt. Reginald Water (*cont.*)
trophy from soldier, 135; avoids
mortar explosion, 139–40; arrested
for drunkenness, 140–1; court
martial, 144, 149; sentenced and
transferred, 158–9
Bradley, Sgt J., 189
Bray-sur-Somme, 92–4, 97–9, 107, 126,
140, 161, 178, 180, 184
British Army Formations:
DIVISIONS: 7th, 45, 48n, 49, 57n,
77, 109; 30th, xviii
MANCHESTER REGIMENT:
CCM enlists in, xvi; embarks
for France, xviii; King's Colours
presented in ceremony (1920),
226
Battalions: 16th Service (1st 'City'),
xvii; 20th, xvii; 21st, xvii, 28n,
91n, 93n; 22nd ('7th City Pals'),
at Battle of the Somme, xxiv–
xxv; as 'Pals Battalion', xxii;
formed and trained, xvi–xviii, 1,
28n, 34, 91n, 93n, 159, 219n, 224;
moves to Lark Hill, 1n; in
France, 28, 34; 22nd, 1n
OTHER REGIMENTS: Border,
156, 200; Dorsetshire, 205; East
Lancashire, 26–8, 31–4, 75;
Gordon Highlanders, 62; Loyal
North Lancashire, 202; Queen's
Own Cameron Highlanders, 74;
Queen's Royal West Sussex,
48n, 57, 61, 77, 112, 150, 152;
Royal Berkshire, 184; Royal East

Kent ('the Buffs'), 171; Royal
Hampshire, 25; Royal Irish
Fusiliers, 25; Royal Norfolk, 94,
98; Royal Warwickshire, 200;
Royal Welch, 77; South
Lancashire, 146; South
Staffordshire, 48n, 77, 145, 155,
170; York and Lancaster, 171, 205
VARIOUS: King Edward's Horse
(territorial unit), xvi–xviii;
London Mounted Brigade, xvi;
Accrington Pals Battalion, 26n;
Machine Gun Corps, 184; Royal
Engineers, 106
British Expeditionary Force (BEF),
xvi, 27n, 171n
Brocklehurst, Capt. Thomas
Pownall, 184–5
Brownlow, Adelaide, Countess, 4
Brucamps, xx
Brunt, 2nd Lt William Edward, 205;
killed in action, 225
Brusilov, Gen. Aleksei, 201n
Bulgar Point: attack on, 188–91, 196
Bull, Pte William, 105, 113
bully beef, 86n
Bunting, Pte Arthur: as CCM's
batman, xxii, 26, 118, 197; drunken
escapade, 52, 54; with CCM at
death, 218–9; correspondence with
Maude following CCM's death,
220–2; later service and death, 225
Bunting, Effie, 219, 225
Burchill, 2nd Lt Vivian, 65, 104 & n,
189 & n, 190 & n

266

Kirchner, Ernest Ludwig, 143 & n
Kitchener, Field Marshal Horatio
   Herbert, 1st Earl: creates New
   Army, xvi–xvii; death, 195 & n
Knowles, Sgt Maj. Frederick Charles:
   conducts drill in France, 66; at
   Minden Post, 122n; on controlling
   weather, 129; exasperated by
   Merriman, 130n; arrested for drunk-
   enness, 140–1; court-martialled and
   reduced to sergeant, 142, 144; trans-
   ferred to Ramsbottom, 145; killed
   in action, 225
Knudsen, 2nd Lt Orric Joures, 3
Kut al Amara (Mesopotamia), xxi,
   164 & n, 175n

La Boisselle, xxiv, 208
La Houssoy, 159
Lake, Sir Percival, 164n
Lambert, Col. Thomas Stanton,
   28n
La Nouvelle, 159
Lark Hill, Wiltshire, xxii, 1
Le Fayel, 70, 72, 92
Le Quesnoy-sur-Airaines, 54–6, 87, 89
Lloyd, Capt. Charles Mostyn: takes
   temporary command of D
   Company, 22n; visits Amiens, 63;
   kept out of line with CCM, 161–2,
   178; wounded in leg, 166, 168n,
   178; returns to front, 180; on
   Bonham-Carter's staff posting,
   200; in 1916 offensive, 214; later
   journalistic career, 225

Longbourne, Lt Col. Francis Cecil,
   177
Loos, Battle of (1915), xviii: xxi, 45n,
   59–61, 200
Lusitania, RMS, 206

McClintock, Capt., 185n
McGregor, Lt Dr George Barbour
   ('Doc'): comradeship, xxii; on
   march in France, 9–10; at Minden
   Post, 122n; helps build dug-out,
   136; sleeps through barrage, 140;
   visits Heilly with CCM, 140, 150;
   shares mess with CCM, 199; sings
   at reunion, 207; survives war, 225
Maiden, Lt Earl Langford, 96, 199
Mametz, 162, 202, 208, 210, 212–3
Mametz, Battle of (1916), xxiv–xxv
Manchester: CCM moves to, xvi
Manchester Cathedral: Derby chapel
   dedicated to Manchester
   Regiment, 226–7
Manchester Guardian, xxvii, 222
Mansfield, Maj., 59
Maricourt, xxiv, 96–7
May, (Bessie) Maude (*née* Holl;
   CCM's wife; *later* Earles):
   marriage, xvi, xxiii, 80; and CCM's
   departure for France, xx; CCM's
   love for, xxiii; CCM visits on
   home leave, 98n; Tawney and
   wife visit, 172; final letters to and
   from CCM, 214–6; correspondence
   with Bunting on CCM's death,
   220–1; gives clock to Bunting's